Celtic

v Rangers

Celtic

v Rangers
The Bhoys Greatest Old Firm Victories

David Potter

First published by Pitch Publishing, 2019

Pitch Publishing
A2 Yeoman Gate
Yeoman Way
Worthing
Sussex
BN13 3QZ
www.pitchpublishing.co.uk
info@pitchpublishing.co.uk

A CIP catalogue record is available for this book
from the British Library.

ISBN 978 1 78531 567 1

Typesetting and origination by Pitch Publishing
Printed and bound in India by Replika Press Pvt. Ltd.

Contents

INTRODUCTION

RANGERS! The very name conjures up all sorts of emotions – shivers down the spine, a cold sweat, a sudden and compulsive desire to shout and swear, and certainly a willingness to see them beaten, humiliated, degraded, hammered – all these things!

And of course we all got our desires in 2012 when they went bust. It came as a shock to me the first time I heard the song about us having a party when Rangers die, for I did not think that it was possible for anyone to believe that Rangers could actually die. Yet Third Lanark died. So did Leith Athletic, Airdrieonians, Clydebank and a few more. But Rangers? Could it happen?

It certainly did. What about the team that now play in blue at Ibrox. Are they Rangers? Technically, I suppose not, but they look awfully like the old Rangers to me with their colours, their supporters, and their offensive songs, so call them Sevco, Newco if you want, but it sounds so much better if we can say that 'we beat Rangers' or even 'the Rangers'!

The desire to beat Rangers is visceral, and this has been the case since the early days, although it is probably true to say that in the 1890s the real Glasgow rivals were Queen's Park. But Queen's Park refused to enter the Scottish League at the start, and Rangers became the main target, especially when they showed that they too could amass a big support and win things. By the 1920s, a new dynamic had entered the equation in the shape of sectarianism when Rangers (incredibly to modern eyes) refused to employ Roman Catholics.

The passion of these games is all-encompassing. I recall back in the late 1950s and early 1960s, when I was as yet too young to go to such games, the sheer gut-rending tension of the occasion, and the sheer fear to put on the radio to listen to a commentary of the games. I recall the New Year's Day game in 1962 being postponed. What a relief! I could enjoy New Year without the gnawing away at my vitals of the thought that, sooner or later, I would have to face listening to the score! Older people said, 'You take that football far too seriously' – but so did they! Indeed the passion was, and remains, shared by millions throughout the world.

Several years ago I heard the story of one of Celtic's greatest-ever players who, after he retired, could not bring himself to watch or listen to an Old Firm game. and his trick, on New Year's Day, for example, when the second half was broadcast on the radio, was to take the dog for a long walk and then to watch for returning supporters' buses to judge by the demeanour of the passengers how the game had gone. Sadly, we are talking here about the awful days of the early 1960s, and so often it was the Rangers buses who were singing and flag-waving, while the Celtic buses were enveloped in gloomy, morbid, brooding, introspective silence!

And yet, we sometimes do everyone a disservice when we concentrate to an excessive extent on Rangers. They are, after all, just one club, and Jock Stein was always at pains to indicate that the points that Celtic got for beating St Johnstone, Partick Thistle and Falkirk were just as valuable as those for beating Rangers. One recalls, for example, the 1969 season when Rangers beat Celtic twice (they only played each other twice in the league in those days), yet Celtic won the league!

There is, of course, one major flaw in that argument, and it is that the other teams in the Scottish League, although quite capable of having their moments of glory, nevertheless seldom make an impact on the Scottish League. 1985 was the last year that any team other than Celtic or Rangers won the Scottish League, and that statistic needs no amplification!

So, yes, beating Rangers is important, and this book is an effort to put together 50 of the best victories over Rangers. Some will be vexed that their favourite game is not there, but I have attempted to include as many from the old days as are appropriate. Why? Because I have a recurrent nightmare that the day will come when Celtic supporters don't know who Sandy McMahon or Jimmy Quinn were. They were as important in their day as James Forrest and Odsonne Edouard are today.

Speaking personally, although I attend games against Rangers, they are not my favourite games. There is just too much hatred there directed towards people who, although of a different tradition perhaps and wearing different colours, look perfectly ordinary sort of people. Bile and hatred can, on occasion, go too far but there is the amusing side to it as well when we realise that some of 'them' actually may well live in the same street as 'us', or work alongside 'us' in the factory or the office, and certainly breathe the same air as we do. One recalls the tribute paid to a grand old Celtic supporter of whom it was said that the word 'Celtic' was written on his heart in such large letters that there was no room for hatred or rancour towards anyone else.

Some of my best friends support Rangers. This sounds like a patronising cliché to show how broad-minded I am, but in fact there is little choice. There are loads of Rangers supporters around, not all of them worthy of the now offensive 'H' word (some are however worthy of being so named, as everyone in Manchester in 2008 would have told you) and if I were to exclude from my circle of friends all those with whom I disagree, I would have no friends left!

None of this, however, should be allowed to detract from the rivalry, passion and excitement that Old Firm games engender. They should be looked forward to, and a win should be celebrated by singing and flag-waving, while a defeat should be taken with equanimity and calmness. There is a place for depression and despair for a good half hour after the final whistle. After that, the questions should be 'Who do we play next week?' and 'When do we play them again?'

ONE

ON THE WAY TO THE FINAL

Celtic 5 Rangers 3	**Scottish Cup Semi-Final**
Old Celtic Park	**6 February 1892**

Celtic: Cullen, Reynolds and Doyle; Maley, Kelly and Dowds; McCallum, Cunningham, Brady, McMahon and Campbell

Rangers: Haddow, Hodge and Dunbar; Marshall, McCreadie and Mitchell; Watt, Henderson, Law, McPherson and Kerr

Referee: Mr G. Sneddon, Queen's Park

THERE was little doubt that the early success of the Celtic Football Club in three and a half years had been little short of phenomenal. In the calendar year of 1891, the club had won the Glasgow Cup twice (in February for the 1890/91 season and in December for the 1891/92 season) and there was a noticeable increase in attendance and certainly excitement whenever and wherever they played. Not only that, but there was ambition in the East End of Glasgow with the new stadium being built (to a large extent by volunteer labour) with the express intention of hosting Scotland v England games. It was not that there was anything all that wrong with their existing ground – just that the club was growing too big for it.

There was as yet something missing, however, and that was the Scottish Cup. The 'blue riband' was what everyone wanted. The Scottish League, started last year and shared between Rangers and Dumbarton, was all very well, but the Scottish Cup was the thing that everyone coveted. Hibernian had won it in 1887, and it was possibly that one event that persuaded the Irish in Glasgow that a football team might not be a bad idea. In the first year of their existence, Celtic had reached the final, only to fall to Third Lanark, although some felt that it was only the bad weather that prevented them winning.

In 1889/90, they had gone out to Queen's Park at the first time of asking, and in 1890/91 bad weather in midwinter against the very good Dumbarton side at Boghead (hence the origin of the phrase 'fatal Boghead') was their nemesis.

This year, however, had seen wins over St Mirren, Kilmarnock Athletic and Cowlairs in the Scottish Cup, as a solid team began to emerge at Celtic Park. There was Dan Doyle, controversial, quixotic, unstable, but by some distance the best defender in the country, half-backs Willie Maley and James Kelly, reliable and steady, and in the forward line the two friends Sandy McMahon and Johnny Campbell. That was the backbone of the side, but the thing that marked out this young team was their enthusiasm and their playing for each other. Energised by a vocal and voluble support on the other side of the rope, the green-and-white stripes were a sight to behold.

The Scottish Cup semi-final draw paired Celtic against Rangers at Old Celtic Park (no neutral venues for semi-finals for another 20 years). The other semi-final had yet to be played, for on that same day of 6 February, Hearts and Renton were playing their second quarter-final replay at neutral Hampden Park while Queen's Park awaited the winners. It was widely expected that there would be a large crowd at Celtic Park, and indeed there was. Twelve thousand lined the ropes; there was a certain amount of crushing at the pay boxes and at the end of the game. Fortunately, no one was seriously injured but clearly the Celtic committee's decision to build a new and larger ground was totally vindicated as a result.

Rangers, founded in 1874, were a large club with a big support, but were chronic underachievers in several respects. Although they had gained a share in last year's Scottish League championship with Dumbarton, they had yet to win the Scottish Cup, famously in 1879 having failed to turn up for the replayed final against Vale of Leven because they felt that they were not getting their own way! In addition, in spite of having played Celtic on several occasions in several competitions and friendlies since 1888, they had yet to beat them! It was beginning to develop into a sort of a complex, but it has to be stressed that in 1892 the clubs remained on good terms with each other, and there was as yet no discernible religious or sectarian element. It was accepted that Celtic were 'the

Glasgow Irishmen', in the same way as, for example, there was a rugby team called 'the London Scots'. A few nasty remarks had been heard at grounds in Paisley and Edinburgh about 'Papists!' and 'Fenians!', but from Rangers, not yet.

On the playing side, Celtic's form had been good, apart from New Year's Day, when they had gone down 0-8 to Dumbarton! Admittedly, it was a friendly and there was a slightly weakened team – Tommy Duff played in the goal, and a chap called Cherry of Clyde was given a game at centre-half – and it was all explained away by too much alcohol the night before. Indeed, there was a certain levity about it all – 'the Celtic players drank plenty but ate nothing' – but it was still a disappointment to the large crowd, and the spectators certainly felt that they were owed something.

Today, Johnny Madden 'the rooter' was out, and for his replacement Celtic turned not to Johnny Coleman, as might have been expected, but to a virtual unknown called John Cunningham. Other than that they were at full strength. The pitch was heavy after a lot of rain in midweek, but it was a fine dry day for February with a strong sun and a drying southerly wind. Old Celtic Park ran from north to south, and Celtic, having lost the toss, found themselves at 3.15pm when the game kicked off, playing against the sun and the wind in the first half.

Not that it seemed to bother them, for at half-time they were 4-0 up. *The Scottish Referee*, an excellent publication that appeared every Monday, talks about a crowd of 12,000 'about six deep in places' enjoying the game in a happy, friendly atmosphere. There was no segregation in the crowd, and although there were arguments and banter and jokes, one never saw an angry man, even though one or two had clearly spent a little too long in the alehouses before coming to the game. 'Considering the condition of the ground, the game was a great one, full of excitement from start to finish and both teams are to be complimented on the entire absence of anything approaching unfair play. The Rangers and Celtic have always been the best of friends. We feel confident that Saturday's game will increase the already good feeling existing between the clubs. Good Ould Celts! Plucky Light Blues!'

Quite a few things there that will surprise the 21st-century reader! The reports of the game talk of Rangers playing well in the first half with Dan Doyle being prominent in breaking up their attacks. Even so Rangers hit the post and had a goal chalked off for offside. But CUNNINGHAM scored for Celtic in 15 minutes with a shot from a distance, and then a lovely move involving McMahon and Campbell saw McCALLUM finish it off. A couple of minutes after that Alec BRADY did likewise, once again McMahon being involved in the build-up. Then not long before the break McMAHON himself added a fourth 'from a scrimmage', and at half-time, now that Celtic had the conditions in their favour, a 'barrowload' of goals was expected.

But whether it was the legendary half-time 'team talk' or simply that Celtic relaxed, Rangers fought back and began to play some good football. Yet it was Celtic who went five ahead when BRADY, from a McCallum pass, seemed to put the game totally beyond Rangers' reach. But Law, Henderson and Kerr all scored. When the third goal went in, there might just have been a little panic, but it was at this point that the leadership qualities of Maley and Kelly came to the fore, and they were able to break up attacks and prevent any further damage being done.

Mr Sneddon's final whistle brought delight to the Celtic section of the crowd. Handshakes were exchanged, and 'three cheers' were raised for each side, as custom demanded, but as the Celtic men trooped off, the realisation grew that they were actually in the final of the Scottish Cup. Rangers began to wonder if they would ever win that trophy, or indeed if they could ever defeat this 'eager-beaver' Celtic team.

Great was the rejoicing in the Celtic heartlands of the city that night, in the various Irish villages dotted around Scotland, and in the Irish communities of Edinburgh and Dundee. Songs were sung, drinks were drunk, and hopes expressed for a good performance in the final. Renton had beaten Hearts in the quarter-final, so everyone knew that it was either Queen's Park (last year's winners and nine times overall) or Renton (winners in 1885 and 1888 and of course the former team of James Kelly and a few others) in the final. It was something to be looked forward to and to be talked about as the volunteer labourers turned up for their unpaid work on Sunday (shocking for Presbyterian Scotland, but a great deal less so for the Irish) at the new Celtic Park. There was even talk of a General Election soon. The Liberals might win, and that might even mean Home Rule for Ireland! Home Rule and the Scottish Cup in the same year? Now that would be something to dream about, would it not?

TWO

REVENGE IS SWEET

Celtic 3 Rangers 2	**Scottish League**
Celtic Park	**24 February 1894**

Celtic: Reynolds, Dunbar and Doyle; Curran, Kelly and McEleney; Madden, Blessington, Cassidy, McMahon and Divers

Rangers: Haddow, Smith and Drummond; Marshall, A. McCreadie and Johnston; Steel, H. McCreadie, Gray, McPherson and Barker

Referee: Mr J. Baillie, St Bernards

A DEFEAT in a Scottish Cup Final is never easy to accept, but at least on this occasion, there was an immediate chance of revenge. Last week at Hampden, Rangers had beaten Celtic 3-1 to win the Scottish Cup, and the general opinion, even from Celtic sources, was that on this occasion the better team had won. It had been Rangers' first-ever capturing of the Scottish Cup, and yet they had been in existence for 21 years (they were born almost at the same time as the Scottish Cup itself). Their failure to win the Scottish Cup (they once, incredibly, in 1879 failed to turn up for a Scottish Cup Final replay!) had been a matter of some distress to their fans.

But now that monkey was off their back, although their slowness in winning the Cup means that they are the first winners of the Cup whose name does not appear on it. There was simply not enough room on the Cup itself, and their name appears on the plinth. For Celtic this defeat was a matter of some concern. They had, of course, won the Scottish Cup in 1892, but had now lost three finals in 1889, 1893 and now 1894. But there was still the Scottish League to be won in this the first season after the legalisation of professionalism.

Celtic had been behind that move, and eventually John H McLaughlin won his point. Being paid for playing football may have been abhorrent to the Victorian middle classes, but it had been going on for a long, long time, the favourite way of payment being a few coins slipped into the shoes, and if a player was seen to limp out of the stadium after the game, well, he had picked up an injury, had he not? The official legalising of professionalism merely regularised a practice that had been rampant. There was now no need for hypocrisy, and it also brought Scotland into line with England where the practice had been legalised since 1886.

In the public perception, the Scottish League paled into insignificance in comparison with the Scottish Cup. The Cup was older, and the final was rightly looked upon as the highlight of the Scottish domestic season. The Scottish League, on the other hand, was a newcomer, ignored by Queen's Park who still saw themselves as the leaders of Scottish football, and was often referred to contemptuously as being what teams played in every Saturday when there was no Scottish Cup nor internationals. In 1894 the Scottish League consisted of ten clubs – Celtic, Rangers, Hearts, Third Lanark, Dumbarton, St Mirren, St Bernards, Leith Athletic, Dundee and Renton. Normally it would be expected that the league would be finished by the turn of the year unless, as this season, bad weather brought postponements.

Celtic's league form had been very good. They had won every game except for one defeat and one draw. The draw was 0-0 against Dumbarton but the defeat was an inexplicable 0-5 hammering from Rangers at Ibrox. The only possible excuse was that Sandy McMahon and Willie Maley were out that day, but that could hardly excuse the five-goal deficit. Apart from that, in other games against other opposition, form had been very good with loads of goals being scored by Sandy McMahon, Johnny Campbell, Jimmy Blessington and Joe Cassidy, and Celtic were well worth their place at the top.

The fly in the ointment was Rangers. Not only was there that 0-5 beating, there was also the 0-1 defeat in the Glasgow Cup semi-final, and now the defeat in the Scottish Cup Final. It seemed that Rangers could beat Celtic at will, and there was a danger that Celtic might develop an inferiority complex about them. Although Celtic still had another two league games left, today might be the best day to do it and retain the league flag that they had won last year. Rangers themselves were more or less out of the league race, having had several bad results.

The day was not untypical of late February. There was still snow around, but coming from the west it tended to come in showers, then we might get a period of sun, then more sleet, rain or snow. The pitch was damp. It was windy and unpleasant, but nevertheless some 10,000 made their way to New Celtic Park to see another Rangers v Celtic clash. This was the second season that New Celtic Park had been opened. It was not yet the finished article, but it was well on its way, and it had been awarded the Scotland v England international this year, something that the Celtic Committee had been hankering for. It was spacious and comfortable, with a new feature called a press box, so that the journalists (always a good breed to have on your side) could see the game in comfort as they sat at their desks with inkwells in them, and a telephone which, sadly, could not always be relied upon to work.

New Celtic Park held the 10,000 crowd with no bother. Celtic were without the ill Willie Maley, and this week they also dropped Johnny Campbell who had looked distinctly out of touch last week. Replacing Maley was Charlie McEleney, and Campbell's place was filled by John Divers. But the star man was, as always, 'the Duke' – Sandy McMahon, the best footballing artist of the day. He was a tall, ungainly sort of man with a distinctive style of running, but he was a complete football player who could score goals, could make goals for others, and, as important as anything, he had the correct attitude, always willing to encourage youngsters and despising any dressing-room cliques. Off the field, he was a scholar with a wide knowledge of Shakespeare and Burns.

Rangers won the toss and chose to play towards what is now called the Lisbon Lions end of the ground, with the sun hovering intermittently over where the Main Stand is now. The play was fast and furious, but generally in favour of Celtic, and after a few close things at either end, McMAHON put Celtic ahead. Details are scarce about the details of the goal, other than that it was 'capital', and then Rangers equalised just on the half-time whistle with a goal that came as a result of a scrimmage, with the goal being attributed to Gray. Thus, the teams crossed over with the score at 1-1. A draw would not have guaranteed Celtic the league, for Hearts, who were second, might just have equalled that total. A win was required.

Celtic now had the wind behind them, and early in the second half they took the lead. It came from a drive down the left wing by John Divers, then a shot which was only parried to Jimmy BLESSINGTON who 'running in, sent the ball through'. For a while Celtic were well on top, and Dan Doyle showed everyone just why he was rated the best defender in the United Kingdom with his clearing and ability to set up another Celtic attack. It was ironic, therefore, that it was a mistake by Dan that led to the second goal.

He and Tommy Dunbar the right-back went for the same ball, and collided with each other, then after a certain amount of panic in the Celtic goalmouth, the ball came to Barker of Rangers, who equalised. This could have been disaster for Celtic, for only ten minutes remained to be played, but Celtic responded immediately. Doyle, clearly upset by his part in the equalising goal, charged down the left wing, crossed immediately and Joe CASSIDY was there waiting to score the winner, to the delight of the Celtic section of the crowd. No further goals were scored, and the full-time score remained Celtic 3 Rangers 2.

Thus, Celtic won the Scottish League for the second year in a row. There was a distinct lack of fanfare of trumpets or pyrotechnics or ticker tape or any of the modern celebrations of the Scottish League winning day. In fact, quite a few of the newspapers in their report of the game failed to mention that the league was now won by this Celtic victory. To a certain extent this can be explained away by the natural Victorian reserve at showing emotion, but it also reflects the way in which the Scottish League was regarded. We find several references to the league being a good 'consolation' for not winning the Cup as far as Celtic were concerned, and *The Dundee Courier* goes as far to describe the league as 'infantile' in comparison to the Scottish Cup. Times have changed since 1894.

What has not changed, however, is the joy felt by Celtic fans because of a victory over Rangers. This was a hard-fought win, and it did a lot to make them feel better after their disappointment the week before.

THREE

SIX OF THE BEST

Celtic 6 Rangers 2	Scottish League
Celtic Park	14 December 1895

Celtic: McArthur, Meehan and Doyle; King, Kelly and Battles; Morrison, Blessington, Martin, McMahon and Ferguson

Rangers: McLeod, N. Smith and Drummond; Marshall, Gibson and Mitchell; Barker, McCreadie, Oswald, McPherson and A. Smith

Referee: Mr Dickson

THE weather was not the best. The snow of the last week had gone, but it had been replaced by rain, hard, relentless, typically Glasgow rain. Incredibly the rain did not deter the fans from attending, and 25,000 passed through the Celtic Park pay boxes and turnstiles that day (and a few more, no doubt, hopped over the wall when the policemen weren't looking!), paying sixpence for adults and three pence for boys (and more for the stands) to give receipts of £713 four shillings and threepence. It was both the record attendance and the record receipts at any Scottish football game, apart from the international against England.

This was the game in which Celtic could win the league. In Victorian times, the Scottish League was normally completed by or soon after the New Year to leave room for the Scottish Cup, international matches and prestigious friendlies, all of which were given higher esteem than the Scottish League, which was however now gradually (as evidenced by the large crowd that came to Celtic Park that day) gaining in importance. The crowd may have been huge by 1895 standards, but there was still loads of 'elbow room' at Celtic Park, which, after all, had been built with the intention of housing the Scotland v England international fixtures.

Celtic had had a marvellous few months in late 1895. Not only had they won the Glasgow Cup by beating Queen's Park 6-3, but three weeks before they had defeated Hearts, last year's league winners, at Tynecastle 4-1, the supporters famously travelling to Edinburgh in large numbers and escorting the players to and from the ground, lest they be 'molested by Edinburgh ruffians'. The next week the horse-drawn brake clubs were out in force at Paisley to see them beat St Mirren, and then a 2-1 win (slightly disappointing, in the eyes of some supporters!) over St Bernards at Celtic Park meant that the league could be clinched today against Glasgow rivals Rangers.

The reason for all this good form lay in Sandy McMahon, who had now clearly recovered his full fitness after he had been out for so long last season. Tall, intelligent, well read and sociable, he was a popular man among the Celtic Park faithful, but the main reason for his popularity was his ability to score goals and to make them for others. A modest gentleman who would always praise those around him, he was an ideal team man, and he loved the club and all that it stood for. He seemed to specialise in headed goals, using his height to rise above the opposition defenders.

But there were others as well. Centre-half and captain James Kelly was now nearing the end of his playing career, but he was still a source of inspiration to everyone. Down the left flank, Celtic had Dan Doyle at left-back, the wild rover and commonly referred to as simply 'Dan', so well known was he in Victorian Scotland, while there was an equally committed and occasionally wild character at left-half by the name of Barney Battles. He was well named, for he did not usually hold back and it was not unknown for him to fall foul of referees. Both he and Doyle needed the calming, restraining, sensible influences of men like Kelly and McMahon to keep them in line.

Another great player was Jimmy Blessington, a forceful inside-right, and in the centre was Allan Martin, who had joined the club from Hibs that year. The team hotched with talent, but it also had two other things that great Celtic teams need – one is an ability to get on with each other, and the other is an ability to relate to the huge and growing support. Celtic had not made the mistake that Hibs had made in restricting their catchment area to men of Irish Catholic descent. They therefore were slowly beginning to attract some passive support from Scottish football fans in general who, as one man put it to me well over 100 years later, 'liked the way that Celtic played football' – a statement that was as true in 1895 as it is today.

Rangers were not having a good season. They had shared the Scottish League with Dumbarton in 1891 and won the Scottish Cup in 1894, but had not had any great recent success. Nevertheless, they were still well supported, and clearly on this day quite a few of their fans had made the trek from the west of Glasgow over to the east. They were, however, heavily outnumbered by those who loved the Celtic, prepared to stand in the wind and the rain in inadequate clothing to see the green-and-white vertical stripes which meant so much to them and had done so much to help them make sense of life over the last few years.

Celtic started playing toward what was then referred to as the 'country' end of the ground (the Lisbon Lions stand end as it is known today) as distinct from the other or 'city' end. The rain had eased temporarily but there was a crosswind blowing from the south, something that made life tricky for the players. To general consternation, it was Rangers who scored first through Alec Smith. But Celtic, spurred on by their huge support, fought back and equalised – some sources say MARTIN, others say BLESSINGTON – and then just before half-time, McMAHON with a 'smart header' from a corner kick hit the post but then the ball crossed the line before it could be 'bundled clear' by Rangers' defenders. But referee Mr Dickson was on the spot and awarded the goal 'to the joy of the Celtic following'.

Mr Dickson had already had cause to call the players together and tell them that he was not happy about some of the tackling, and then at half-time he made another decision to simply turn the players around and to keep playing, for he feared that, as the clouds were gathering ominously in the background, daylight might be a problem. The game had started at 2pm but this was December, and although some clubs (Celtic included) had tried experiments with primitive forms of floodlights, the real things were still some 60 years away in the distant future.

'Nothing but disaster followed Rangers in the second half,' says the *Daily Record and Mail*. Already struggling with injuries to Drummond and McPherson, Rangers were simply overrun in the second half as Celtic showed them and the world just why they deserved to be the champions of Scotland. BLESSINGTON, BATTLES, McMAHON and MARTIN all scored in the gathering gloom and then the heavy rain. The elements did nothing to dampen the spirits of the Celtic fans, who cheered, shouted and sang throughout, and even gave a sporting cheer to McCreadie of Rangers when he scored a late consolation goal. Mr Dickson probably used his discretion and ended things a few minutes early as it was now becoming virtually impossible to see the players, certainly from a distance, and no one seemed to mind with Rangers players, even those who had been guilty of a few rough tackles during the game, sportingly offering their congratulations.

The *Daily Record and Mail* is in no doubt about who the star man was – 'Celtic's one and only Duke' (Duke being the nickname of Sandy McMahon). He was 'courageous and plucky throughout', 'his heading was a treat' and in dribbling 'he wriggled with eel-like grace'. The *Glasgow Observer*, unashamedly pro-Celtic as it was the newspaper for the Catholic community in Scotland, uses the Irish war cry 'Faugh a Ballagh' (Clear the Way) to describe the Celtic forward line, and compares them to the way the Irish Brigade defeated the serried ranks of the Saxons in the Battle of Fontenoy in 1745 in the War of the Austrian Succession!

McMahon and company were presumably flattered by such a comparison, even though it might just have been above the heads of many of the supporters and readers of the *Glasgow Observer*. But this did not in any way stop the parties that proliferated throughout the east end of Glasgow that night, even in the rain, described in one report as 'Biblical'.

The team had now pulled itself round. Season 1894/95 had not been a good season, with internal strife, injuries to key players and resultant poor performances on the field. But now with key man McMahon back on form, there had been a total reversal of roles. Two trophies, the Glasgow Cup and the Scottish League had been won, and the year had not even turned yet! It was the third time that Celtic had won the Scottish League – Dumbarton and Hearts had won it once each outright and in 1891 it had been shared – and it was a great feeling to be the champions of Scotland. Now in the new year, the Scottish Cup approached and not only that, but the Scotland v England international match was scheduled for Celtic Park. The club which had been in existence for considerably less than a decade had done well – huge ground, success in competitions and a tremendous support which seemed to follow them everywhere, and in all weathers. This was what it meant to be Celtic in 1895!

FOUR

SAVING THE SEASON

Celtic 2 Rangers 0   **Scottish Cup Final**
Old Hampden Park   **22 April 1899**

Celtic: McArthur, Welford and Storrier; Battles, Marshall and King; Hodge, Campbell, Divers, McMahon and Bell

Rangers: Dickie, N. Smith and Crawford; Gibson, Neill and Mitchell; Campbell, McPherson, Hamilton, Miller and A. Smith

Referee: Mr T. Robertson, Queen's Park

THERE seems to be little point in denying that in 1899 Rangers had a splendid team. The facts speak for themselves. They won the Scottish League with a 100 per cent record, the only team ever to have done that. Granted, the Scottish League was a lot smaller with only ten teams and 18 games, but nevertheless it was a considerable achievement. Celtic lost to them 0-4 and 1-4 and were also removed from the Glasgow Cup by the men from Ibrox. Celtic this time were clearly playing second fiddle.

Yet it was not entirely true that Celtic were having a bad season. Willie Maley had been in his job as secretary/manager for two years now and had worked tirelessly to build up a team that could challenge the men from the west of Glasgow. His major coup had been the bringing back of Barney Battles to Celtic, and this had made a huge difference to the side and the support who had been visibly energised by his reappearance. He had been 'exiled' following his part in the strike of 1896, but, now repentant and determined, he was playing his part in the fight back. Centre-forward John Divers had also been one of the rebels, but he too had made his peace with the club.

And, of course, up front Celtic had someone special in Sandy McMahon. He was a great goalscorer, but he was also a fine player. Now playing in the inside-left position with his old friend Johnny Campbell at inside-right, the forward line was beginning to click. The path to the Scottish Cup Final had featured a game against

Queen's Park at Celtic Park in late February, and McMahon had scored the two goals in the 2-1 victory. This had actually been a replay of sorts, because the first game had been stopped by 'bad light', something more common in cricket than in football! Full-backs James Welford and Davie Storrier would have been familiar with that, for they were both cricketers, Welford a professional with Warwickshire and Storrier an amateur with Arbroath and Forfarshire.

The Scottish Cup was the important competition in Victorian football. Celtic were uncomfortably aware that since their triumph in 1892 they had not won the trophy. In that time they had won the Scottish League four times, but in the Scottish Cup they had lost (painfully) in the finals of 1893 and 1894, and no one mentioned 1897 without a shiver running up their spine. That was the year in which Celtic had managed to lose to Arthurlie.

Celtic had two English Cup winners in their team. Full-back James Welford had won it with Aston Villa in 1895 and Johnny Campbell with the same club in 1897, but they did not have many Scottish Cup winners – only McMahon and Campbell having survived since 1892. Rangers, on the other hand, had won the Scottish Cup for the last two seasons and were determined to do 'three in a row' to equal the achievements set by Queen's Park and Vale of Leven in the 1870s.

Celtic reached the final when they disposed of Port Glasgow Athletic on 18 March, and then they had a fair wait until 15 April to find out who their opponents would be. Rangers duly beat St Mirren in their semi-final, and thus the Scottish Cup Final was set for April 22 at Hampden Park. Concern was expressed about the suitability of Hampden as a venue for this fixture. Hampden Park, as we know it, had not yet been built and this ground was the one that became known as Cathkin, the home of Third Lanark in later years. The problem was that it was simply not big enough, and warnings were issued about getting there early.

Glasgow talked about little else than the Scottish Cup Final in the week leading up to it. Most people thought that Rangers would win simply through their all-round strength and the fact that they had certainly had the upper hand over Celtic this year.

On the other hand, Celtic could play with a great deal of flair, and had improved immensely since their mediocre start. *The Scottish Referee* refuse to predict a winner, but says that it looks like being one of the best finals since the Scottish Cup began in 1874.

The weather was lovely. It was a beautiful spring day, not too warm and with only a hint of a breeze – just perfect for playing football, in fact. The game was due to kick off at 4pm but at 3.30pm the SFA took the decision to close the gates, for already the ground was packed. This decision caused no little anger outside the ground. Some of the disappointed went home, but more stayed outside to follow the game by listening to the roar of the crowd and hoping perhaps to be able to jump the wall when the policemen weren't looking! The admission price was one shilling, when the usual admission to a football match in 1899 was about half of that, and sometimes less. Many of those waiting outside simply did not have the money to get in, and those of the middle classes arriving in their horse-drawn taxis were warned to beware of pickpockets.

The game started a few minutes early (all the crowd were in, so why not?) and the first half was very even, with neither side able to gain any significant advantage over the other. It was a game, however, where some of the tackling was a little fierce and several players on each side were spoken to by referee Mr Robertson. The worst culprits were Nick Smith, the fair-haired right-back of Rangers, and Barney Battles of Celtic, whose methods were always on the robust side.

Things took a distinct turn for the worse when, early in the second half, Smith once again fouled Jack Bell, Celtic's left-winger. Smith was lucky not to suffer the 'long, lonely walk' to the pavilion for that one, but it meant that Bell was now virtually a passenger. He would, however, still play a part in this game.

Gradually, Celtic, now with the slight breeze behind them, gained the upper hand and forced many corners as Campbell and McMahon began to take control of the situation. It was from one of these corners that John Hodge sent over a high ball which at first glance looked too high for everyone, but not for Sandy McMAHON. Timing his jump perfectly, 'the Duke' (as he was called) rose like a bird to connect, and the green-and-white verticals were one up, amidst 'great cheering and waving of rattles'.

From then on, Celtic never looked back. The team had spent the few days before the match training at Loch Katrine, and a great bond of togetherness had been formed, and this now showed on the park. Full-backs Welford and Storrier made sure that goalkeeper McArthur was never troubled, while the half-back line of Battles, Marshall and King dominated proceedings to such an extent that many of the crowd, including some Rangers supporters, wondered why Rangers had been unbeaten in the league.

But with Celtic, there was also an element of good tactical nous. McMahon, having scored the goal, now dropped back, knowing that in so doing he would take at least one disorientated Rangers player with him, and all the while encouraging some of the other defenders to go forward and try their luck against the now tiring Rangers defence.

It was then that the injured Jack Bell played his part. The game had virtually passed Jack by, but suddenly the ball came to him, having spun off a Rangers defender. Jack managed to keep the ball in play, and then with his one serviceable foot, punted the ball in the general direction of the Rangers goal. By chance, it came to the unmarked John HODGE, who gathered the ball, ran on and scored, as the Rangers defence appealed unconvincingly for offside.

Once again, the Celtic section of the crowd went mad with delight while some of the Rangers sympathisers departed. When the exit gates were opened for them, hundreds of supporters who had been trapped outside rushed in and were able to see the last few minutes of this now rather mundane cup final. Full time came, and sporting handshakes were exchanged between the two sets of players and the directors. Celtic had won the Scottish Cup for the second time.

The Scottish Cup in those days was not presented to the winning captain after the game, but to the winning chairman at a post-match banquet – something that one would imagine to be an excruciatingly painful experience for the players on the losing side. However, not for Celtic's chairman, the mighty

John H McLaughlin who at the Bath Street Hotel that night graciously accepted the Scottish Cup from the SFA chairman, Mr McCulloch of Dundee, and then went on to declare that sectarianism in Scottish football was a 'dead letter' and that Celtic would continue to sign anyone 'regardless of sect'. He then went on to talk of the pleasant and happy relationship between the two clubs, and hoped that it would continue.

FIVE

CORONATION QUINN

Celtic 3 Rangers 2 aet   **British League Cup Final**
First Cathkin Park   **17 June 1902**

Celtic: McPherson, Davidson and Battles; Loney, Marshall and Orr; Crawford, Campbell, Quinn, McDermott and Hamilton

Rangers: Dickie, N. Smith and Crawford; Gibson, Stark and Robertson; Lennie, Walker, Hamilton, Speedie and A. Smith

Referee: Mr J. Hay, Greenock

THE year 1902 was an unusual and eventful year in the history and politics of Great Britain, and indeed of Scottish football. The major disaster, of course, in Scottish football was what happened at Ibrox on 5 April when 26 people lost their lives when a stand collapsed during the Scotland v England game. It was also the year when the mild-mannered, gentlemanly, almost saintly, Sandy McMahon was outrageously sent off by a drunk referee at Celtic Park on New Year's Day in the game when Rangers won the Scottish League, and it was also the year in which Hibs won the Scottish Cup, beating Celtic 1-0. It would take them another 114 years before they could do it again!

But things were happening on the broader world stage as well. The Boer War came to an end. There were those who saw it as a great example of Imperialist derring-do, and others who saw it as a piece of Imperialist bullying leading to all kinds of unnecessary slaughter.

We are mildly surprised to read that Celtic FC tended to support this war, hoping presumably that the grateful British Empire would then grant Home Rule for Ireland, but progressive opinion like Lloyd George and Ramsay MacDonald were against this silly South African adventure. We are also perturbed to read about the large amount of young Glasgow men who tried to enlist in the Army to go to South Africa only to be turned down because they were not fit or healthy enough, such was the malnutrition in the slums, where even medieval manifestations like the bubonic plague were not unknown!

1902 was also the Coronation. King Edward VII was due to be crowned on 26 June. Flags were flying everywhere since early in the year, as distinct from 1901 where everything tended to be black in view of the death of Queen Victoria. Her son, Bertie, a dissolute roue, who smoked, drank, ate to excess and womanised endlessly, was also a man determined to do things to bring about world peace. Edward VII, in some ways far more human and likeable than his stuffy, moody mother, did however have some fairly severe and, to a very large extent, self-inflicted health problems.

All these factors played a part in this rather remarkable football match on 17 June. What do we call this tournament? Some call it the Glasgow Exhibition Cup, some call it the British League Cup, others call it the Ibrox Disaster Cup and others call it the Coronation Cup. Each one of these contenders has a case. It was a strange competition, but no less keenly contested and indeed recalled with enthusiastic reminiscence by all who saw it.

There had been a Glasgow Exhibition in 1901. A football tournament was held as part of this event, and Rangers won it. Immediately after the Ibrox Disaster, Rangers put the trophy up for the purpose of raising funds, and invited the top two teams of Scotland and England to take part, namely Rangers, Celtic, Sunderland and Everton.

Celtic may have finished up second in the league to Rangers and runners-up in the Scottish Cup, but that was considered a poor season. Their attempt to win the Scottish Cup had received a great boost when they heard that the Scottish Cup Final was to be played at Parkhead. Ibrox was clearly out of action after the disaster on 5 April, and there was no other place big enough. Hibs moaned a little about that, but it was they who duly won the Cup thanks to an Andy McGeachan back-heeler over a very poor Celtic side in an awful game.

This one-off tournament, however, would give Celtic a chance to win something this year. The semi-final saw Sunderland at Celtic Park on the Wednesday after the Scottish Cup final. Only 4,000 turned up to see the English League winners, a reflection on how disgusted Celtic fans were by their team's Saturday performance, but those who were there saw a tremendous Celtic display. They won 5-1 and Johnny Campbell scored four of them and the other was scored by Harry 'Beef' Marshall. Campbell had been out of the team on Saturday, and his return made all the difference as the English League winners (full of Scotsmen, including Scotland international goalkeeper Ned Doig) were simply swept aside.

In the other semi-final, Rangers beat Everton, but then there was a huge gap until the final. Some of the delay can be put down to the enlarged Glasgow Charity Cup, which this year contained the Edinburgh teams to help raise funds for the Ibrox Disaster fund, but it is difficult to explain why the final of the British League Cup was not played until 17 June. Possibly the idea was for it to be as near to the Coronation as possible, but in any case the final was set for Cathkin Park, Govanhill (not the later Cathkin Park on which Third Lanark played). The final, played on a beautiful summer evening, drew a crowd of about 10,000 – a large crowd for 1902, considering that it was out of season. They saw a remarkable game.

Celtic's now ageing talisman Sandy McMahon was out with his chronic knee problem, and Maley decided to play young Jimmy Quinn in the centre. The youngster from Croy was a strange youth. He had been with the club for a couple of years now and had played mainly on the left wing with only sporadic success. Yet Maley felt that he had something, even though some of the directors made it clear that they would not be averse to selling him. He was reserved, shy and socially gauche – not necessarily great attributes for a footballer, but tonight he was given the role of centre-forward for the green-and-white vertical stripes. This would also allow Celtic to play another promising youngster called David Hamilton on the left wing.

Celtic started off well, and with Johnny Campbell dictating things in the centre of the field, they hemmed Rangers back. In seven minutes, 'after a prolonged siege' (as Willie Maley put it), the ball rebounded to young QUINN who hammered the ball into the Rangers net. After another ten minutes of Celtic dominance,

QUINN scored again, this time after a rebound from the bar. Loud was the cheering and the noise of the rattles of the Celtic supporters after this, but there was still a long time to go on this warm midsummer night.

In fact, the young Celts had not paced themselves very well in the heat (which was, of course, totally foreign to the conditions they normally played in) and the more experienced Rangers came back into the game. They were, after all, the league champions for the past four years, and by half-time they were level with goals scored by Bob Hamilton and Finlay Speedie. Celtic must have felt a little depressed by this as they sucked their half-time oranges, but they also knew that this game could be won.

The sun was slowly setting and it became more of a problem for the players in the second half. No goals were scored but Celtic had real hard luck in the last minute when Dickie kicked away a drive from Harry Marshall that looked goal bound. The referee blew for full time, and it seemed to be a draw. Many of the newspaper reporters finished their report and gave them to the boy cyclists to take the report to the office (there were no telegraphic facilities at Cathkin in 1902) and some of the crowd went home. But then after a brief delay the players came out again to play ten minutes each way to see if they could get a winner. It seems to have been a decision taken there and then and agreed to by both clubs. This was too late for the press, and many newspapers appeared on the streets the following morning to say that the game was a 2-2 draw. Maley himself in his reminiscences gets confused, for he seems to think there was a replay. There wasn't. Extra time was played and with it came an immortal moment in Celtic's early history.

The first period brought no goals, and time was running out in the second half. Even the light was now beginning to fade when right-winger Andy Crawford picked up a ball from Willie Loney, made space down the right, and sent over a ball which looked too high for Tommy McDermott. But then Tommy heard a cry of 'Stey whaur ye are, Tommy!' and up popped Jimmy Quinn to use McDermott's shoulders to get up high and head the ball gloriously into the net. It was an unusual, although perfectly legal, way of scoring a goal. Some of these details may owe a little to romantic exaggeration in the memories of some players and spectators, but QUINN it was who scored what turned out to be the winning goal of the Glasgow Exhibition Cup, the British League Cup or the Coronation Cup, call it what you will. The point was that Celtic had won the trophy and a star was born!

You may call it the Coronation Cup, but if you do, please call it Coronation Cup number one. There was, of course, another in 1953. And in any case, there was no Coronation a week later in 1902. King Edward took ill and had to have his appendix removed – a dangerous operation in 1902 – and the Coronation was postponed until August. As Celtic had not won any Scottish trophy since 1900, this trophy was much prized and talked about.

'Some say that Rangers are stars at fitba',
That Lennie and Dickie and Speedie are bra',
But Jimmy Quinn, he diddled them a'
At the Glasgow Exhibition o!'

SIX

QUINN, QUINN AND NOTHING BUT QUINN

Celtic 3 Rangers 2	**Scottish Cup Final**
New Hampden Park	**16 April 1904**

Celtic: Adams, McLeod and Orr; Young, Loney and Hay; Muir, McMenemy, Quinn, Somers and Hamilton

Rangers: Watson, N. Smith and Drummond; Henderson, Stark and Robertson; Walker, Speedie, Mackie, Donnachie and A. Smith

Referee: Mr T. Robertson, Queen's Park

WILLIE Maley was in a quandary. In front of him was his centre-forward Alec Bennett, more or less in tears and very upset. Alec was being pestered by family and friends because he played for Celtic, and they all wanted him to play for Rangers. Indeed, Rangers had made an offer to him for next season. Bennett, normally a very level-headed young man, was not coping with this. His particular fear was that, as centre-forward, he would get loads of chances to score in the coming Scottish Cup Final. If he scored, his family would not be pleased; if he fluffed them, he would be accused of all sorts of things by the Celtic fans.

Maley decided reluctantly that Bennett was in no fit emotional condition to play, and that the centre-forward position would go to the sometimes erratic but nevertheless determined character called Jimmy Quinn. Quinn, the miner boy from Croy, had once before scored a hat-trick for Celtic against Rangers, two years ago in that funny Coronation Cup tournament played in midsummer and now ridiculed by some. It would be nice, mused Maley, if he could do the same again, and this time in a real competition.

Maley had been quite happy with the improvement in the team this year. There could be no doubt that Third Lanark deserved the Scottish League and the Glasgow Cup this year, but it was rewarding to beat them in the Scottish Cup semi-final. The Celtic team was still young, but there were undeniably some fine tricky players – McMenemy and Somers, for example, were great inside men, and that half-back line of Young, Loney and Hay could take a grip of games. But what he liked about them was their enthusiasm and their ability to play together. He felt they had a great future ahead of them.

But this year's cup final was against Rangers. Possibly Rangers' moment had passed. Their four league titles in a row from 1899 to 1902 had been impressive, and they had won the Scottish Cup last year, but this year they had not been so good. But they were still Rangers, a team with a massive support and a good manager in William Wilton, a close friend of Maley. It looked like an even contest for this year's Scottish Cup at New Hampden.

Celtic had had the honour of opening the stadium this year at the end of October. It was massive, and although it was not yet totally ready (the eastern end in particular still needed some work) it was already bigger than Celtic Park and there were intentions to make it able to contain a mind-boggling 100,000 spectators. As it happened, 65,000 turned up to see this Scottish Cup Final, and that was considered to be a huge crowd – not quite a world record, currently held by the Crystal Palace in London, but still a massive amount of people, and quite clearly a record for a Scottish domestic game that was not an international. Both sets of supporters were there in good voice, but mingling happily together with loads of banter. The hatred between Celtic and Rangers supporters had not yet developed, although the seeds had been planted.

The weather was fine, and the crowd would see a memorable and indeed famous contest. Celtic lost the toss and thus Quinn started the game for Celtic, playing towards the western terrace against the slight, almost negligible breeze. Celtic had a bright first ten minutes, with Peter Somers in particular looking good, but then things began to go wrong.

Rangers scored. The hero was Alex 'Cutty' Smith who ran down the left wing and crossed for the head of Finlay Speedie, who was visibly vexed with himself as he headed straight into the hands of goalkeeper Davie Adams. It was Adams's first touch of the ball, but riddled with nerves he dropped the ball and the ball squirmed over the line into the net. Rangers were one up.

This was bad enough, but a few minutes after this it was two. A corner from Alex Smith missed everyone except Finlay Speedie, curiously unmarked, and he scored again with many Celtic supporters feeling once again that Davie Adams could have done better. The final had thus started disastrously and Rangers were feeling good about themselves. They had won the cup last year after two replays against Hearts. Maybe they were going to do the job at the first attempt this time.

But this was the day of the mighty Quinn. His first goal brought Celtic back into the game, and it was a goal which according to the writer of the *Dundee Courier* was worth 'any football enthusiast travelling any amount of miles to see'. It involved three players running together in a parallel line to get a long ball, which had gone over the heads of everyone – Stark and Nick Smith of Rangers and Quinn of Celtic. It was like a sprint, but it was QUINN who got there first to edge the ball past goalkeeper Watson.

Now the wearers of the green-and-white rosettes, who had been silent for a while, became more animated. Their team was still behind but now back in the game. There was still a long time to go. And then just before half-time Celtic were back on level terms. This time, part of the credit goes to right-winger Bobby Muir, a Kilmarnock boy who had joined Celtic from Bristol Rovers at the same time as his fellow townsman Sunny Jim Young last year. Muir had been good enough this season, but not outstanding. Today, however, he did enough to earn a place in Celtic immortality when he picked up a ball just inside the Rangers half on the far side of the pitch from the stand and charged towards the corner flag, beating Drummond and Robertson on the way. He then crossed perfectly and Jimmy QUINN was there to hammer the ball past Watson.

Half-time came soon after that, and Celtic trotted off quite satisfied. They had convinced themselves that they were a faster, fitter and generally a better team than Rangers were, and their supporters shared that opinion. Rangers for their part felt robbed.

They had been ahead but had thrown their lead away. The interval was a long one to allow men with white sheets to collect coins thrown at them for the relatives of those who had been injured in the collapse of a stand at the Perthshire v Forfarshire cricket match last summer. No one had been killed, but several were so badly injured that they could not work – and that, in these evil pre-Welfare State days, could mean the Poor House for relatives!

The game resumed and the huge crowd enjoyed some fine play by both sides, although it was now clear that Celtic were playing the better football. Muir had a good chance but was bundled off the ball by Drummond, and the same player used his hand to stop a Quinn drive getting past him. These offences would have been dealt with a great deal more harshly 100 years later, but this was 1904.

About 15 minutes from time came the winner. Willie Orr won a ball from Nick Smith, and passed to James Hay. Hay lofted the ball forward to QUINN, who flicked the ball past Stark and charged in on goal. Converging on him were the two Rangers full-backs, Smith and Drummond, but Jimmy kept his nerve even when goalkeeper Watson came out of his goal as well. Just as the two full-backs were about to collide with him, he released the ball, having the maturity not to blast the ball, but to lob it gently over the advancing Watson and into the net!

This was football at its best, and Jimmy Quinn became the hero of all Celtic fans that day – a status which he held until his death in 1945, and well beyond. Celtic had now won the Scottish Cup for the fourth time, and once again the Celtic heartlands of the Gorbals, the Garngad, Holytown, Leith in Edinburgh and Lochee in Dundee celebrated all night. And that was not to mention Jimmy Quinn's own Croy! Jimmy, painfully shy, may well have found this embarrassing, but he would also have permitted himself a small smile. He was certainly the hero of the hour.

The significance of this game would be long-lasting. It was the springboard for Celtic's six league titles in a row and in that respect was not dissimilar to McNeill's goal against Dunfermline in the Scottish Cup Final of 1965. It is also worth considering the long-term effect it had on Rangers. They would not win the Scottish

League again until 1911, nor the Scottish Cup until 1928. Their inferiority complex was just about to begin.

But the main significance was in Jimmy Quinn himself. The hero of Celtic, and the hero of Scotland on many occasions as well, Jimmy was now commonly referred to in newspaper reports as 'Jimmie', 'Jamie,' 'Jeemie', 'Jamie the Silent' or 'the bhoy from Croy', and everyone knew who he was. People would get off the train at Croy and wait there for the next one just on the off chance of seeing him, and there was the well-documented story of two youngsters who stole a couple of pebbles from his garden – and boasted about it! For Celtic, he was the replacement for Sandy McMahon, and the second in the line of personality goalscorers that the Celtic support always craved and still does. Everyone in Scotland knew who Jimmy Quinn was.

SEVEN

THE PLAY-OFF

Celtic 2 Rangers 1   **Scottish League Play-Off**
Hampden Park   **6 May 1905**

Celtic: Adams, Watson and Orr; McNair, Loney and Hay; Bennett, McMenemy, Quinn, Somers and Hamilton

Rangers: Sinclair, Fraser and Craig; Gourlay, Stark and May; Robertson, Speedie, McColl, Donnachie and Smith

Referee: Mr F. Kirkham, Preston

THE Scottish League did not, in its early years of existence, seem to have any policy of what to do if two teams finished equal on points in any given year. In 1891, the first year of the competition's existence, the two teams who finished top, Rangers and Dumbarton, were both declared joint winners after a play-off, which ended 2-2. Between 1891 and 1905, all winners were clear-cut on points, but 1905 saw a tie between Celtic and Rangers. Had either goal difference or goal average been in vogue in 1905, Rangers would have won the title because their goals were 83-28, as distinct from Celtic's 68-31.

But this year, after some deliberation (one got the impression that, in the early years, the Scottish League more or less made it all up as they went along!), the Scottish League decided on a play-off. It so happened that a slot was available, for Celtic and Rangers were due to play each other in the Glasgow League (a little-valued competition, sometimes called contemptuously 'the supplementary' and which was not fated to last very long) on Saturday, 6 May 1905. With the agreement of the Glasgow authorities, the game was moved to New Hampden and was billed as a league decider as well. What is not clear is what would have happened if the game had been a draw. Presumably, on the precedent of 1891 they would have been declared joint champions.

The Scottish League in 1905 was still not considered anything like as important as the Scottish Cup. This was seen in the way that Scottish Cup fixtures were always given precedence. Celtic had finished their Scottish League campaign on 4 March with a 6-2 win over Motherwell, whereas for Rangers it was as late as 29 April before they beat Morton 2-0 to finish off their league campaign. The reason for this was the Scottish Cup. After a very contentious semi-final at Celtic Park, in which Jimmy Quinn had been sent off and which had had to be abandoned because of crowd trouble, Rangers had lost the Scottish Cup Final to Third Lanark after a replay, both of them held on Saturdays. There had also been the Scotland v England international on a Saturday, and generally speaking the Scottish League was at the bottom of the queue.

The main item in the build-up to this game had been the fall-out from the semi-final of the Scottish Cup on 25 March at Celtic Park. The sending-off of Jimmy Quinn had been disputed by Celtic, but there could be no excuse for the behaviour of some of their young fans, who had rioted and prevented the game from being finished. Celtic had conceded the tie (Rangers were 2-0 up and would probably have won in any case), and this perhaps took the sting out of things, but they also took up the cause of Quinn and were supported by a letter from Rangers' Alec Craig who confirmed that Quinn did not kick him, merely tried to shake Craig off when Craig had held on to him to prevent falling on the wet and slippery ground. This letter from the honest and gentlemanly Craig cut little ice, and Quinn was suspended for a month.

But fortunately his suspension had been served before 6 May and he was available for the league decider. Of course, it was Quinn who had scored a hat-trick in the Scottish Cup Final the previous year in 1904. The Scottish League was sufficiently worried about trouble to appoint an Englishman, Mr Fred Kirkham of Preston, generally regarded as being the best in the world, to be the referee and they also appointed two neutral linesmen in Mr McGill of Thornliebank and Mr Jeff of Govan, an unusual and expensive step in 1905.

The crowd was a rather disappointing 30,000 on a fine sunny day, but there were several reasons for this. One was the fear of hooliganism after the events of 25 March in the Scottish Cup semi-final, another was the disillusion of the Rangers support who were disappointed at their team's performance in the Scottish Cup Final against Third Lanark, yet another was that the Celtic support, whose team had played their last league game about two months ago, had lost interest, but the main thing was that this play-off was seen by many people as yet another attempt to get more money out of them. This argument seemed particularly valid on a nice summer afternoon when there were so many other things to do which did not cost money.

The month of May was generally believed in 1905 to be the month when football should stop. Granted, there was the Glasgow Charity Cup played that month, but that was indeed for charity and worthy causes, and players were meant (theoretically at least) to play for free, and the tournament had a light-hearted atmosphere about it. But this was the Scottish League, taking over and hijacking a meaningless Glasgow League fixture which would otherwise have been played by the reserves of both sides.

Celtic were without Sunny Jim Young at right-half (he had injured himself in a Glasgow League match on the Monday before) and Alec McNair played there. The great thing about 'Eck' was that he was at home almost anywhere, and he would never let the club down. Willie Orr at left-back was the only player on the Celtic side who had been around in 1898, the last time that Celtic had won a Scottish League championship, whereas Rangers had several players who had won medals from 1899 to 1902. But Celtic were a young side, and many reports testify to their fitness and eagerness.

The Scottish Referee tells us that Celtic kicked off with the breeze on their backs, but by half-time no goals had been scored, although the closest chance came when Jimmy Quinn embarked on a 'dodgy' (that word meant something a great deal different in 1905 than it does today!) run down the left wing before crossing for Alec Bennett, but Bennett could not quite reach the ball and the chance went a-begging. Several times Celtic were called for offside, to the wrath of the supporters, but the half finished with Rangers on the attack and Donnachie trying to shoulder charge

Davie Adams into the back of the net. But Adams, now having regained his confidence after his horror Scottish Cup Final of the previous year, was a big strong boy and Donnachie bounced off him!

The wind had intensified in the second half and Celtic found themselves facing quite a stiff breeze. This was where the brain and composure of men like Alec McNair and Jimmy McMenemy came to the fore. Concentration on short balls was the order of the day, and their patience would eventually pay great dividends. Rangers, on the other hand, were now prepared to shoot from a distance and several efforts went over the bar.

But then it all happened for Celtic in a couple of minutes around about the halfway point of the second half when a shot from Davie Hamilton, which may have been going past the post, was blocked by left-half May and the ball bounced out to Jimmy McMENEMY, who had one of his easiest of tasks to prod the ball home from about two yards. Scarcely had the cheering died down from that goal when Celtic scored again, and this time it was a shot from Davie HAMILTON which seemed to dip and deceive Tommy Sinclair in the Rangers goal.

The Celtic supporters were now 'dancing on the cinders' of the Hampden terracing, as their team were well on top. They remained so until, with about five minutes to go, Robertson tried a snap shot which beat Davie Adams. Thereupon Rangers piled in the pressure, but Celtic's half-back line of McNair, Loney and Hay resisted it all, and their stranglehold of the game meant that full time came with the score 2-1, and Celtic had won their fifth league championship to join those of 1893, 1894, 1896 and 1898.

This Celtic team was not yet the finished article, but it soon would be. It is interesting to speculate just what would have happened if Rangers had won this game, or if the Scottish League had been decided on goal average or goal difference. Celtic would never have won their six titles in a row, the thing which marked them out as being a special team.

So much of this success goes down to manager Willie Maley who had painstakingly built this team. Appointed as secretary/manager in 1897, he realised in about 1900 that a major influx of talent was required and spared no effort in scouring the British Isles for talent. Last year he had won the Scottish Cup, and Maley was wise enough to realise that, although the Scottish Cup carried more prestige, the Scottish League really proved who the best team in Scotland was. Between now and 1910, there would be no doubt who this was.

EIGHT

QUINN COMES BACK
TO HAUNT THEM

Rangers 0 Celtic 3	**Scottish Cup Quarter-Final**
Ibrox Stadium	**9 March 1907**

Rangers: Newbigging, Campbell and Hendry; Gray, Stark and May; Dickie, Livingstone, Kyle, Spiers and Smith

Celtic: Adams, McLeod and Orr; Young, McNair and Hay; Bennett, McMenemy, Quinn, Somers and Hamilton

Referee: Mr J. Lewis, Blackburn

THERE could be little doubt about who was the most talked-about man in Scotland in early 1907. Indeed, he had been much talked about before 1907 as well. It was none other than Jimmy Quinn, the quiet, almost introverted 'bhoy from Croy', who was Scotland's most famous goalscorer. The 'Quinn case' of January 1907 had divided opinion almost as much as the Dreyfus case in France had done. Quinn had been suspended by the SFA for two months after an incident at Ibrox on New Year's Day.

Basically the case was brought after Quinn had been sent off by referee Mr Kirkham of Burslem, it being the habit to appoint referees from England for this fixture. The referee's version was that Quinn had kicked Joe Hendry in the face when Hendry was lying on the ground. Quinn's version was that he ran over to remonstrate with Hendry after the latter had fouled a Celtic colleague (some say Bennett, others McMenemy) and skidded on the wet ground while trying to avoid contact. Hendry was taken off with blood running from his face, and Quinn was then sent off for 'violent conduct'. The SFA accepted the referee's version and Quinn was suspended for two months.

This decision did not meet with any favour whatsoever in the Celtic community, and it did seem draconian especially as there was some doubt about Quinn's intention. It was probably from here that the perception that the SFA was implacably anti-Celtic originated. This belief has proved difficult to eradicate in some minds over the past 110 years! Quinn, however, now became even more of a legend and hero, with concerts being held to raise funds for him and to compensate him for lost earnings.

And then, irony of ironies, the first game that Quinn would be allowed to play in was, of all things, a Scottish Cup tie against Rangers at Ibrox on Saturday, 9 March 1907. The draw could not have been more controversial in its outcome. It was as if fate was going to give Quinn another chance when the SFA wouldn't.

There were other issues as well, notably whether Celtic could become the first team to do the 'double' and win the Scottish League and the Scottish Cup in the same season. In spite of being without 'Jimmie', 'Jeemie' or 'Jamie' (everyone knew who you meant!) the team had made progress towards the Scottish League, although in the Scottish Cup they clearly missed Quinn and took an unconscionable time to get the better of Morton until another two Jimmies, McMenemy and Hay, did the job at the third attempt. But the mighty man would return for Ibrox.

The crowd at Ibrox was given as 65,000 – it was probably a lot more than that – and that was no surprise, for the game had caught the attention of the Scottish public almost as much as the annual 'international' (between Scotland and England) usually did, and much was the talk in Glasgow of what Quinn was going to do to Rangers to get his revenge.

Quinn was probably embarrassed by all this. Although the Celtic support and indeed most of the Scottish footballing public endowed Jimmy with some sort of supernatural power, Jimmy himself knew that he was simply a miner boy who got on the train from Croy every morning with a suitcase containing his football boots, wearing a gaberdine overcoat and a bonnet. He travelled to Glasgow for training at Parkhead, and then back home again in the afternoon. The fact that he could score goals did not alter that. Yet, nevertheless, he was burning with desire to get back at Rangers for what he saw as their part in getting him suspended. In 1905, in a similar situation, a letter from Rangers' Alec Craig, a decent man, had attempted to exonerate Quinn to a certain extent; no such letter had been sent by Joe Hendry.

But Quinn also knew the best way to get his revenge. So, too, did Willie Maley. At a pre-game meeting, a plan was formulated. Rangers, in fact, were afraid of Jimmy Quinn. They had vivid and painful memories of the Glasgow Exhibition Cup Final of 1902 and the Scottish Cup Final of 1904. They would therefore mark him closely. (In the event, three defenders shadowed him constantly.) Quinn was therefore encouraged to run about in every direction, while all the time ignoring provocation which would definitely be offered. In this way he could pull the Rangers defence all over the place and allow loads of space and opportunities for the other attackers to do the business.

The plan could not have worked better. Ibrox, much changed and renovated since the disaster of 1902, presented an astonishing sight. It had never housed such a crowd (international matches had been given to Celtic Park and Hampden since 1902) and green and blue rosettes were seen in the crowd, but everyone in good humour and prepared to stand beside each other. No doubt there was banter between the two sets of supporters about Jimmy Quinn and other players, and maybe the odd remark about 'Irishmen' and religion (even the newspapers referred to Celtic as 'the Irishmen' although every single one of them was now Scottish!), but the sectarian edge, which would become so prevalent in the 1920s, was not yet there.

The weather was cold and snow threatened. Prices had been raised for the game, particularly for the Main Stand, but that did not seem to deter the supporters who had gathered outside the ground since the morning. The suspension of the Boys Gate was explained away as an attempt to dissuade youngsters from attending, on the grounds of their personal safety, but that fooled no one. It was all about making more money! By 3pm Ibrox was well filled for the 4pm kick-off and the players came out to find a 'cheering, shouting, singing crowd' awaiting them. A considerable portion of the crowd had got in for nothing, when an exit gate had been burst open 'either by accident or design', and mounted police had to be deployed to prevent chaos and injuries.

Other than long-term absentee Willie Loney, Celtic had no injury problems, and Rangers were at full strength. The referee was another Englishman, a Mr Lewis from Blackburn, and it would be generally agreed that 'his control was impeccable'.

The greatest cheer from the green-and-white sympathisers came whenever Jimmy Quinn touched the ball even in the pre-match warm-up. But when the game started, we had the extraordinary spectacle of three defenders marking Quinn, who wandered aimlessly up and down the field with his three shadows, one of them always being Joe Hendry. Taking advantage of one of the holes in the Rangers defence, Peter SOMERS, 'the powder monkey' (a reference to the small boy on board ship who stuffed the ammunition down the inside of the cannon) popped up to score in the first few minutes after good work from McMenemy.

It was soon after that that Quinn was put to the test. *The Dundee Courier* talks blandly about a 'regrettable accident' but then talks unconvincingly about Hendry 'getting his uplifted foot into Quinn's stomach in the act of clearing'. Celtic supporters saw it differently. For all the world, it looked to them like Hendry deliberately 'back-heeled' Quinn in the abdominal area, let us say. This was Quinn's acid test. He might have retaliated and earned an even more severe suspension than the one he had just returned from. Instead, Jimmy just walked away, earning the plaudits from the press for doing so. And how nice it was to see that the dirty tactics of the Rangers did not succeed!

Celtic now simply took command. The injury to Quinn had impaired his mobility but Rangers still thought that he had to be marked heavily, and thus Celtic dominated. Sunny Jim Young had a great game, as did 'Napoleon' McMenemy, and before half-time Celtic were two up. After a bombardment of the Rangers goal, the ball broke to the intelligent Jimmy HAY. Instead of simply lashing the ball back into the goalmouth, the intelligent 'Dun', noticing that goalkeeper Newbigging was off his line, simply 'lobbed a drooper' into the net.

Half-time was spent with the Celtic supporters in the crowd in uproar, and halfway through the second half they scored another, this time a fine well-timed bullet header by Davie HAMILTON off an Alec Bennett cross. Jimmy Quinn himself also scored but the goal was chalked off, but in truth the 3-0 scoreline was a very satisfactory one for Celtic, who had now clearly proved that they were the best team in Scotland.

The only threat to the game came from snow which fell fairly heavily from about the 70th minute. Some of the crowd departed, the Rangers ones wanting the game to be abandoned. But the game continued until the end, and Celtic now found themselves in the draw for the semi-final alongside Hibs, Hearts and Queen's Park. With Quinn now available and Rangers defeated, what was to stop them?

NINE

HAPPY BIRTHDAY, MR MALEY!

Rangers 0 Celtic 1	**Scottish League First Division**
Ibrox Stadium	**25 April 1908**

Rangers: Newbigging, Law and Sharp; May, Taylor and Galt; Noble, McDonald, Campbell, Livingstone and Smith

Celtic: Adams, McNair and Weir; Young, Loney and Hay; Bennett, McMenemy, Quinn, Somers and Hamilton

Referee: Mr J.A. Faichnie, Falkirk

WILLIE Maley was 40 on 25 April 1908. He had been born in Newry, Ireland, on this date in 1868, the son of a soldier. He had had an eventful 40 years, especially since that day in 1888 when two Celtic committee men had called to invite his brother Tom to join the new club and one of them had said, more or less as an afterthought, to Willie, 'Why don't you come along too?'

He had played with honour and distinction for the club, and then in April 1897 he had been appointed 'secretary and manager'. In theory, he did not pick the team to play the game, but such was the strength of his personality and general knowledge of football that in fact he did just that. It had taken him time, but he had now built his new young side, having scoured the length and breadth of Great Britain to do so, and not being afraid to enlist the services of non-Catholics if he had to.

In the current squad, Adams, McNair, Weir, Young, Hay and Bennett were all serving the Celtic from a non-Catholic background, and helping to make nonsense of the abuse about Fenians and Papists that one heard from the lunatic fringe at Paisley, Greenock and Airdrie, or perhaps the more subtle form of prejudice when the newspapers occasionally talked about 'the Irishmen' – a name that was ludicrously inappropriate. 'Celtic' meant Ireland AND Scotland.

Last week the team had won the Scottish Cup for the sixth time. Maley had played in 1892 and had been heavily involved as a manager in 1899, 1900, 1904 and 1907. Now today they had the chance to win the Scottish League as well. They had already won the Glasgow Cup, and if they could win the league and the Glasgow Charity Cup, it would be a clean sweep. Last year, they had lifted everything except the Charity Cup. This year it was the intention to go one better.

Maley rejoiced in the triumphs of his young side. There was nothing better than reading what the newspapers said about the 'fast, attractive football', the 'pretty passing', the strength of his half-back line of Young, Loney and Hay, the brilliant thoughtful football of Jimmy McMenemy and the thrusts and goalscoring of Jimmy Quinn. Maley had reason to be happy with himself, and just occasionally his pride was given another boost when he was referred to as 'Mr Celtic', something that tickled his vanity.

All this came at a price. It was no secret that his home life was not happy, but he was prepared to spend all his life with his team, 'without whom my life would have been an empty existence'. He lived for his club, but he also contributed to football in the broader sense, always being willing to give talks on 'The Game of Football' to church organisations, political groups and any gathering that showed any interest. He was also a great personal friend of William Wilton, his opposite number at Rangers Football Club.

His friendship, however, did nothing to diminish the keen rivalry that existed between the two sides who had emerged as the leading lights of Scotland, now that professionalism had seen the end of the hegemony of Queen's Park. Not without cause were the two teams called 'the Old Firm' for their seemingly relentless ability to generate money.

Today, 40,000 appeared at Ibrox. The Rangers support were obviously keen to see Jim Sharp, the left-back who had recently joined the club from Woolwich Arsenal, and Celtic supporters, still on a very high note after their Scottish Cup success the previous week, knew that even a draw would secure the fourth Scottish League championship in a row. The weather was cold but dry, the unseasonal snow of midweek having melted in Glasgow, as distinct from Edinburgh where it delayed the start of the cricket season. The wind was blowing from the east and deserved the Scottish word 'snell' to describe it.

Celtic had already beaten Rangers three times that season, having defeated them in the Glasgow Cup Final at the third attempt (the first two drawn finals doing little to dispel the rumours in Glasgow that the two of them were 'at it'). They then removed Rangers from the Scottish Cup a couple of months previously, this time at the first attempt at Ibrox, and also got the better of them at Celtic Park on New Year's Day.

There was also a sub-plot about Jimmy Quinn. Jimmy Quinn was, of course, the talk of Edwardian Britain, with even the English newspapers talking about his goalscoring prowess. He had scored four in Dublin for Scotland a month ago, and was dubbed the 'uncrowned king of Scotland' and even the 'uncrowned king of Ireland' by some of the Irish press, who had clearly forgotten their own Charles Stewart Parnell. When the ship docked at the Broomielaw the following day, he was given a hero's welcome by thousands. Jimmy looked more than ever 'just like an ordinary man' as he calmly walked to the railway station to get his train to Croy.

But Jimmy had twice in recent years been sent off in games against Rangers. Both occasions were held to be grossly unfair by Celtic supporters, but there seemed to be little doubt that Rangers would try to provoke him today. In fact, they did more than that, for after several severe tackles by various Rangers defenders, notably Jimmy Galt, Quinn was seen to be limping. It is hard to believe that this was not a deliberate attempt to crock the great man, but in this case it failed to work.

This particular Celtic forward line was very good at swapping positions, usually for short periods. Now it was Alec Bennett with whom Jimmy Quinn changed positions for the rest of the game. This did not really impair the effectiveness of the Celtic forward line, for Bennett was an accomplished centre-forward. Maley, sitting in the stand, chuckled to himself as he recalled that 1904 Scottish Cup Final when Bennett, being tapped by Rangers and not wanting to play in the game, had to be dropped from the centre-forward position in favour of Jimmy Quinn. That had started something!

But today, soon after the exchange of places, Alec BENNETT scored the only goal of the game. Normally called 'the artful dodger' because of his ability to trick defenders, on this occasion, a sudden 'bolt away caught Taylor napping' and although Sharp came across to try to take the ball off him, Alec beat him too and then slid the ball past Newbigging in the Rangers goal. It was a great goal, and the Celtic fans reacted joyfully.

The second half saw no further scoring but some superb ball control and ball possession from Celtic, with captain James 'Dun' Hay being singled out for his ball winning and passing, and wee Davie Hamilton in the forward line also catching the approving eye of the writer of *The Scottish Referee*. And as for Quinn, he limped along his wing doing his best, but mainly Jimmy was a passenger.

It was at the full-time whistle, though, that Quinn excelled as a man. The full-time whistle came to loud rejoicing among the Celtic fans, with Sunny Jim Young's paean of delight heard all over the ground. But it was the quiet dignity of Jimmy Quinn that won the day. When he might have had a few angry words with those who had tried to maim him, May, Taylor and Galt in particular, Jimmy quietly limped up to the referee, Mr Faichnie of Falkirk, shook his hand, then calmly turned to every Rangers player and shook hands with them. No retaliation, no angry words, no vengeance. He had won his point by the fact that his team had now won the Scottish League for the fourth year running.

The team would go on and win the Glasgow Charity Cup in May, and thus for the first time won all four trophies that they had entered. The next Celtic team to do that would be the team of 1967, and so on that basis we must assume that these two teams were of comparable standard. It is highly flattering for both teams to be mentioned in the same breath as the other!

And so Mr Maley did indeed enjoy his birthday. His contribution to Celtic had barely started, however, for he had a long way to go. He had many comparisons to Jock Stein in his leadership qualities and ability to motivate his players. Both men were totally dedicated to the job, and it would be a brave historian who would ever dare to compare the pair of them or to say which was the better. Curiously, they both enjoyed the love and respect of their best players, but neither was quite so popular with their 'fringe' players. Several of the 1967 *squad* (not the actual 11 Lisbon Lions) had their criticisms of Jock, in the same way as men like Davie McLean, who was a good centre-forward but never really able to replace Quinn, had a well-documented contempt for Maley.

Maley's joy of this particular day was slightly tempered by the knowledge that Alec Bennett was once again angling for a move to Rangers, and this time he would indeed go. Alec was a Rangers supporter, but everyone agreed that his best football was played for Celtic, and this day was one such example.

TEN

QUINN DOES IT AGAIN

Celtic 1 Rangers 0	Glasgow Cup Final
Hampden Park	9 October 1909

Celtic: Adams, McNair and Weir; Young, Loney and Hay; Kivlichan, McMenemy, Quinn, Johnstone and Hamilton

Rangers: Lock, Law and McKenzie; Gordon, Stark and Galt; Hogg, Gilchrist, Reid, McPherson and Hunter

Referee: Mr J.T. Ibbotson, Derby

THE year 1909 had not been without its trauma in Scottish football. It was the year of the riot at the replayed Scottish Cup Final in April between Celtic and Rangers which had wrecked large parts of Hampden Park. The ostensible cause was that the crowd felt cheated out of extra time when the second game ended in a draw. No clear decision appears to have been made or at least to have been communicated to the spectators about whether extra time would be allowed. In the confusion, things got out of hand, and although there was no great damage done to anyone's person, there certainly was to property.

There was more to it than met the eye, however. It all stemmed from the widespread perception that sometimes cup ties were deliberately drawn at the first attempt, so that another large crowd could turn up next week to see the replay. An examination of games around this time, particularly Glasgow Cup finals involving Celtic and Rangers, does reveal a disturbing amount of games falling into this pattern, and the press are not above making a snide insinuation or two about a draw being 'good for the coffers of each club' and 'smiles on the faces of the directors as they shook hands with each other at full time'.

It could not be proved, of course, but it didn't matter, for the important thing was that some people believed that this sort of thing was going on. Sociologists will make comments about poor housing, poverty and shocking living conditions – and these are all valid as well – but one thing that the 1909 riot was NOT was a sectarian disturbance. Football was far more important than sectarianism to the good people of Glasgow in 1909.

What this riot, shameful and destructive as it was, tended to hide was how well Celtic did in its aftermath to win the Scottish League by playing eight games in 12 days. The withholding of the Scottish Cup also prevented Celtic from winning the cup three years in a row, something they did not do until 2019.

However all that may be, Hampden had now been repaired and it was all set for the Glasgow Cup Final which, as luck would have it, was between Celtic and Rangers. Police were there in strength to prevent any repetition of the events of April, and it was generally agreed by all concerned that a draw in this game would be tactless, to put it mildly! (The semi-final between Celtic and Queen's Park had been a draw on the first occasion, doing little to play down the general cynicism of the public.) Nevertheless, 55,000 turned up on a pleasant autumn afternoon, spoiled only to a certain extent by a stiff breeze blowing from the west.

Celtic had had better starts to the season than this one, for they had already lost to both Morton and Hibs in the league. The team was still substantially the same as previous years, although a strapping fellow from Fife called Peter Johnstone had now replaced Peter Somers at inside-left, and of course Willie Kivlichan was on the right wing because Alec Bennet had departed to Rangers in 1908. Bennett was not playing for Rangers today, presumably injured, perhaps dropped because Rangers' start to the league campaign had been even worse than that of Celtic. It was probably true to say that Bennett's form for Rangers was never as good as when he played for Celtic.

It is important that modern eyes do not undervalue the Glasgow Cup. It is a beautifully ornate trophy and was in its day something of great prestige. Indeed, it was older than the Scottish League (but not the Scottish Cup), something that allowed it to claim precedence over Scottish League fixtures. It had begun in 1877/78, and 'Bauldie' of *The Scottish Referee* claimed to have seen all 23 Glasgow Cup finals. With the characteristic tendency of most older people to romanticise the past, 'Bauldie' said that this one was not as good as some of the previous ones he had seen. It was good enough though to please the crowd, and it was Celtic's ninth triumph in this competition. This final was considered important enough for the Glasgow FA to appoint two neutral linesmen to officiate and help the English referee Mr Ibbotson. Mr Colquhoun of Clyde and Mr Allison of Queen's Park did the honours.

The game started with Celtic using the advantage of the wind, but it was Rangers who almost scored in the very first minute when McPherson was through on goal but 'shot wildly'. The first half saw loads of good football, with the ball going back 'to and fro to the excitement of the spectators', and the Celtic crowd were particularly delighted to see the ability of Peter Johnstone to trap a ball and then immediately distribute. The only bad point of the first half was that McMenemy seemed to have picked up a knock in a collision with Jimmy Galt, the legendary 'dirty Galt', and Celtic supporters found it hard to believe that it was any kind of an accident. If McMenemy was injured, that could spell trouble for Celtic. He did not have to withdraw from the contest, but his value to the side was seriously impaired.

Into the second half it was becoming apparent that the struggle was between Celtic's forward line and the defence of Rangers, for only very occasionally were Rangers able to get through the half-back line that had been the mainstay of Celtic's excellent team for several years now – Young, Loney and Hay – and even if they did, there was still Eck McNair and Jamie Weir before they got close to Davie Adams. Hogg was having a good game on the right wing for Rangers, but Willie Reid in the centre was well policed by Willie Loney, who was now nicknamed 'No Road This Way' for his ability to gobble up everything that came down the middle.

It was also true that the game became rather rough, with several men on either side not shrinking from any tackles. Mr Ibbotson, the referee, was praised for his control of the game in that he blew his whistle quickly, talked severely to some players and clearly indicated that he would not be reluctant to use the ultimate sanction of dismissal if necessary. The *Glasgow Herald* describes the game as 'keenly contested to the point of fierceness'.

The only goal came halfway through the second half and it was scored, to no one's surprise, by the man generally reckoned by most English journalists, let alone Scottish ones, to be the best in UK football. This was, of course, 'the bhoy from Croy', Jimmy Quinn. A few minutes before the goal, QUINN was seen to be limping, but he soon ran it off, and then when Rangers left-back McKenzie miskicked a ball, Jimmy was on it like a flash, rounded the right-back Law, then beat McKenzie (who had now recovered) again, before rounding goalkeeper Herbert Lock to score. This goal was reported in some quarters as being scored 'with a Ranger hanging from each leg' but I think one can put this down to an element of rhetorical and romantic exaggeration.

Hampden erupted at the brilliance of all this, with even some of those who had confessed to a soft spot for the Light Blues being seen to join in the applause. This was, after all, Jimmy Quinn – that enigmatic figure who more or less gave his name to that decade of Edwardian football, and whom everyone talked about.

Rangers were not yet out of the game, for there was only the one goal in it, but they never really looked like breaching the Celtic citadel. McNair was organised, Weir had probably his best game for the club, and Rangers had no battering ram to get through Willie Loney. Mr Ibbotson, having allowed a generous amount of time for injuries and stoppages, blew for full time to the great paeans of delight from the lovers of the green and white.

The cup was presented immediately after the game – unusual for the times – but not to Celtic's captain. The tradition was that it should be presented to Celtic's president or chairman James Kelly. The president of the Glasgow FA, Sir John Ure Primrose, was unavailable, so his vice president, Mr Colquhoun, who had just acted as linesman (or 'touch judge' as he was described in *The Scottish Referee*) did the job for him. The 'drinking from the cup' would take place at a later stage. This was a quaint tradition by which the winning team would fill the cup with wine or some other liquid and offer a drink to the losing finalists.

The winning of the Glasgow Cup in October set Celtic up well for the rest of the season. They would go on to win the Scottish League for a record-breaking six years in a row, but the absence of key men like Adams, Young and McMenemy meant that they would lose the Scottish Cup semi-final to Clyde.

ELEVEN

QUINN THE INVINCIBLE

Celtic 3 Rangers 0	**Scottish League Division One**
Celtic Park	**1 January 1912**

Celtic: Mulrooney, McNair and Dodds; Young, Loney and Johnstone; McAtee, McMenemy, Quinn, Travers and Brown

Rangers: Lock, Campbell and Richmond; Gordon, Waddell and Hendry; Hogg, Bowie, Reid, Bennett and Smith

Referee: Mr Stark, Airdrie

IT hadn't been Celtic's best year, 1911. True, there had been a Scottish Cup success, but it was far from a convincing one, having come in a replay against Hamilton Academical after a dull, anodyne first game, but the main disappointment in 1911 had been the loss of the Scottish League to Rangers after Celtic had won the title six years on the trot. It hadn't even been close in 1911. Celtic had ended up in fifth place, some 11 points behind Rangers. For a support that had been bred on almost constant success, this was unacceptable.

And then in the summer, captain James Hay had gone to Newcastle United. Why he went, we do not know. Perhaps he had had too much of the tyrannical Maley; perhaps he simply wanted a change; perhaps Newcastle United offered him more money – but for whatever reason, the loss of 'Dun' Hay was a grievous one, and form in the early part of season 1911/12 had not been great. Celtic had gone out of the Glasgow Cup to Partick Thistle, and in the league away form had been awful, with the loss of six fixtures to Dundee, Hearts, Hamilton, Rangers, Motherwell and Third Lanark. It was already depressingly clear that, barring miracles, there would be no strong league challenge this year either, and the Scottish Cup would be the limit of their ambitions in 1912.

The problem was quite simply that one great team had aged and some players had moved on, and another great team had not quite arrived as yet. There were still some fine players. Alec

McNair, Sunny Jim Young, Jimmy 'Napoleon' McMenemy and, above all, the great Jimmy Quinn were as good as you were likely to get anywhere. Others were slowly arriving. Peter Johnstone was beginning to impress at left-half, Andy McAtee likewise on the right wing, and a month ago a debut had been given to a spindle-shanked young Irishman by the name of Patrick Gallacher.

In general terms, outside football, the Celtic community was still obsessed with Home Rule for Ireland. Grudging admiration and support was given to the Liberal Government of Herbert Asquith and David Lloyd George for their prolonged but slowly successful emasculation of the House of Lords, because it was the Lords who had been the major stumbling block to Home Rule throughout the 19th century. But anywhere one looked in Glasgow in particular, there was still poverty. The Liberal reforms were perhaps making a slight difference, but it would take time, and housing, health and education were still, frankly, shocking and a disgrace to a country which was the richest on earth, and called itself 'civilised'.

On a lighter note, everyone was thrilled about the new ship that had been built in Belfast (there was still a residual feeling of jealousy that it had not been built in Glasgow) and was currently undergoing tests of seaworthiness with the intention of having a maiden voyage in April. It was to be called the *Titanic*. In Australia, the Australians had won the First Test Match, but on 30 December S.F. Barnes had taken 5 for 44 to give England a good start in the Second Test.

The weather as 1911 came to an end was cold, but dry and pleasant. Celtic had finished the year depressingly with a defeat at Third Lanark and then two draws against Morton and Airdrie, the Airdrie one ending 0-0, and the Celtic fans who had travelled to Airdrie on Saturday 30 December had not been slow in making their feelings known. The prospect of meeting Rangers was not a happy one.

But it was the New Year. Glasgow celebrated Hogmanay (even though it was a Sunday) and the New Year as it always did, and the pleasant weather encouraged 70,000 to turn up on New Year's Day. This was believed to be a record for Celtic Park, described oddly by *The Scottish Referee* as 'difficult of access', meaning presumably that transport in the form of cabs and trams was less available than usual. Be that as it may, the place was heaving with an excited holiday crowd, and it was noted that there were more ladies there than normal. It was also noted, tragically and sadly, that not everyone wore shoes!

Willie Maley decided not to risk young Pat Gallacher for this game. He felt that the game might just be too big for the slender Irishman, and he turned to Paddy Travers for the inside-left position. Travers had disappointed so far this season, but Maley felt that there was still some football in him. The rest of the team was as expected, but Rangers were without Galt and Law. They were, nevertheless, a strong team, deservedly top of the league. Maley met his old friend William Wilton, his Rangers counterpart before the game, they wished each other a Happy New Year and Maley promised they would meet again after the game in Maley's room for 'something strong to celebrate the New Year'.

There were two Rangers players in particular who Celtic fans did not like. One was Joe Hendry for his part in the Jimmy Quinn suspension of 1907, and the other was Alec Bennett, the man who had jumped ship from Celtic to Rangers in 1908 for reasons that no one could ever understand. He had of course won the Scottish League with Rangers in 1911, but the move had not really been a great success for Alec, who had always played his best football for Celtic, earning the nickname 'the artful dodger'. A sensitive soul, Alec would not have relished the abuse that he got at Celtic Park from those who used to adore him, but then again, like Maurice Johnston and Brendan Rodgers in future years, he had to face the consequences of his own actions. Why did he do it?

Rangers started confidently. They had clearly brought a fair amount of supporters with them, and they played with the enthusiasm that their comfortable league position would have warranted. In the first half hour Willie Reid hit the bar, and several other shots went past the post, and it was a long time before Celtic managed to gain any kind of composure. But gain it they did, and late in the first half they took the lead. It came from a corner on the left taken by John Brown. The ball came to the normally well-marked QUINN, but on this occasion Jimmy had managed to escape the attentions of Hendry and Waddell, made a little space for himself and then hammered the ball home.

It was thus 1-0 for Celtic at half-time, and thus the interval was spent with Celtic Park in an uproar of excitement. Quinn always could get everyone excited with his goals, and had certainly 'lit the candle' for them today. He was generally agreed to be the best in Great Britain for scoring goals, and as he came out for the second half from the old pavilion in the north-east corner he was given a special cheer to himself. And to think that there were those who had gone around saying that he was finished!

The second half saw Celtic take command with two of the lesser-known Celts showing what they could do. Paddy Travers (a man who would go on to have a distinguished managerial career with Aberdeen and then Clyde), clearly worried about losing his place to the young prodigy called Gallacher, took it upon himself to have what was probably his best game for the club, and the same could be said about the young Fife miner called John Brown. Brown had taken the corner which gave Quinn his first goal, and now about halfway through the second half, he sent a long ball across the field to Andy McAtee who slipped a fine ball through to his fellow Crojan (man from Croy) QUINN to put Celtic 2-0 up and to trigger an outburst of cheering, waving of handkerchiefs and rattling of crawmills from those who were wearing the green-and-white rosettes. Late in the game, Brown released QUINN who thus scored his hat-trick. Jimmy was good at scoring hat-tricks against Rangers. Everyone recalled the 1904 Scottish Cup Final and even a few remembered the Glasgow Exhibition Final of 1902.

The celebrations that night in the Celtic strongholds of the East End and the small mining villages like Jimmy Quinn's Croy were intense. Jimmy himself and young McAtee were more or less escorted by adoring fans to the railway station for the journey home. Jimmy was a paradox. Adulated by Celtic supporters everywhere, Jimmy considered himself to be nothing other than a miner boy, lucky enough to be a good football player, playing for the club he adored.

The game in itself did not achieve very much. Rangers did indeed go on to win the Scottish League, but Celtic never again experienced defeat that season (they did have a few miserable draws) and went on to lift the Scottish Cup for the second year in a row. In some ways this was the swansong of Jimmy Quinn – injuries now took longer to heal – but this game was a timely reminder to Rangers that, although Celtic had had a poor season, they were still there. It was almost an act of defiance and it gave their supporters at least one day of happiness. 1912 was well begun.

TWELVE

A CHINK OF LIGHT

Celtic 3 Rangers 2	**Glasgow Charity Cup Final**
Celtic Park	**10 May 1913**

Celtic: Shaw, McNair and Dodds; Young, Loney and McMaster; McAtee, Gallacher, Connolly, Browning and Hill

Rangers: Hempsey, Gordon and Ormond; Brown, Logan and Galt; Paterson, Goodwin, Reid, Bowie and Smith

Referee: Mr J. Bell, Dundee

SEASON 1912/13 had been a shocker. Willie Maley and the directors would have loved to have had something on the sideboard to celebrate the silver jubilee of the club, but it was not to be. Indeed, of the 25 years of football played by the club, this one was generally looked upon as one of the least successful, almost as bad as 1896/97, which still sent shivers of horror down the spine of supporters. Rangers won the league for the third year in a row, and Celtic departed the Scottish Cup at the quarter-final stage to Hearts in March, then went on to lose their next two league games to kill off what little chance they had in the league as well. The Scottish Cup was actually won by Falkirk this year.

Celtic's performances against Rangers had been odd. They had actually won both their league games against Rangers, but had lost the Glasgow Cup Final to them in October. And now they had to play Rangers in the final of the Glasgow Charity Cup. It would be nice to win that one to avoid a completely barren season. The supporters were unhappy, because 1913 was the first year since 1903 that Celtic had not won either of the Scottish trophies.

The truth was that Celtic were not all that bad a side. Injuries to Jimmy Quinn had probably finished his career, and at the end of the season McMenemy was injured as well. The defence was reasonably solid, and just recently Celtic had acquired a new goalkeeper in Charles Shaw from Queens Park Rangers in London. He had previously played for Port Glasgow Athletic.

Goalkeeping had been a problem since the days of Dan McArthur and Davie Adams.

The Glasgow Charity Cup, traditionally played at the end of the season, was often when clubs could try out new players with a view to next season. Maley recalled with pride how a decade earlier he had blooded Sunny Jim Young in these circumstances, and that had been a great success. This year he had acquired Bernard Connolly from Vale of Clyde to ginger up the forward line, and also on the very day of the Charity Cup Final he enlisted Johnny Hill from Dumbarton Harp, apparently on the suggestion of another 'son of the rock' who had joined the club that season called Johnny Browning.

Celtic had beaten Clyde and Third Lanark in the earlier rounds, and won the toss for the venue for the cup final. So Celtic Park it was on Saturday, 10 May. It was a blustery, unpredictable sort of day, with the weather varying between heavy rain and strong sunshine. Some 35,000 turned up to see Celtic's last chance of a trophy. No one could possibly have known it at the time, but with Joe Dodds now recovered from a slight knock, this was the birthday of the immortal 'Shaw, McNair and Dodds', the three names who would start the Celtic line-up for the best part of the next decade. They didn't get off to the best of starts, as it turned out.

Rangers, playing towards the eastern goal (where the Lisbon Lions stand is now), were 2-0 up within the first ten minutes. The first goal was particularly unlucky for Eck McNair, who tried to clear a ball and had the misfortune to clatter the ball straight into Alex Smith, off whom the ball then cannoned to international centre-forward Willie Reid, who had the easiest of tasks to put Rangers 1-0 up. Then a minute later, with the Celtic defence still trying to work out what had gone wrong with the first goal, Rangers scored again, this time a better goal by Willie Reid after he had picked up a Bowie pass. Rangers were thus well on top, and the game had hardly started.

But this Celtic team was not lacking in character, and captain Jimmy Young went around shouting and urging everyone on, particularly the newcomers in the forward line. 'Sunny Jim' of course had clear and vivid memories of the Scottish Cup Final of

1904 when Celtic had been 2-0 down as well, and yet had come back to win 3-2 with Jimmy Quinn's hat-trick. The trouble was that Jimmy Quinn was today sitting nursing his injuries in the gallery of the Celtic Park pavilion alongside his friend Jimmy 'Napoleon' McMenemy. Celtic could have done with these two on the park. Quinn's very presence, however, was a constant reminder that nothing was impossible in football.

Play became a bit rough. It would be facile and dishonest to claim that it all came from the Ibrox men, for Celtic had players, not least 'Sunny Jim' himself, who could give it out as well, but it all stemmed from the Light Blues' determination to hold on to what they had. But Celtic supporters were also beginning to be impressed by Charlie Shaw in their goal. He was a funny character. Small and with jerky movements, sporting a moustache and wearing a bonnet, he did not really look like a goalkeeper, or indeed any kind of football player, but his handling of the ball and command of his penalty box was very impressive. Born in Twechar, Charlie was Celtic through and through.

And of course Celtic had Patsy Gallacher. This young man had been in the team for a season and a half now and was really beginning to impress with his ball control and trickery. By half-time, Celtic had pulled a goal back. In the wake of a free kick, the ball came to Andy McAtee, who just managed to get to the ball before it went out of play and hooked it across where it reached GALLACHER. It was just a little behind him, but Patsy got the ball and in one movement, with his back to goal, swivelled and fired the ball past Hempsey. It was a goal of some brilliance and was duly acclaimed by the crowd. Half-time came soon after, and Celtic were now back in the game. They now had the wind at their back as well.

In addition, Rangers right-back Jimmy Gordon was injured. No substitutes were allowed, of course, for another 50 years, but *The Scottish Referee* is of the opinion that Rangers would have been better playing with ten men rather than what they did, which was to reshuffle their defence and put Gordon on to the right wing, where he was merely a passenger. All this gave Celtic a decisive advantage.

There is the old Scottish adage 'ilka doggie has its day' or the more august 'cometh the hour, cometh the man' or the Andy Warhol aphorism that 'everyone has their half hour of glory'. This was clearly the moment of Bernard Connolly, commonly known as 'Barnie'. One hopes he enjoyed his brief moment in the sun, for he disappeared back to obscurity almost as soon as he hit the highlights.

Celtic equalised soon after the restart when a long clearance saw Connolly and centre-half Logan racing for the ball. Logan seemed to have won the ball, but CONNOLLY robbed him, dashed past him and scored. It was indeed a goal that reminded one of Jimmy Quinn, and Jimmy himself was seen to stand up and applaud what was a good goal.

The winner came after Willie Loney had hit the bar with a 'raking drive' (as *The Scottish Referee* puts it). The ball rebounded to Andy McAtee, who lobbed the ball back into the goalmouth, it was knocked back out again, then Sunny Jim sent the ball in once more. While Logan and goalkeeper Hempsey left the ball to each other, CONNOLLY nipped in between the two of them while they were 'foozling' and levelled the score for Celtic.

Parkhead was now animated and excited, and Celtic now took command of the game. The most encouraging thing was the way that the newcomers played. Shaw was described as a 'complete' goalkeeper, McMaster was given the honour of being described as the best half-back, and when one considers that the other two were Sunny Jim and Willie Loney, that was some compliment, and up front, Connolly won all the glory, but Hill and Browning also played their part.

The best player on the field was Patsy Gallacher, but that was no real surprise. He had not had the greatest of seasons, but his best was clearly yet to come. The fans left the ground with a spring in their step, the likes of which they had not experienced since the Scottish Cup triumph of 1912. There were definite signs that a great new team was developing at Celtic Park, and next year would prove how good they were. But the main thing of importance at the moment was that Celtic's silver jubilee did not lack silver, and Celtic's chairman James Kelly was duly presented with the trophy at the after-match banquet that night. In addition, the 35,000 had made a healthy contribution to Glasgow's charities and both Celtic and Rangers were seen to add to the 'pot' as well.

It had been a great game of football, and a lovely way to end what had hitherto been a rather depressing season.

THIRTEEN

NAPOLEON'S HAPPY NEW YEAR

Celtic 4 Rangers 0	Scottish League
Celtic Park	1 January 1914

Celtic: Shaw, McNair and Dodds; Young, Johnstone and McMaster; McAtee, Gallacher, Owers, McMenemy and Browning

Rangers: Hempsey, Ormond and Fulton; Gordon, Logan and Hendry; Duncan, Bowie, Reid, Bennett and Paterson

Referee: Mr T. Dougray, Belshill

CELTIC supporters toasted New Year 1914 with a spring in their step as they walked round their various towns and villages doing their 'first footing'. They had cause to be happy about their team who were now comfortably at the top of the league, and had not been beaten since they went out of the Glasgow Cup to Third Lanark on 7 October. Not only that, but in that period until the New Year they had conceded only one goal – and that was in a game that they still won, beating Raith Rovers 2-1 at Stark's Park, Kirkcaldy. A few days ago, they had finished 1913 by beating Ayr United 6-0 with four goals coming from Ebenezer Owers, the redheaded Englishman who was being groomed as Jimmy Quinn's successor – if he could prove himself good enough.

Celtic had had a bad 1913 overall, however, but 1914 looked as if it would be a great deal better. Charlie Shaw had bedded in as an excellent goalkeeper, and the half-back line of Young, Johnstone and McMaster had taken on a far more solid look, reminding supporters of Young, Loney and Hay of a few years back. Up front there were two superbly tricky inside-forwards in Patsy Gallacher and Jimmy McMenemy. McMenemy was such a superb tactical genius that he now rejoiced in the name 'Napoleon' after the great French general of 100 years ago. Wee Pat from Donegal had come on in leaps and bounds, and things were looking good for the team.

Rangers, whom Celtic had already beaten at Ibrox 2-0 at the end of October 1913, had won the league championship for the past three years but were beginning to struggle this season. But if anyone was going to stop Celtic's great run for the championship, it would be Rangers. Rangers still had some great players in Jimmy Gordon, a superb wing-half, Willie Reid, a proven goalscorer and of course Alec Bennett, the man who had left his adoring fans at Parkhead to join Rangers in 1908. 'Why, Alec, why?' was still the puzzled cry of the fans. It promised to be a great day at Celtic Park.

The weather had been good for 'first footing' and stayed good for New Year's Day. It was dry, reasonably mild for the time of year, the low 'weary winter sun' that Burns talked about was out, and as the crowd assembled at Celtic Park good cheer was in the air. 1914 was looked upon as the year that Ireland might at long last get Home Rule, something to which the Irish had aspired to for decades. The House of Lords, which had thwarted them so often in the previous century, was now a broken reed and the only problem seemed to be the Orangemen of the North, but there was no reason why they couldn't be talked into it. Yes, life looked good as the trains and the trams headed eastwards to Celtic Park full of excited, animated supporters, but also containing one or two who looked as if they had been celebrating the New Year rather too well and gave the impression that they had not even been to bed!

There were the usual beggars and urchins as the crowd approached the stadium, the plaintive singing of 'The Wearing of the Green' and 'The Rose of Tralee' by those who held out their caps for money, hoping thus perhaps to earn enough to be able to pay their entrance fee for what was regarded by everyone as 'The Greatest Show On Earth'. The crowd was huge – variously reported as 65,000, 70,000 or 80,000 – and people were still flooding in well after the game had started. There was a certain amount of elbow room near the front, but everywhere else was jam-packed, and there was the sight of a few boys being passed over the heads of the crowd so that they could get a better view at the front. For such a huge crowd, it was great to report that there was not a hint of violence or disorder even from those whose New Year celebrations had clearly been excessive!

Rangers started well but suffered a bad blow early on when Joe Hendry was carried off injured and did not return. The cause was a totally accidental kick in the face from Patsy Gallacher. The little Irishman received the ball with his back to the goal and tried an overhead kick at which he usually excelled. Hendry unfortunately had been running forward trying to head clear at the same time, and Patsy's boot collided with him. Patsy was seen to enquire after his health, and when Hendry was led off with blood streaming from his face, he was given a sympathetic round of applause, even though it was Hendry who had played such a despicable part in the suspension of Jimmy Quinn in 1907.

Newspaper reports of the game are all at pains to stress that although this was a handicap to Rangers, Celtic would have still been good enough to win even if Hendry had still been on the field. Celtic took the lead after about 30 minutes, and it was from a strange source – Sunny Jim YOUNG, a man who seldom scored goals. Sunny took a throw-in, the ball was returned to him by Gallacher, and almost from the by-line he sent a high drooping ball into the goalmouth. Ebenezer Owers dived to head the ball but missed totally, and the ball continued its course, bouncing on the goal line itself, and crossed into the net. It was a strange goal, and Rangers goalkeeper Johnnie Hempsey claimed that he had been unsighted by the diving Owers, but as Owers did not actually touch him he could not claim obstruction. 'Brigadier' of the *Daily Record* admitted that it was an unusual goal to score, but there was nothing illegal about it, and Celtic Park celebrated noisily.

But that was nothing compared with the next goal, claimed to be the best goal ever seen at Celtic Park. *The Dundee Courier* describes it thus: 'McMENEMY was the master who aroused the crowd to the highest pitch of enthusiasm by scoring a goal reminiscent of Quinn at his best. Thirty yards out, he got the ball and deceived Gordon by swerving to the centre instead of inclining to the left. Gordon was the first of five deceived and dazzled Light Blues. One after another was left standing agape as the Celt meandered along. Once he was knocked down but up he got, beat his last man with another swerve and gave Hempsey no chance with a swift upward shot that bounced into the net. One is apt to get carried away with the latest thing in goals, as in most other luxuries, but it is safe to say that no finer goal has ever been scored on Celtic Park.' And that was why they called him 'Napoleon'!

There is no answer to that, and when half-time came a few minutes later, the crowd was still stunned at the magnificence of Napoleon who was cheered to the echo as he ran off, and cheered to the echo as he came out again, and every time the ball came near him after that. But the goals had not finished yet. Two more came, both from the foot of left-winger Johnny BROWNING, a wild boy by nature, but a man who came to respect and even enjoy the strict Maley regime of regular diet and training. His first came from a cross sent over by Young to find him at a difficult angle to the goal. Johnny simply belted it past both Ormond and Hempsey to send Parkhead into further delirium. His second came in the aftermath of a McAtee corner, when the ball bobbed about for a spell until it came to BROWNING, who drilled it home from the edge of the box for his second goal and Celtic's fourth.

That completed the scoring but not the entertainment, as Celtic passed the ball about with dazzling accuracy. The Celtic fans were in raptures throughout the second half, even those who only saw the last few minutes because they had come in when the exit gates were opened, not having had the financial wherewithal to come in and see the mighty Celts. From the balcony of the pavilion, Maley was seen to stand up and applaud, and long before full time his old friend William Wilton, the manager of Rangers, was seen to shake his hand, as indeed did the Rangers directors.

Darkness was beginning to fall as the game came to an end and the huge crowd dispersed. It was a lovely end to what had been a lovely day, and 'Happy New Year' hardly came into it as the Celtic enclaves continued their parties until well into the night. It was such a glorious feeling to make so many people happy, especially those who had little else going in their lives. But everyone could be a part of 'the Celtic', and talk fondly and enthusiastically about Gallacher, Browning and, in particular, Jimmy McMenemy, the humble little man from Rutherglen. Bonaparte may have come from Corsica, but Rutherglen was the home of the real Napoleon!

FOURTEEN

IN THE SHADOW
OF A DISASTER

Celtic 3 Rangers 2	**Glasgow Charity Cup Final**
Ibrox Stadium	**8 May 1915**

Rangers: Hempsey, Craig and Muir; Gordon, Pursell and Hendry; Duncan, Cunningham, Reid, Cairns and Paterson

Celtic: Shaw, McNair and McGregor; Young, Johnstone and Dodds; McAtee, Gallacher, McColl, McMenemy and Browning

Referee: Unknown

AS the 40,000 crowd made their way to Ibrox that sunny but rather breezy day, there was one topic of conversation which dominated everything, making even the outcome of this game less important than it would have been in other circumstances. The war was coming even closer with the news that the day before, off the south-west coast of Ireland, the Germans had sunk the Cunard liner RMS *Lusitania*, causing the deaths of over 1,000 passengers, most of them civilians, many of them neutral Americans and many of them children.

This can only be seen as an act of outrageous barbarism on the part of the Germans. The Germans had been demonised in the British press, but this act needed no further demonising. It was totally evil, and can hardly be excused by the fact that the *Lusitania* was also (allegedly) carrying armaments for Britain or that the Germans had taken out an advertisement in some American newspapers advising Americans not to travel into British waters. Amazingly, the USA did not immediately join the war on the British side (they did a couple of years later) but there could be little doubt from then on which side American public opinion would support. Anti-German demonstrations were held in New York and Chicago.

For Glaswegians and shipbuilders, this sort of thing struck home. Bits of the *Lusitania* had been built on the Clyde before its maiden voyage in 1907, and this sort of thing did not in any way help the anti-war cause, espoused so eagerly by men like Ramsay MacDonald and John McLean. Indeed, at Ibrox today the Army made a recruiting speech, telling everyone about the attractions of life in the HLI (Highland Light Infantry) and reminding young men that a mere glance at the morning's newspaper would tell everyone just what sort of people the Germans were.

Indeed, the early editions of the evening newspapers were already out, telling everyone the latest count of the casualties. Some of them were even making the perceptive point that now that stalemate seemed to be the order of the day in Europe, Germany's best hope lay in starving Britain out, something that would seem to have more hope of success than the many foolish fantasies that the British had, like the Dardanelles, for example. It was frightening stuff. The thought of food shortages was a frightening one, especially among people who didn't eat all that well at the best of times.

This would be the second-last game of the season. The following week Celtic (the Scottish League champions) would play the rest of the Scottish League in a game to raise money for Belgian refugees, but this was the final of the Glasgow Merchants' Charity Cup, now simply called the Glasgow Charity Cup. Celtic had failed to win the Glasgow Cup in the autumn, losing to the eventual winners Clyde, and were quite keen to lift the Charity Cup to go with the Scottish League trophy, because in 1915 there had been no Scottish Cup on the grounds of travelling difficulties. There had been an English Cup won by Sheffield United over Chelsea in the final, but that was to be the last English Cup for the duration, and international matches had now been stopped as well.

Football, however, had seemed to have won its battle to stop itself from being closed down entirely. Some of the smaller clubs had gone into abeyance, but the bigger clubs kept going, and the large attendances were proof of the propaganda and 'escapism relief' of football to the hard-working munitions workers and indeed soldiers and sailors home on leave. There were indeed quite a few khaki-dressed spectators in the Ibrox crowd that day.

The Glasgow Charity Cup was traditionally played for in the month of May. Celtic had already beaten Queen's Park and Partick Thistle. The season officially ended at the end of April, and players were, technically, not paid after that. In peace and in war, they were expected to play in this cup as amateurs, for all the proceeds went to charity. To what extent this lofty ideal actually happened in practice we cannot be sure about, but the reporter of the *Daily Record* says that 'easily the best thing about the game' was the £894 raised for charity. The standard of football was not high.

But the commitment was. Clearly there were a few old scores being settled, and the *Daily Record* says that there was too much 'bad temper' and one player ('the wrong one', according to the writer) was threatened with 'his marching orders'. Tantalisingly, the report does not go into many more details than that, but the rough stuff does not seem to have been entirely unconnected with the fact that Patsy Gallacher was off the field at the time when both Rangers goals were scored. The referee, whose name we do not know, was inclined to be lenient as it was all for charity, but between Rangers and Celtic leniency was all a mistake. Celtic were determined to show that their success this season was no fluke, and Rangers, who had had a poor season, finishing in third position way behind Celtic and Hearts, and had been knocked out of the Glasgow Cup in the autumn (Clyde won the trophy this year), were determined to win something.

Rangers opened with the wind behind them, and for a while they were all over Celtic, but it was Celtic who scored first with a good run and shot from Joe DODDS, normally a first-rate left-back but equally effective at left-half in place of the absent McMaster. This was a surprise, but then after the brutal tackle on Celtic's Patsy Gallacher, which saw him taken off, Tommy Cairns of Rangers (who after the war would be the best player in Rangers' very good side of that period) scored with a drive that hit the roof of the net, and then Andy Cunningham, who would also perform well for Rangers in the 1920s, ran in and scored a carbon copy of the goal which Joe Dodds had scored for Celtic earlier in the half.

At 2-1, however, at half-time, there was still a little consolation for Celtic in that they were now to play with the wind which seemed to be intensifying. Further encouragement was given to the lovers of the Celtic when the unmistakable figure of Patsy Gallacher trotted out along with his team-mates, having clearly recovered from his injuries. He was such a talismanic character that anything was believed possible when he was around.

There would be no replay of this game. If the sides were level then they would count corner kicks. They would then go to extra time. The only problem about counting corners was that no one had won one yet, but there was still time for that. Celtic now pressed a little harder with the wind behind them, and as the pressure increased, the ball came to 'smiler' BROWNING, who hammered home and brought Celtic to level terms. He was called 'smiler' simply because he didn't smile very often, but he did on this occasion. He was also responsible for Celtic earning a corner, Rangers having earned one previously.

So, as time was running out, it looked as if, with both teams level and on corners, there would have to be extra time, but then with a couple of minutes left Celtic won a free kick halfway inside the Rangers half. Up stepped captain Sunny Jim Young to take it, and in an instant he summed up the situation and showed why he was captain of Celtic. Rangers defenders expected a high ball, so they marked Jimmy McColl and Peter Johnstone, both of whom they knew to be good headers of the ball. But they forgot about Jimmy McMENEMY. Sunny lobbed the ball in, not quite in the direction that everyone expected but into some free space, and Napoleon ran forward to nod the ball in and to give Celtic the Glasgow Charity Cup for the fourth year in a row. In the remaining two minutes, Rangers managed to get a corner, but had no time to score another goal.

And thus ended one of the strangest of all Old Firm games. The crowd was a decent one, but it was probably true to say that the war had the effect sometimes of blurring the distinction between the sets of fans to a certain extent at least, in that there were many lovers of football there rather than partisan supporters of one side or another. In any case, thoughts of everyone kept returning particularly to what had happened yesterday. The visions of women and children being sunk by torpedoes in the Atlantic Ocean were vivid and chilling. Just what sort of an enemy were we fighting?

But Celtic fans both at home and in the trenches (Maley always made sure that results were sent in a telegram to the War Office for distribution as quickly as possible) rejoiced at the thought that their team were still the holders of the Glasgow Charity Cup as well as champions of Scotland.

FIFTEEN

'...DEPARTING IN DROVES'
AND IT WAS ONLY 2-1!

Celtic 2 Rangers 1   **Glasgow Cup Final**
Hampden Park   **9 October 1915**

Celtic: Shaw, McNair and Dodds; Young, Johnstone and McMaster; McAtee, Gallacher, McColl, McMenemy and Browning

Rangers: Lock, Craig and Muir; Gordon, Pursell and Bowie; Duncan, Cunningham, Reid, Cairns and Paterson

Referee: Mr A. Allan, Glasgow

IN some ways, this was the most bizarre Celtic v Rangers game of them all. The *Sunday Post* claims that this game took place before a crowd of 80,000. Other sources are a little more conservative, but most agree on 70,000. Even at 70,000, this was a remarkable attendance for war-time football, and there was a large number of soldiers in uniform, who were therefore admitted for free. Already in 1915 there were also a fair number of war-disabled soldiers as well, most of whom were helped to privileged places in the stand, or in the area immediately in front of the stand where the blind would be given a running commentary on the game by a volunteer.

And the war had now struck Celtic themselves. In the background was the Battle of Loos. It did not take any huge experience in unravelling the art of telling lies to work out that the 'success' reported in the newspapers was in fact no such thing. Sir John French, for example, assured everyone 'the German counter-attack was a failure'. Maybe so, but those who could read between the lines were able to figure out that if the British attack had been a 'success', there could not have been any German counter-attack!

In any case, British casualties had been enormous, not least to the families of Jimmy McMenemy and Joe Dodds. Both these men had lost a brother in the week leading up to this game, and rumours spread around Glasgow to the effect that neither McMenemy nor Dodds would play. But this was when the man-management skills of manager Willie Maley came to the fore. He called both men into his office, sympathised, listened to what they knew about their brothers' deaths, asked kindly about the rest of each family, and then said that he would leave it up to them whether they wanted to play in this game or not. He hoped they would, however, for he said that it might even be therapeutic to their grief and pointed out the example of Eck McNair, who had lost his wife to illness a few weeks ago. He was now back playing and doing a great job.

Both men listened to the man who was their hero as well as their boss and said that, yes, they wanted to play. In 1915 there was no monopoly in suffering, they reckoned, and many of the Celtic supporters were similarly bereaved. They deserved some sort of lift as well. Maley smiled and said, 'That's the spirit, boys! Now go out and do it!'

The team was playing superbly. Eight games played so far this season, and eight games won. Rangers, not for the first nor the last time in their history, buckled when they saw that. The day of the game was a beautiful autumn day, with a light, almost negligible breeze, and not even a hint of an autumn chill. The conditions were in total contrast to the horror of what was going on in the war at the time. If Loos was not going to be a success, how long might the war go on?

The crowd contained a fair number of people from outwith Glasgow. Many soldiers and workers from England and Ireland were based on the Clyde, and curiosity drove them to watch this game. Not a few Belgian refugees were there as well, some of them now with jobs in the shipbuilding or munitions industries, and they too were curious to see this game called 'football' which seemed to dominate Scottish life.

The *Sunday Post* was appalled at some of the play, claiming that some of the players were encouraged by their fans to do some things that were not 'legitimate'. Sunny Jim Young in particular was lectured by the referee for his treatment of Jimmy Paterson, whom he treated 'like an enemy, rather than an opponent'. Two other

Jimmies, McMenemy and Gordon, both Scotland internationals, both good friends normally and arguably the best players of their respective teams, were seen to confront each other after a nasty foul by Gordon on McMenemy. It is often claimed that James 'Napoleon' McMenemy, normally placid and mild-mannered, was not given to retaliation. That is generally correct, but he also knew how to 'dish out the verbals', as they might have put it a century later. Mr Allan intervened and awarded Celtic a free kick, but a minute or two later he pointed in the other direction when Johnny Browning fouled Scott Duncan mercilessly.

It was that sort of a game. Both teams were about equal in the 'He-Man' primitive sort of stuff, but in regard to arts of ball play, ball control and movement, Celtic were streets ahead. Celtic went ahead through Patsy GALLACHER. Following a sustained amount of Celtic pressure in which Rangers' goalkeeper Herbert Lock was outstanding, Celtic forced a corner on the right. Andy McAtee took it and the ball came straight to Browning, who, instead of trying to drive the ball through a ruck of players, calmly slipped it back to the unmarked Patsy Gallacher. Patsy had time to pick his spot, and to send the Celtic section of the crowd into raptures.

Rangers, however, fought back, and Duncan scored with a shot which Charlie Shaw got his hand to, but he could not prevent it from entering the net. This was undeserved on the balance of play, but before half-time Celtic restored their lead. The goal came after some brilliant half-back play when Young, Johnstone and McMaster charged forward, passing the ball to each other at speed, then feeding Andy McAtee on the right. He 'of the billiard table legs' swung over a ball to BROWNING who shot hard and beat 'Lock to the wide', a phrase which seems to mean the ball was well out of the goalkeeper's reach. It was a brilliant goal.

That was the position at half-time, the interval being celebrated noisily by the men in green on the terracing singing 'God Save Ireland', 'The Wearing o' the Green' and 'A Nation Once Again'. It was a clear message to those who were prepared to hear it that Ireland was in the war along with Great Britain at the moment, but that 'the grand old dame Britannia' would be well advised not to take anything for granted!

The second half saw Celtic on top the whole time, and the wonder was that no more goals were scored. Celtic simply knew how to pass the ball to each other 'full of fine football' and the attack was 'brainy', especially Gallacher, McMenemy and Browning. Captain McNair showed everyone why he was called 'the icicle', but the best man on the park was the grossly underrated left-half called Johnny McMaster. By no means a handsome man with his lantern jaw and perpetually melancholic countenance, Johnny was quick to the ball, passed superbly and created loads of opportunities for the forwards, who really should have scored a great deal more goals, and would have done so, had it not been for the inspirational Herbert Lock in the Rangers goal.

In the other goal, Charlie Shaw might well have not been there, and it was one of those games where everyone joked about him going off for a cup of tea, going out for an evening newspaper or even off to see his mythical lady friend rumoured to be an actress at the Pavilion Theatre. These were jokes, but what was definitely true was the departure of the Rangers fans. The *Glasgow Herald* talks about 'thousands passing through the exit gates nearly half an hour before the finish', yet the score was only 2-1! So outclassed were the Rangers that some of them, notably centre-forward Willie Reid, a Scotland internationalist, and inside-left Tommy Cairns, arguably to become the greatest Ranger of them all after the war, hardly got a kick of the ball.

This was the stuff to give the troops, and Maley was, as usual, quick off his mark to send a telegram to the War Office with the score to distribute to Scottish and Irish troops, particularly those who were involved at Loos. Assuming the War Office did its job, the troops would have known the result only a matter of about an hour after Tom White, the Celtic director, took possession of the lovely old trophy from Mr Maguire of the Glasgow FA. Celtic had not done so well in this trophy of late – they had last won it in 1909/10 – but this was an important success in 1915, especially as there had been no Scottish Cup since the commencement of hostilities.

It did not heal the grief and pain of those who had lost so much at Loos, but it did mean that if Jimmy McMenemy or Joe Dodds went to visit their distressed and bereaved sisters-in-law that weekend, they had another medal to show them. It also meant that so many supporters could face Monday morning in the shipyards, the munitions factories, the blacksmith's forge or the bakery (and the younger ones could go to school) with a smile on their faces.

SIXTEEN

THE CASSIDY CAVALCADE

Rangers 0 Celtic 2   **Scottish League**
Ibrox Stadium   **1 January 1921**

Rangers: Robb, Manderson and McCandless; Meiklejohn, Dixon and Muirhead; Archibald, Cunningham, Henderson, Cairns and Morton

Celtic: Shaw, McNair and McStay; Gilchrist, Cringan and McMaster; McAtee, Gallacher, McInally, Cassidy and McLean

Referee: Mr T. Dougray, Bellshill

NEW Year's Day 1921 was a fine day. New Year celebrations, as usual, had been long and intense, but soon after midday there was a general movement to the west end of Glasgow to Ibrox to see the game that everyone had been talking about for weeks, the Old Firm derby between Rangers and Celtic. Rangers were undefeated in the league, but Celtic were not all that far behind them, and were the winners of the then-prestigious Glasgow Cup, in which they had beaten Rangers in the semi-final and Clyde in the final.

This Old Firm game was, of course, more than a football match, for it must be seen in the background of what was going on in Ireland at this time. The picture was confused, and the British newspapers grossly misrepresented what was actually going on, portraying the Irish patriots as criminals and thugs and ignoring or playing down the activities of the real criminals, the Auxiliaries, commonly known as the Black and Tans recruited to a large extent from the prisons of Dartmoor and Peterhead. But the rest of the world was not so impressed, and people wondered, for example, why the Lord Mayor of Cork, the educated and urbane Terence McSweeney, had died on hunger strike in Brixton Prison, London, and why the Royal Irish Constabulary and Auxiliaries had opened fire on the crowd at a Gaelic football match at Croke Park.

The political situation was no clearer. Ireland had voted overwhelmingly in favour of De Valera's Sinn Fein in the December 1918 General Election, and when independence was not immediately granted, Sinn Fein had unilaterally seceded to form a Dail in Dublin. The problem was the minority in the North who feared independence, and there was now a disturbing trend in Glasgow that Rangers were beginning to identify with that minority. Both full-backs, Bert Manderson and Billy McCandless, were Ulstermen, and now that Harland and Wolff's shipbuilding concern were active on the Clyde, loads of Ulstermen had moved to Glasgow and had begun to support Rangers, with their offensive songs and ridiculous beliefs that the Battle of the Somme could have been won if it had been left to the Ulstermen, for example.

All this was certainly in the air that New Year's Day. 1920 had seen a change at the top of Rangers as well. William Wilton had sadly perished in a boating accident on the Clyde near Gourock in early May, and he had been replaced by William Struth, called, not without cause, 'ruthless Struth', and he was not slow to realise the changing nature of the Rangers support and tap into its potential. Willie Maley of Celtic claimed to have been a close friend of William Wilton. He never made the same claim about his relationship with Struth.

The teams seemed equally balanced. Both had sound defences and good attacking footballers in their forward line, but Rangers were more reliable, if a little less flamboyant than the champagne football of which Patsy Gallacher and Tommy McInally were capable. It was a game which promised a great deal. The crowd was excited and animated, but one of the differences between this crowd and those before the war was that the Rangers fans tended to congregate at one end (the end nearest the subway) and the Celtic fans at the other. Supporters also dressed more in the colours of their side, wearing rosettes and waving wooden 'crawmills' to make a noisy sound. And there were some who appeared wearing captured German helmets with slogans like 'good old Rangers' or 'Celts for ever' written upon them.

There was also the sad sight of the disabled. They were normally admitted free, and were given a special enclosure in front of the Main Stand where volunteers supplied them with tea and biscuits. The blind were a special case. They sat in one section of the enclosure and had the game described to them by volunteer 'commentators'.

When the game started, it was clear that Rangers were probably having the better of the play, although their star left-winger Alan Morton, who had joined the club from Queen's Park in 1920, was not making much of the determined and steady Alec McNair, and the same could be said of centre-forward George Henderson, who was up against Willie Cringan. Tommy Cairns was a tricky little player, however, and he was backed up by the sheer solidity of Tommy Muirhead and Davie Meiklejohn behind him. But even when they did get forward, they found Celtic's ever-reliable Charlie Shaw in the goal and Alec McNair to stop them, as well as Willie McStay, a war veteran and a very impressive left-back.

Celtic, for their part, seemed to be trying to involve Patsy Gallacher as much as possible, and this was understandable, for Patsy who on song was the best in the world. It was often rumoured that he and the 'boy wonder' Tommy McInally did not get on, for they were two of a kind, both in their style of play and general personality, but there was none of this on show today, and the Celtic forward line played as a cohesive unit.

The first half was heading towards its close – time had passed so quickly – when Celtic took the lead. It was a long through ball to Joe CASSIDY who ran on and scored, giving goalkeeper Robb no chance. It was all the more effective because it was unexpected, but it was also a great tribute to the ever-alert Joe Cassidy. Cassidy was the proud possessor of the Military Medal since his days in the Black Watch and the Highland Light Infantry in the war. He had been a key element of Celtic since leaving the Army, but this was to be the first time that he was ever to come close to heroic status.

Half-time was spent in glorious appreciation of that goal and eager anticipation of the second half, with the real belief growing that today could mark the end of Rangers' unbeaten league run. Certainly, the noise from the Celtic supporters was far greater in volume than the noise from the other end.

As the second half commenced, the play intensified. Charlie Shaw once again pulled off several fine saves as Rangers pressed to preserve their undefeated record, and then Celtic would run up the field and try to add to the lead. It was great entertainment, and the crowd, which had now swelled to such an extent that there was very little room for anyone else, thoroughly enjoyed it. But Celtic were now the better side, and about halfway through the second half came the moment which confirmed Celtic's victory and destroyed Rangers' undefeated record.

Patsy Gallacher made ground on the right of the park, defeating a couple of opponents, then he passed an inch-perfect ball to Tommy McInally, with Cassidy lurking behind him. In a brilliant piece of work, McInally shaped to shoot, but then suddenly jumped over the ball and shouted 'Joe!' so loudly that it was heard in the press box in the stand over the noise of the crowd. It was a brilliant dummy, and all Joe CASSIDY had to do was dribble the ball around McCandless and then goalkeeper Robb, to score what was a genuinely brilliant goal. The Celtic end lit up in appreciation of all this, and the volume never diminished until the game ended with 'Erin's Green Valleys' being belted out, to the unashamed joy of the writer of the *Glasgow Observer*, who, one imagines, broke the so-called neutrality of the press box by joining in!

It was a tremendous victory for Celtic, and much feted throughout the Irish Diaspora, not only in Scotland and Glasgow itself. The Paisley Road after the game was full of horse-drawn and motorised Supporters Brake Clubs travelling in both directions, with supporters waving flags and blowing bugles and singing their songs of victory. Each brake had some sort of inscription on it, recently produced by chalk. The obvious one was Celtic 2 Rangers 0, but there were variations along the lines of Cassidy 2 Meiklejohn 0, Maley 2 Struth 0, Rebels 2 Black and Tans 0 as well as the more oblique and opaque ones of 'Good Old Joe', 'Sinn Fein Abu' and 'Glasgow is Irish'.

1921 was thus well begun, but the form of the team was not quite consistent enough to win the Scottish League, nor the Scottish Cup. They would win the Glasgow Charity Cup at the end of the season, beating Rangers again, but that was all. Rangers would win the Scottish League but would lose out in the final of the Scottish Cup to Partick Thistle, for whom Celtic veteran

Jimmy McMenemy now played. The game was played at Celtic Park, Napoleon's old stamping ground, and many Celtic fans turned up that day to support Thistle.

New Year's Day 1921 would remain in the hearts of Celtic supporters for a long time. It would have to. Not until 1983 (62 years later) would Celtic again defeat Rangers at Ibrox when the fixture was played on New Year's Day.

SEVENTEEN

'WE BEAT THE RANGERS IN THE CUP...'

Celtic 5 Rangers 0	**Scottish Cup Semi-Final**
Hampden Park	**21 March 1925**

Celtic: Shevlin, W. McStay and Hilley; Wilson, J. McStay and McFarlane; Connolly, Thomson, McGrory, Gallacher and McLean

Rangers: Robb, Manderson and McCandless; Meiklejohn, Dixon and Craig; Archibald, Cunningham, Henderson, Cairns and Morton

Referee: Mr P. Craigmyle, Aberdeen

CELTIC were an annoying team to watch in the mid-1920s. They were a curious mixture of men like Patsy Gallacher, as great a player as anyone had ever seen, and youngsters like Peter Wilson, Alec Thomson – both good, emerging players – and a prodigiously talented young goalscorer called James McGrory. Yet they never seemed to be able to string together any consistent form. Since the war they had won the Scottish Cup only once, in 1923, and the Scottish League twice, in 1919 and 1922. For a club of Celtic's pedigree and for supporters who recalled the great Celtic teams of before the war, this was all very disappointing.

It was probably true to say that Rangers, man for man, were better than Celtic in those days. A solid defence, some good midfielders (although that area of the field was possibly their weak link), a talented forward line which included Alan Morton 'The Wee Blue Deil' and Tommy Cairns 'Tireless Tommy' – all added to a grim Presbyterian determination to win, whatever the cost, meant that they had won the league for the previous two years (and would do so this year as well) to the delight of their manager, the tyrannical and terrifying Willie Struth.

But two things had changed about Rangers of late. One was the now blatant identification with the cause of Protestantism and the equally blatant (although never overtly stated) policy of refusing to employ anyone of the Roman Catholic faith. This policy brought them great credit in the eyes of all those who feared that Roman Catholics were about to take over the country, a belief that even found root in the Church of Scotland, whose 1923 blood-curdling denunciations of that other Christian faith are quite astonishing for anyone in the modern world to read. But because the Church of Scotland said what it said, and because Rangers did not employ Roman Catholics, bigots found a home at Ibrox. It must, however, also be stressed that the Rangers support also contained many decent people, attracted by success and the undeniably good players that Rangers possessed.

The other thing about Rangers was their growing obsession with the Scottish Cup, and their need to win it. 1903 had been their last success in that tournament, and although some of these intervening years had seen the Great War, 22 years was still a long time. Since 1903, Celtic had won the Scottish Cup in 1904, 1907, 1908, 1911, 1912, 1914 and 1923, and Rangers had appeared in five finals, losing in 1904, 1905, 1921 and 1922, while the 1909 final had been abandoned after the Hampden riot. It was a poor record, and the Glasgow music halls (of which there was a veritable plethora in the 1920s) had much fun at Rangers' expense.

Rangers had reason to believe, however, that this could be their year. They had beaten Celtic three times that season already, and assuming they beat Celtic today they did not expect a great deal of bother from the winner of Dundee and Hamilton Academical in the Scottish Cup Final. They approached today's match with a degree of confidence, bordering on arrogance. They were, after all, Rangers, and Mr Struth was always very good at telling them how good they were.

Celtic had needed three games to get the better of St Mirren in the quarter-final, and even then the game had ended controversially. But Jimmy McGrory had scored the only goal of the game, and Celtic had only a few days to prepare themselves for Rangers. But they had Patsy Gallacher, not only the best player of them all, but also a superb tactician and in this case a motivator of others.

At Hampden, Celtic used the dressing room on the right as you entered the Main Stand. This was because it was nearer the east, where Celtic's ground was, and of course in the 1920s it was not unknown for players to turn up in dribs and drabs accompanied by and escorted by their fans. From this, Patsy Gallacher got an idea of just how much the supporters wanted to win a trophy and exactly what it meant to so many.

Patsy allowed Mr Maley to say his piece, and then captain Willie McStay said his bit before he, with the full blessing of Maley, took the floor. He said that he was a great believer in hoodoos and jinxes and that they should remind the Rangers players of their jinx in the Scottish Cup. Rangers full-backs Manderson and McCandless, fellow Irishmen and possibly, said Patsy with a twinkle in his eye, more given to supernatural beliefs, might be susceptible to being reminded of such things. Dixon and Craig were the two weak links, Morton and Cairns could be neutralised by effective marking by Willie McStay and Peter Wilson, while Henderson in the centre was a provincial who had simply overreached himself. He also suggested that Celtic should lie back, take things easy and not try anything silly for the first quarter of an hour at least. The longer the game went on without Rangers scoring, the more they would become nervous, as indeed would their fans in the massive crowd.

The crowd was given as 101,714, a record for a game that was not an international in Scotland, and the first time that a six-figure crowd had been recorded for a domestic game. The day was bright and sunny but with a coldish east wind blowing towards the Mount Florida goal, the goal that Celtic defended in the first half. Celtic had already surprised Rangers by winning the toss and choosing to play against the wind, then Celtic did as Patsy had suggested, allowing Rangers to come to them up to a point, but then crowding them out and not allowing a shot at goal. Rangers were clearly bewildered by all this, for they had expected Celtic to come at them out of the traps. But it never happened, and then in the 30th minute Celtic went ahead. Paddy Connolly, not without cause called 'the greyhound', sprinted down the right wing, lofted a ball over to young McGRORY who finished things off with little bother.

Half-time came and Celtic left the field with a spring in their step. They had weathered the worst of the storm, they would now have the wind at their backs, and, more importantly, they had Patsy Gallacher!

At the start of the second half came Rangers' big chance. It was a double chance, in fact. Davie Meiklejohn hammered the ball against the Celtic bar with Shevlin beaten and the ball rebounded to Tommy Cairns with the goal at his mercy and plenty of time for him to choose his spot. Incredibly, to the relief of the green-and-white hordes behind that goal, 'Tireless Tommy' headed weakly into the arms of Peter Shevlin.

It was Rangers' only real chance in the game, for Celtic now took the game by the scruff of the neck and pressed forward on the attack. Soon 'Erin's Green Valleys' was being belted forth from the King's Park end of the ground as the goals began to go in. A Connolly corner kick looked destined for McGrory, but McGrory was simply the decoy, taking Meiklejohn and Dixon with him while Adam McLEAN headed home. The third goal was a delight to watch. McGRORY swung a ball out to the feet of Connolly and charged forward to take the return ball, delivered with astonishing precision by 'the greyhound'.

Twenty minutes remained and the exit gates at the Mount Florida end opened to allow home the bewildered Rangers supporters. Some of them were out of the ground when they heard another roar from the deliriously happy Celts at the other end – goalkeeper Willie Robb had fisted a cross ball out to Alec THOMSON who made it four, and then Celtic went 'nap' when Robb made a further mistake in a pass back from Bert Manderson, and Adam McLEAN nipped in to score his second.

Full time came and Hampden presented an amazing scene. Half the 101,714 crowd had gone home or were going, while the other half stayed and cheered on their favourites, with all the old familiar songs being churned out by fans with tears in their eyes. In the stand, old heroes like Quinn and McMenemy stood to applaud their successors, and Maley looked like the cat who had got all the cream!

Apart from anything else, this win had given Celtic the opportunity to win the Scottish Cup for the 11th time on 11 April. Their opponents would be Dundee, and once again Patsy Gallacher would play his part in winning this game. But for the moment, Glasgow belonged to Celtic, and the song to commemorate this game lasted on the terracings of Celtic Park for 40 years after this:

> 'Hello, Hello, we are the Tim Malloys
> Hello, Hello, you'll know us by the noise
> We f***ed the Rangers in the Cup
> Twas great to be alive,
> Not one, not two, not three, not four, but five!'

EIGHTEEN

AN IBROX WIN AT LAST

Rangers 1 Celtic 2	**Scottish League**
Ibrox Stadium	**21 September 1935**

Rangers: Dawson, Gray and McDonald; Meiklejohn, Simpson and Winning; Main, Brown, Smith, Gillick and Roberts

Celtic: Kennaway, Hogg and McGonagle; Geatons, Lyon and Paterson; Delaney, Buchan, Crum, MacDonald and Murphy

Referee: Mr M.C. Hutton, Glasgow

IT had been a long time since 1921. New Year's Day 1921 was the last time that Celtic had won at Ibrox, the goals being scored on that famous occasion by Joe Cassidy. Since then Celtic had beaten Rangers at Celtic Park and at Hampden, but never at Ibrox. Too often Celtic had gone there expecting a defeat, and, of course, getting one as a result. It was what was called the self-fulfilling prophecy.

More pertinently perhaps, it was now almost a decade ago since Celtic had won the Scottish League. Since Tommy McInally and company had delivered the goods in 1926, Rangers had had it all their own way with only Motherwell in 1932 breaking the depressing sequence. Celtic had won the Scottish Cup three times in the last decade and the Glasgow competitions now and again but had always seemed to lack the consistency required to win the league.

The problem lay, to a certain extent, with Willie Maley himself. Still a giant of the Scottish game and therefore virtually irreplaceable at Celtic Park, Maley had become awkward, curmudgeonly, aloof, hypochondriacal, obsessed with money and forever talking about 'the Celts of old' and comparing the present-day players unfavourably with them, an attitude which hardly helped or encouraged the current squad. There is a suggestion that he even suffered a little from depression in the wake of the tragic early deaths of Sunny Jim Young, John

Thomson and Peter Scarff, but in any case his time, it was felt, had passed.

But there was now a difference. Last October, Celtic had appointed as trainer Jimmy McMenemy, one of the 'Celts of old', and arguably the best of them all. Jimmy was an unassuming man and not really cut out for the harsh side of football management, but there was no one who knew the game of football, its tactics and its dynamics as well as McMenemy. That was why he was called Napoleon, the greatest general of them all. Patsy Gallacher was possibly the better player, but Napoleon was the better tactician.

Good at tactics, and also good at tact! A clever man, Napoleon knew how to run the team while all the time deferring to Maley and allowing him to think that it was he who was making the decisions. For his part, Maley loved McMenemy, whom he had recruited as long ago as 1902, and Celtic Park began to blossom in rare harmony and trust. It was a combination which would deliver.

The key to the success of the great forward line in which McMenemy had starred 30 years previously was their ability to interchange position and to understand each other. Napoleon now worked hard at doing likewise with this bunch of forwards, and he certainly had the raw material to do so. McGrory was, of course, McGrory, but there were also two lively wingers in Jimmy Delaney, clearly one of the best around, and the grossly undervalued Frank Murphy. Johnny Crum was fast developing, as indeed was Willie Buchan.

Today, however, Celtic had a familiar problem in that Jimmy McGrory was injured – something that was happening with a great deal more frequency these days as Jimmy was getting older – so a reshuffle was required. Crum moved to centre-forward and at inside-left we saw the introduction of Malky MacDonald, commonly known as 'Callum'. He had not as yet made a huge impact at Celtic Park, but his great strength was his versatility. He had played at centre-half, right-half and inside-right (where he would have his moments of glory) but today he was asked to play. at inside-left. Not that it mattered. In this Celtic set-up, nominal positions counted for very little.

Rangers were also without one of their star men in Bob McPhail. A crowd of 71,000 turned up at Ibrox on a fine dry day, and they saw a good but goalless first half in which, according to Rex Kingsley who then (calling himself simply 'Rex') wrote for the *Sunday Post* (after the war he would be more identified with the *Sunday Mail*), Celtic were 'the prettier sight' with their neat passing. Chick Geatons and George Paterson were singled out for their good work. The only problem about that was that Celtic had frequently been acknowledged as the better team in the past 15 years in their games against Rangers, but had ended up with nothing to show for it.

Things then took a distinctive turn for the worse at the start of the second half when, with four minutes gone, Jimmy Smith, Rangers' centre-forward, scored. He had been well shadowed by Willie Lyon and seemed to have been diverted from the centre of the goal with the ball when he suddenly turned and scored what one would have to admit was a great goal from a distance.

Spirits sank behind the Celtic goal, for there was a distinct feeling that we have been here before and that Celtic would now subside. Not a bit of it! Celtic were soon back in the game, and it was the two wingers who made the goal. Jimmy Delaney ran down his wing, won a corner kick, then took it himself and fired a glorious cross over the heads of the Rangers defence, and Frank MURPHY came charging in to head past an astonished Dawson. The *Sunday Post* then says that Murphy 'was kissed so enthusiastically by his joyous team-mates that the Garbo won't mean a thing to him now' – a strange piece of writing and something that would not be likely to be written today.

But irrespective of the charms of Greta Garbo, Celtic were now on level terms and for a long time after that pressed hard until, with about 15 minutes to go, Johnny CRUM put Celtic ahead after a wonderful Celtic move, starting with George Paterson and involving Malky MacDonald and Willie Buchan, who swung over a ball to find Crum 'as much on his own as a cross-eyed flapper at a dance'. Crum trapped the ball and picked his spot.

Joy abounded at the Celtic end and a few misguided youths tried to invade the field to congratulate the players, but the game was not finished yet. The desperate Rangers threw everything at Celtic, but lacked the guile to get through a well-organised defence. They resorted to cross balls, but Joe Kennaway, Celtic's Canadian goalkeeper, was well up to the challenge, rising above everyone to clutch the ball. But this was 1935 when shoulder charging was legal, and twice the coarse Jimmy Smith charged him hoping to knock him into the back of the net. But Smith came off second best and Kennaway was just going to kick the ball upfield when he saw Davie Meiklejohn about to charge him. Instinctively he threw out a hand to protect himself, but this was not allowed and referee Mr Hutton, correctly in terms of the prevailing laws of the game, immediately awarded a penalty kick. It was an awful law, meaning that shoulder charging was allowed but the goalkeeper was not allowed to defend himself! It was legal, however, and Rangers now, late in the game, had a chance to equalise.

Meiklejohn himself prepared to take the penalty. He was a man who almost personified Rangers in the 1920s and 1930s in the same way as John Greig fulfilled a similar role for them in the 1960s and 1970s. Meiklejohn was a decent man who had conducted himself with total dignity in the tragedy of John Thomson in 1931 even to the extent of reading the lesson at John's memorial service, but he was also the man who had scored the famous penalty which set Rangers on their way to victory in the 1928 Scottish Cup Final to give them their first Scottish Cup in 25 years.

But now he had another penalty to take. *The Scotsman* captures the moment: 'In almost unnatural stillness and with five minutes to go, Meiklejohn stepped up and placed the ball to the right of Kennaway.' But it was too close to Kennaway, and not really hit with enough power. Joe simply moved to his right, dropped to his knee and pushed the ball away with his hand. The ball was cleared and Joe was surrounded by exultant team-mates as the Celtic supporters went mad with joy. Their joy was sustained for the next five minutes until Mr Hutton, 'almost the perfect official', as the *Sunday Post* says, blew for time up and triggered another pitch invasion from Celtic supporters.

This was the eighth game in a row that Celtic had won this season. They had lost at Pittodrie on the first day but since then had shown splendid form. The significance of this game was that it showed Celtic that they could beat Rangers, even at Ibrox. Hitherto, one had got the impression that they didn't feel that they were allowed to win there, and those who watched Celtic in the early 1960s will know what I am talking about! But Celtic now went on to win the Scottish League in 1935/36. It was a league campaign characterised by the goalscoring exploits of Jimmy McGrory, but it might not have happened if it hadn't been for this early-season defeat of Rangers at Ibrox.

NINETEEN

'DON'T LET IT GO TO YOUR HEAD, SON'

Celtic 4 Rangers 2	**Glasgow Charity Cup Final**
Hampden Park	**9 May 1936**

Celtic: Kennaway, Hogg and Morrison; Geatons, Lyon and Paterson; Delaney, Buchan, McGrory, Crum and Murphy

Rangers: Dawson, Gray and Cheyne; Meiklejohn, Simpson and Winning; Ross, Venters, Smith, McPhail and Turnbull

Referee: Mr M. C. Hutton, Glasgow

THIS Glasgow Charity Cup Final was in a sense the unofficial play-off for the championship of Scotland. Celtic had won the Scottish League that season for the first time in a decade, but Rangers had won the Scottish Cup, Celtic having unaccountably lost 0-2 to St Johnstone at Celtic Park in an early round. But that was just a small blip in an otherwise great season for the Parkhead club.

Jimmy 'Napoleon' McMenemy was now the trainer at Celtic Park. The ageing Maley, now increasingly prone to bouts of depression and psychosomatic illnesses, was seen less often at Celtic Park than previously and in practice, although Maley did the administration and the public relations, McMenemy was the manager of the football side. Maley loved and trusted McMenemy and was quite happy to allow him to run that side of things, especially when, fairly obviously, the system was working well. Napoleon was far too diffident to claim any of the credit, and that suited everyone as well, for Maley was always very happy to use words like 'I' and 'my' and 'we' when talking about Celtic.

The players found Maley's behaviour inconsistent. Sometimes brusque and rude and certainly not a man to approach if you had a problem of any kind, other times he would be friendly, affable, talking to players with tears in his eyes about John Thomson,

Sunny Jim, Dan Doyle and Sandy McMahon and other Celtic players who had died before their time.

McMenemy's plan was to replicate 'the Celts of old', as Maley used to call them. This was the great team in which he himself had played 30 years previously. That great team depended on several things – one or two really great players, teamwork, dedication, speed, camaraderie and in particular the ability of the forwards to constantly change position. He was particularly fortunate in having loads of great players who would have graced a Celtic team at any point in history, with two in particular standing out – Jimmy McGrory, whom everyone knew about and who had scored 50 goals that season, and the other Jimmy, Jimmy Delaney, the lad from Cleland who had made such an impact recently.

Captain Willie Lyon was an inspiration. He was an Englishman, but that meant nothing at all, for in the same way that Celtic could open its doors to all religions, so too could it accept people of different nationalities. He was naturally a leader, and knew how to comfort and cajole when required. He was also an excellent player and frequently we find the opinion expressed that if he had been Scottish he would have been a strong candidate for a Scottish cap. Goalkeeper Joe Kennaway was Canadian, the replacement for John Thomson, and he was a superb clutcher of the ball with great positional sense. Chick Geatons, the right-half, had been around for some time. A Fifer from Lochgelly, Chick had suffered a little after fellow Fifer John Thomson had died, but had recovered now with the breath of fresh air that had come with the arrival of Napoleon. He had also changed position from right-half to left-half.

Rangers, on the other hand, had seemed a spent force, or at least a team which was going through a transition period. Having more or less won every league title since the war (they had lost only to Celtic in 1919, 1922, 1926 and Motherwell in 1932), they had now lost out in 1936 to this new Celtic team, and their own supporters were of the belief that they had been lucky to win the Scottish Cup. On the other hand, they still had men like Dougie Gray, Davie Meiklejohn, Jimmy Simpson, Jimmy Smith and, above all, Bob McPhail, commonly known as 'Greetin 'Boab' (especially now that he was growing old) but arguably still one of the best players around.

1936 was generally a good year. The recession, or at least the worst of it, had passed, and although Hitler and Mussolini caused more than a little worry, the general outlook seemed a lot better than it had done a few years before. The old King, George V, had died in January and his son Edward VIII was on the throne. He was young, personable, headstrong yet well liked by everyone, although rumours did circulate about some of his lady friends. The Prince of Wales was still the most eligible bachelor around, with many well-documented occasions when he would arrive at a railway station, ignore the town councillors and the official welcoming party, and go and talk to poorly dressed women and their young children.

A total of 43,165 had paid £2,224 to Glasgow charities to see this game and they saw a cracker. The weather was fine, the pitch was in good condition and the play was fast. Celtic's first goal was a tribute to the training methods of Jimmy McMenemy. Celtic broke down the left with Frank Murphy, a grossly underrated player in the opinion of many supporters, who felt that if it had not been for Jimmy Delaney doing even better on the right, Murphy would have been rated as the star on the left. However that may be, Murphy's cross was aimed at McGrory, but McGrory immediately ran in another direction taking about three defenders with him and in popped the other Jimmy – DELANEY – to put Celtic one ahead. It was a move which had clearly originated in the training ground, and was much appreciated by the supporters.

Celtic remained on top until near the half-time interval when Rangers won a corner kick on the left. Jim Turnbull took it and the ball came to Bob McPhail, who was not marked as tightly as he should have been by the Celtic defence, and McPhail made no mistake as he levelled the scores. Twenty minutes after the interval, it was Jim Turnbull himself who put Rangers ahead. This time it came from a free kick foolishly conceded by Celtic's left-back Jock Morrison on Rangers' Jimmy Smith when he was nowhere near the goal and not likely to do anyone any damage. It was about 30 yards out, and instead of someone trying to go for goal and glory, captain Meiklejohn himself took the kick and floated it across the goalmouth for Turnbull to score.

Thus Celtic were now in a losing position but this Celtic team could fight, and amidst great excitement Frank Murphy charged down the left wing leaving a trail of Rangers defenders in his wake, then drove across a simple enough cross for DELANEY to score with a tap-in; 2-2 and the game was now levelled. It all now looked as if it would go down to the counting of corners – something that they did then before the idea of a penalty shoot-out.

Five minutes remained, but Celtic were now in the ascendancy, and Jimmy DELANEY proved his class once again when he picked up a ball on the right wing and, instead of charging down the wing towards the corner flag, he cut inside and ran in a mazy diagonal with Rangers players unable to tackle him, until Jerry Dawson came out of his goal and Jimmy calmly lobbed the ball over his head to put Celtic 3-2 up. This was pure class, and the Celtic end was a sea of acclamation for this piece of brilliance.

Rangers were now a beaten team, and the Celtic victory was complete in the last minute when Jimmy McGRORY headed number four, and the celebrations began in earnest. Celtic had now won the Glasgow Charity Cup for the 21st time. Significantly, the last time they had won the Glasgow Charity Cup was in 1926, the last time they had won the Scottish League.

There was a postscript to this occasion. Jimmy Delaney himself told the story of how he came off the field feeling quite pleased with himself, as well he might. He had received the congratulations of his team-mates, trainer McMenemy, and even from the Rangers players, and then he met his manager Willie Maley. Maley made as if to pass him, and then turned to him and growled 'Don't let that go to your head, son!' and moved on.

If this story is true, it is hardly surprising that so many of Maley's younger players did not like him. He may have had his tongue in his cheek at that point and the young Delaney did not realise it, but there are also quite a lot of other stories of some of Maley's players being unwilling to sit on the same tram as he did, and resenting his autocratic and inexplicable diktat that they were not allowed to own a motor car. Yet he was still very well respected in Scottish football – as indeed he deserved to be – and was very proud of his team winning another trophy. The Scottish Cup would follow next year, and then in 1938 the Scottish League again and the winning of the Empire Exhibition Trophy. Maley was not yet a spent force.

TWENTY

STARTING THE
NEW YEAR WELL

Celtic 3 Rangers 0	Scottish League
Celtic Park	1 January 1938

Celtic: Kennaway, Hogg and Morrison; Lynch, Lyon and Paterson; Carruth, MacDonald, Crum, Divers and Murphy

Rangers: Jenkins, Gray and Winning; McKillop, Simpson and Brown; Fiddes, Venters, Smith, McPhail, Kinnear

Referee: Mr M.C. Hutton, Glasgow

JUST quite why attendances at football matches were so high at this time in history, no one has quite been able to explain. Last April, Hampden Park hosted in successive weeks two crowds of over 147,000, one for the Scotland v England international match and the other for the Celtic v Aberdeen semi-final, and attendances continued to be high this 1937/38 season. Today the crowd was given as 92,000 and quoted as the record attendance for Celtic Park, but the evidence for this is not strong. However, even if the attendance was a little short of that (most sources tend to go for something like 83,500), it was still an enormous crowd.

Nor was it only at Celtic Park that the crowds were huge; 37,600 were at Easter Road to see the Edinburgh derby, and at Stark's Park, Kirkcaldy, 19,700 were crammed in to see the Fife derby – and that was in the Second Division! The gates at Celtic Park today had to be closed, and those who could not get in shrugged their shoulders and went off to see Queen's Park v Third Lanark at Hampden and 25,000 attended that game as a result.

The reason often adduced for the phenomenal attendances in this era is the approach and even imminence of war, something that made everyone determined to enjoy life as long as they could. There is merit in that suggestion, but the real reason perhaps was an offshoot of the 'imminence of war' theory. The fact that war was possible, and even likely, meant that the economic depression was gone. Everyone now had a job, everyone was now needed to make armaments, ships, uniforms, boots, etc., and therefore there was a great deal of money in pockets to allow folk to travel on trains and buses and to attend football matches.

In addition, the product was good. Scotland felt good about itself once again. They had defeated England in 1935 and 1937 and earned a draw in 1936. They had even defeated Nazi Germany in 1936 when Jimmy Delaney scored the two goals on the day that the swastika was shamefully allowed to fly at Ibrox. Such things were important, and still are. It meant that everyone talked about football, and the newspapers reflected that, with loads of space devoted to it.

In Celtic's case, the product was very good. McGrory had now gone to become manager of Kilmarnock, but he had been replaced seamlessly by Johnny Crum, and what had seemed like a shoddy example of asset stripping in the selling of Willie Buchan to Blackpool for £10,000 was in fact a brilliant piece of business, for he was replaced almost immediately by Malky MacDonald ('Callum'), a man who had been used as a permanent utility man because of his versatility. He now became one of the best inside-rights that Celtic had ever had.

Today's crushing at Celtic Park could have been a great deal worse in terms of casualties, but several times play had to be suspended until such time as the crowd were ushered back onto the terracing. The St Andrew's Ambulance Service was kept busy dealing with people who had fainted in the crush, particularly during the swaying at the west end of the terracing. It was generally good humoured, but it was worrying. The weather was as clement as one might have hoped for on New Year's Day, and given the huge crowd the turnstiles had to be closed before kick-off. Just to prove that there was no discrimination in those who were allowed in and those who weren't, Celtic's great right-winger of about a decade ago, Paddy Connolly, 'the greyhound' was one of those who were denied admission!

For Celtic, Geatons and Delaney were injured, but the replacements, Matt Lynch and Joe Carruth (commonly known as 'the mad monk' for some reason) were more than adequate, and they played their part in Celtic producing today one of their best results against Rangers for some time. The *Glasgow Herald*, generally regarded as the most impartial of all the newspapers (apart from a pronounced, wistfully nostalgic liking for the amateur Queen's Park) is in no doubt about who the better team was. 'Steadfast in defence, mobile and thrustful at half-back, fast and daring in attack, Celtic reduced Rangers to a sad plight indeed and in doing so impressed everyone by their wonderful team spirit and apparently endless reserves of stamina.'

It was probably true that this Rangers team was not as good as some of the teams that they had had in the early 1930s, but they still had Bob McPhail, arguably their best-ever player, who on one occasion looked certain to score with a fierce drive, but Celtic's Canadian goalkeeper Joe Kennaway 'brought the house down' with a magnificent save, while Jenkins, Rangers' goalkeeper, at the other end also earned plaudits by his good keeping.

The major surprise was that it took Celtic 38 minutes to go ahead, so superior had they been in every respect. But the goal was a great one. A corner on the right was taken by Joe Carruth – Carruth found Crum who in turn slipped the ball through to John Divers. DIVERS controlled the ball cleverly, neatly side stepped an opponent, evaded the challenge of another and hammered the ball home – the eruptions of joy on the terracing causing serious and dangerous swaying as people lost their footing. After this, some women and children were seen to be taken out of the terracing and allowed to watch the rest of the game sitting on the running track.

This John Divers, incidentally, is commonly referred to as John Divers II by Celtic historians to distinguish him from his son John Divers III who played in the early 1960s and John Divers I (no relation as far as can be ascertained) who played in the 1890s. It is probably true to say that John Divers II was the best of the three of them.

Half-time saw the Celtic supporters on the western terracing and, in what would come to be called the Jungle in later years, in a permanent state of excitement, anticipating the second half while the Rangers fans, grossly outnumbered but still a significant part of the crowd, naturally disappointed with their team's performance but hoping for better things. Meanwhile, the police inspector in charge of the game just hoped that they could get through the game without any serious accidents. He was seen to be in earnest conversation with some of the Celtic directors and the referee as the players ran out for the second half.

The second goal came from the penalty spot, and it was conceded by Rangers' centre-half Jimmy Simpson with a save of which his son Ronnie would have been proud in years to come. Jimmy had had a terrible game today, having no idea how to get the better of the ubiquitous Johnny Crum, whose leading of the Celtic forward line today was a thing to behold, and earned the obvious approval of Jimmy Quinn in the stand. On this occasion, George Paterson tried to lob the ball over Simpson's head to get to Crum, and would have done so, but Simpson decided to play rugby or basketball and a penalty kick was awarded. Nowadays there might have been a red card as well, but this was 1938, and Malky MacDONALD converted the penalty. People who were there recalled the huge hush, then the explosion of sound as the ball hit the net, followed by the predictable bedlam on the terracing.

It was a similar tactic which brought the third goal in the 70th minute, but this time it was the gallus Crum who lobbed Simpson to find DIVERS. Divers read the situation as if it were an Agatha Christie detective novel and darted in Lennox-like to pick up the ball, dash past a static Rangers defender and hammer the ball into the net before the Rangers goalkeeper could realise what was going on.

Once again, delirium, but this time the pressure was eased with the departure of the Rangers support. The segregation was by no means as rigid as it would become after the war, and the crowd did contain a great deal of neutrals in any case, but the departure of the Rangers supporters meant that more of the crowd could breathe! They could also sing with a great deal more comfort, and 'Erin's Green Valleys' was belted out with passion and volume, and only those with a precociously enquiring kind of mind inclined to wonder how it was that Erin's green valleys could possibly look down on Parkhead!

Full time came with the fans still in full flow, and to everyone's relief, all supporters managed to leave the ground unscathed and lived to tell the tale – and what a tale it was! It was the springboard to winning the Scottish League, and also the all-British Empire Exhibition Trophy. Pity about the Scottish Cup, though. Celtic went out to Jimmy McGrory's Kilmarnock, thereby perhaps creating the dangerous illusion that Jimmy McGrory was a good manager, but Kilmarnock themselves would lose in the final to – of all teams – East Fife. Meanwhile, nothing happened to stay the imminence of the inevitable war.

TWENTY ONE

HOGAN, BODEN, WEIR AND TULLY, THE LADS THAT RAN THE RANGERS SULLY

Celtic 3 Rangers 1	**Scottish League Cup**
Celtic Park	**25 September 1948**

Celtic: Miller, Milne and Mallan; Evans, Boden and McAuley; Weir, W. Gallacher, J. Gallacher, Tully, Paton

Rangers: Brown, Lindsay and Shaw; McColl, Young and Cox; Waddell, Findlay, Thornton, Duncanson and Gillick

Referee: Mr R.G. Benzie, Irvine

FOR Celtic, 1948 was a dreadful year. In fact, the whole decade since 1938 had been disastrous. Celtic had had a dreadful Second World War with only a very few bright spots and a few starts like Jimmy Delaney to give any sort of succour and comfort to the troops and those at home who were suffering terribly. Without Willie Maley, the man who made Celtic, the team was rudderless and unable (often even seeming *unwilling*) to stand up to Rangers. April 1948 had seen Celtic perilously close to relegation, needing a late-season victory at Dens Park to save them, even though that particular game was not quite what it seemed to be. Dundee, according to those with eyes to see, shall we say, 'collaborated' (to use an unpleasant 1940s word with all its associations with French and Norwegian collaborators with the Nazis) to keep Celtic in Division 'A'!

But in summer 1948, two men arrived who would make a difference. One was a new coach called Jimmy Hogan who had worked all over Europe, and the other was an Irishman from Belfast Celtic by the name of Charles Patrick Tully. The story of Belfast Celtic is a sad and tragic one. Indeed, they would soon be forced out of existence after violence against them from Linfield supporters, but Charlie Tully was one of their best-ever players, and he very soon transferred his talents to Glasgow Celtic, where he very soon became a cult hero.

And how Celtic needed a cult hero in 1948! The war was over, and already there were a few signs of post-war recovery as the energetic Labour Government of the day set about creating the National Health Service and the Welfare State. This would, however, take time, and the creation of a good Celtic team was also looking as if it would need time. The mantle of the principal challengers to Rangers seemed to have fallen on Hibs, at least temporarily, for little was happening at Celtic Park to encourage anyone.

And yet the passion for the club remained constant. Attendances were huge, with supporters, now in an era of full employment with a little more money in their pockets, prepared to travel the length and breadth of Scotland to follow them. What they saw on the pitch may have discouraged them, but backed by the Celtic traditions and memories, they kept going. Most of them still remembered McGrory as a player, and the great Empire Exhibition Trophy team of 1938, and of course there were still a large amount of the support who could recall Tommy McInally and Patsy Gallacher and the great days of Jimmy Quinn. When was this going to happen again?

There were two Gallachers in the team. One was Willie, the son of Patsy, and the other was John or Jackie, the son of Hughie of Newcastle United fame. With respect to both sons, neither was a patch on their illustrious fathers. Patsy (regularly) and Hughie (occasionally, for he now lived in Newcastle) were seen at Celtic Park to watch their sons, but frequently left shaking their heads. It was into this set-up that young Charlie Tully entered, and indeed there were a few signs that he was making a difference. In the Scottish League Cup, a new competition instigated after World War Two, Celtic had beaten Hibs and Clyde in their group section and now faced Rangers at Celtic Park.

And Rangers! They had had a good war against little opposition, and still radiated arrogance and self-assurance. The ever-elegant Willie Struth was still in charge, their policy of religious discrimination still unchallenged, and in recent months the phrase 'Iron Curtain' had been used to describe their defence. It had been Winston Churchill who had coined that phrase a year ago to describe the tyranny of the Soviet Union and how impenetrable it was, and as Rangers had defenders like Jock Shaw, George Young, Willie Woodburn and Sammy Cox, it seemed an appropriate description.

But not today, however. Tully had played since the start of the season, but although it was obvious that he was a bit above the average Celtic player, he had not yet really turned it on, and it was today that he showed how good he really was. The *Sunday Post* finds it difficult to contain its enthusiasm, calling him 'the Pied Piper of Belfast' and talks about the 'other 21 players dancing to his Irish jig'.

A crowd of 65,000 turned up at Celtic Park to see this game, and they were well entertained. The weather was dull but dry. It was actually Rangers who took the lead, when Celtic's goalkeeper Willie Miller, making one of his very rare mistakes, dropped the ball for Findlay to put Rangers ahead and to reduce the Celtic fans to despair as they exchanged 'Here we go again' glances with each other. That was after ten minutes. Was this the prelude to another 'lie down' in the face of the seemingly unstoppable Rangers juggernaut?

But for one man, it might have been. Just on the half-hour mark, Tully with a superb pass found Johnny Paton after having signalled to him, with the ball at his feet, where exactly he wanted him to go. Paton then found the unmarked Jackie GALLACHER who finished the job with no bother. There was a bizarre note to this goal, for a linesman was seen to flag for offside when both Paton and Gallacher were clearly onside, and not even the Rangers defenders protested about the goal. Referee Mr Benzie waved the linesman down and the goal was given.

Just before half-time, with the Celtic fans now glowing with anticipation every time Tully got the ball, cheeky Charlie released the other GALLACHER, Willie, to put Celtic ahead. He did it this time with a header as he ran through and scored from a delicate Tully lob, giving goalkeeper Bobby Brown no chance. Half-time was thus spent with the Celtic end in uproar. It had been a long time since football of this calibre had been seen at Celtic Park.

The wizardry continued in the second half. The wonder was that Celtic did not score sooner but in fact they scored twice in a minute about halfway through the second half. Both were contentious involving offside (this was likely to happen, for the iron curtain defence employed an offside trap). One was given, and one wasn't. The first goal came from Jock WEIR, often called Celtic's 'utility man', a conscious echo of the 'make do and mend' culture of post-war austerity Britain. Rangers' protest was that Johnny Paton was in an offside position. Indeed he was, but as he was lying on the ground injured, referee Benzie ruled that he was 'not interfering with play' and the goal was given, to the intense fury of Rangers and their dervishes behind the goal who immediately then assumed that Mr Benzie was a Roman Catholic!

Whatever his religious beliefs, Mr Benzie was wrong (in the opinion of the *Sunday Post*) a minute later when he thought that Jackie GALLACHER was offside as he picked up a Tully pass and scored. Not that it mattered, for the Rangers end 'emptied as if by magic' as Celtic and Tully remained in total control to give the supporters a great result to celebrate.

And it did not stop there, for a couple of days later on the Glasgow Holiday Monday, Celtic beat Third Lanark 3-1 at Hampden to win the Glasgow Cup for the first time since 1940 before an astonishing crowd of 87,000 – something that clearly showed the size of the Celtic support. Once again it was Tully on song, and his name was much feted in all the impromptu street parties that were held that night. It was not often in the 1940s that there was dancing in the streets of the Gorbals (the last one had been VE Night in 1945), but this was one such occasion with everyone now convinced that Celtic were on the way back, and Charlie Tully was being openly compared to Patsy Gallacher of old.

Sadly, it did not turn out that way. Celtic had too many players who were little better than ordinary, and, in general, consistency was seldom a word that anyone applied to Celtic. Having won the first three games of their League Cup section, they then managed to lose the next three and were duly eliminated. They were nowhere in the league, and managed to lose to Second Division Dundee United (most of whose supporters cheerfully admitted that they supported Celtic as well) at the primitive Tannadice Park in the Scottish Cup in January.

But 25 to 27 September was a glorious weekend, hinting at what things might yet be. Charlie Tully would indeed have many more games like this one – although, because of the general ambience of the club at this time, not as many as we would have liked.

TWENTY TWO

A BOXING DAY CRACKER

Celtic 5 Rangers 3	Glasgow Cup Final Replay
Hampden Park	26 December 1955

Celtic: Beattie, Haughney and Fallon; Evans, Stein and Peacock; Smith, Fernie, Sharkey, Collins and Mochan

Rangers: Niven, Caldow and Little; McColl, Young and Rae; Scott, Simpson, Kichenbrand, Baird and Hubbard

Referee: Mr J. Mowat, Rutherglen

SCOTTISH football did not normally have football matches on Boxing Day in the 1950s. England certainly did – in fact, it was one of its biggest days of the year – but in Scotland where Christmas Day itself wasn't a public holiday until 1958, there would have been little point. But on this occasion, after the Glasgow Cup Final between Celtic and Rangers had been drawn in September, and no other date immediately suggested itself, the replay was arranged for Hampden this Boxing Day Monday with a 1.30pm kick-off to allow for the possibility of extra time before darkness fell. (Hampden would not have floodlights for a few years yet.)

It turned out to be an excellent idea, for the tie attracted a crowd of 39,000. They saw a good game of football and (something of great importance in the 1950s) everyone seemed to behave. In a week's time, the two teams would meet again for their New Year fixture. That would be less successful for Celtic, but today saw Celtic win 5-3 and lift their first Glasgow Cup since 1948.

One says that Christmas wasn't a public holiday. This was true but more and more employers were beginning to bow to realism and to give their workers a day off or to turn a blind eye to absenteeism. Certainly Santa Claus was beginning to have an effect on consumers, as the economy was now beginning to pick up. The bad old days of poverty seemed to be on the way out, and one of the side effects of this was a rise in the importance of

Christmas. Within a few years, you would begin to hear the cliché of 'Christmas being too commercialised'!

The game took place on a dullish Boxing Day and with a wind that the *Evening Times* describes as 'snell', meaning very cold. Quite a few of the Celtic team, and certainly manager Jimmy McGrory himself, knew of the serious illness of Tommy McInally, Celtic's flawed genius of the 1920s. Tommy would die on the Thursday, and one hopes that someone told Tommy of Celtic's fine win that day. Tommy had himself starred in the Glasgow Cup on many occasions, and won four Glasgow Cup medals.

Celtic surprisingly dropped Jimmy Walsh from the right-wing position and brought in Eric Smith for that job. Charlie Tully was out long term, and many of us wondered whether we would see him again very often, for he was now clearly ageing. He was far from finished, though. An odd feature of the team selection was that both centre-forwards were playing their first Old Firm game – Jim Sharkey for Celtic and South African Don Kichenbrand for Rangers. Sharkey was a good striker (as it would be proved today) yet grossly underestimated by the Celtic Establishment, while Kichenbrand did not last long for Rangers either, his cause not helped when news leaked out that his wife was a practising Roman Catholic and that he sometimes went along with her!

George Young of Rangers won the toss for ends and chose to play with the biting east wind in the first half, something that meant that Celtic were playing towards their own supporters in the first half. Rain was now coming on as well and conditions were far from pleasant, but the two teams served up some fine football.

It was probably true to say that neither team was satisfying their supporters at the moment. Neither had won a Scottish trophy in season 1954/55 (and that doesn't happen very often!) and Rangers' last tournament success had been as long ago as 1953. George Young, on whom so much had rested for so long, was now clearly beginning to show the signs of age, and Rangers form had been inconsistent. Celtic really should have won the Scottish Cup in May 1955 when they lost out to Clyde in a replay, and probably had the better players, but they were bedevilled by management which persisted in making unnecessary changes in the team, today's dropping of the excellent Walsh being a case in point.

At half-time the score was 2-2, both Rangers goals coming from goalkeeping errors and both being scored by South Africans! Both Celtic goals had come from the combination of Jim Sharkey and Bobby Collins. Rangers scored first and it was Kichenbrand. A floating cross from Sammy Baird found the South African who headed beautifully into the net, but the Celtic end was rather upset to watch Beattie being rooted to the spot and not making any great effort to get to the ball. Celtic equalised soon after when the nippy Sharkey got the better of the cumbersome Young and slipped the ball to Bobby COLLINS to score. Collins himself, 'the wee barra', was having a very good game, then he got to a ball before George Young did and slipped the ball to SHARKEY to put Celtic ahead.

Celtic were well worth this 2-1 lead, controlling the ball against the wind very successfully, and they had every right to consider themselves ill-done by Lady Luck when Rangers got a penalty, foolishly conceded by goalkeeper Dick Beattie for holding on to Kichenbrand's ankles in a goalmouth scrimmage, long after the immediate danger had passed. Mr Mowat, eagle-eyed and generally regarded as the best referee around in the 1950s, had no hesitation in pointing to the spot. John Hubbard, Rangers' other South African, was not called 'Johnny on the Spot' for nothing. He was phenomenally successful at penalty taking, and on this occasion he made no mistake.

The Celtic supporters worried about Dick Beattie. A cheerful, extroverted character who often wore an orange (!) jockey cap, he was generally reckoned to be agile enough for a goalkeeper, but did not always make the right decisions. In later years, when he was with Portsmouth, he was 'done' for accepting bribes to throw games, and in retrospect one has often looked at a few of the goals he conceded and wondered. It is important, however, to stress that no evidence exists of any dark dealings in his time at Celtic Park, nor was it ever a major topic of conversation among the support at the time. The worry at this stage was about his competence, not his probity.

The pace did not slacken in the second half. Following a narrow miss by Kichenbrand, and then the booking of Billy Simpson for a bad tackle on Bobby Collins, Jim SHARKEY once again made his mark on the game by dribbling his way around a few Rangers players and shooting past George Niven to put Celtic 3-2 up. But no, scarcely had the green-and-white scarves from the King's Park end been put back round necks than Rangers equalised. This time it was a total fluke. A shot from Baird was going past the post, but Sean Fallon could not get out of the way of it and the ball rebounded into the Celtic net.

This was simply too bad for Celtic. Celtic had scored three good, crisp, clear goals, whereas Rangers' goals had been a goalkeeping error, a penalty kick and now an own goal! It was not necessarily that Rangers did not deserve to be on level terms, but the way that they had got their goals was just so frustrating!

But now another problem was beginning to appear. It was called darkness. Although it was not yet 3pm, this was a midwinter day, and one with very bad weather. The 90 minutes would probably be seen in daylight, but where would that leave the half hour of extra time? Almost certainly, they could not play 30 minutes, so what was the position? Would there be a third game? Would they count corners, as they did in the Glasgow Charity Cup? Or would the cup simply have to be shared? It was a shame that penalty shoot-outs were still many years in the future!

Fortunately, Celtic solved the Glasgow FA's problem for them by scoring twice in the dying minutes of the match. Jim Sharkey, going for Celtic's winner and what would have been his hat-trick, shot from a distance and hit the bar to his intense chagrin, but the ball rebounded to Bobby COLLINS who picked his spot. Then, with the stadium becoming even more crepuscular, Mr Mowat looking at his watch and the Celtic end in an uproar of scarf waving and singing, Celtic put the issue beyond any doubt when Eric Smith, who had had a quiet game up to this point, sent over a perfect cross to avoid the now tired men of Rangers and to find the head of Willie FERNIE who finished the job!

Around about 3.15pm, Mr Mowat pointed to the pavilion, everyone shook hands, delirium took over the Celtic end, captain

Jock Stein was presented with the large handsome trophy, and everyone went home in the dark.

It is tempting to dismiss this trophy as being 'just' the Glasgow Cup, but it was a trophy much coveted and sought after in the 1950s, and it did mean that Celtic finished the calendar year of 1955 with something in the cabinet. 1956 would bring its own challenges, beginning with a disappointment on New Year's Day, but that was some time and place in the future. Celtic supporters enjoyed the immediate present!

TWENTY THREE

SEVENTH HEAVEN

Celtic 7 Rangers 1	**Scottish League Cup Final**
Hampden Park	**19 October 1957**

Celtic: Beattie, Donnelly and Fallon; Fernie, Evans and Peacock; Tully, Collins, McPhail, Wilson and Mochan

Rangers: Niven, Shearer and Caldow; McColl, Valentine and Davis; Scott, Simpson, Murray, Baird and Hubbard

Referee: Mr J. Mowat, Rutherglen

THIS game is probably the second most famous game of Celtic's long and distinguished history. Lisbon is obviously number one, but this game runs it close. Several songs and a book have been written about this game, so it is clearly well documented. What kept it so alive in people's memories was that it was, in fact, isolated. It was a beacon standing almost alone in a decade of dire underachievements. Almost immediately after this game, the dark ages descended with a vengeance, and vengeance was indeed an appropriate term, for Rangers were able to get back at Celtic on many occasions, and the only ammunition we had to throw back at the chortlers was '7-1', but, sadly, it only happened the once.

It ought to have happened a lot more often than once, for Celtic at that time had loads of great players, and man for man they were a lot better than anyone else. Bobby Evans, Bertie Peacock, Willie Fernie, Bobby Collins, Neil Mochan and Charlie Tully were as naturally gifted as one would find, but the team was badly managed. Jock Stein's playing career had now ended. If he had been manager of that team at that time, Celtic would have won many leagues and cups.

As it was, it was not entirely a barren time. Celtic were the current holders of the Scottish League Cup, and the double of 1954 was not yet a distant memory. It was just that it could have been a lot more. This was the day, however, in which the whole team came good, and the world saw Celtic at their best. It was almost an apology from the players to the fans for their previous underperformance.

Captain Bertie Peacock was the ideal man to deal with one particular problem in the week leading up to the final. It concerned fisticuffs in the dressing room. Bobby Evans and Charlie Tully did not get on all the time. Tully thought Evans was stuffy and humourless, and Evans resented Tully's constant showing off, often to the detriment of the team. On this occasion, Tully had 'ghosted' an article for a newspaper on the subject of a recent Scotland international, in which he said that only a few players were worth going to the World Cup. He named them, and Evans wasn't one of them. Evans did not accept the 'everybody's entitled to their opinion' line, and after a few intemperate words fists were raised. Fortunately, other players stepped between them, and no damage was done ... but captain Bertie Peacock had to 'have a word' with the pair of them, and equally important, to ensure that the whole business went no further.

In this, the charming Irishman succeeded to such an extent that no one else suspected any problem. It was certainly not apparent from the performance on the day. It was a sunny day, but the crowd was a low one of 82,000, something that was blamed on a rather unseasonal flu epidemic that had hit central Scotland over the past few weeks and was blamed, according to one letter writer to a newspaper, on the Russians who had sent their Sputnik into space!

None of the players seemed to have been affected for this, the first-ever League Cup final between the two sides and the first national final between them since 1928. Celtic were possibly the slight favourites, having beaten Rangers at Ibrox a month ago – the first league victory there since 1935! – and had a more settled side. Rangers seemed to have problems replacing centre-half George Young, who had retired in the summer. For this game they had chosen John Valentine, whom they had signed from Queen's Park. Up front they had the ageing Sammy Baird, the under-performing Maxie Murray, and their best forward appeared to be the Ulsterman Billy Simpson. Their recent form had not been great, and not all Rangers supporters were as optimistic as their raucous battle hymns would have suggested.

Celtic started off playing towards their own supporters, and almost immediately were on the attack. They had hit the woodwork on at least two occasions and it was a major surprise that they were not ahead. Indeed, the pessimistic of the green-and-white hordes were beginning to fear that their moment had passed, but not a bit of it. Billy McPhail headed down for Sammy WILSON to bang the ball home. Wilson had joined the club in the summer on a free transfer from St Mirren. His career had not exactly been coming along in leaps and bounds but today was his day. Then as half-time approached, and everyone was remarking how lucky Rangers were to be going in only 0-1 down, Celtic struck again. This time it was Neil MOCHAN who made ground on the left, racing past Bobby Shearer as if he wasn't there, and when everyone expected a cross, he ran on himself and scored from an incredibly tight angle.

Half-time was spent in glorious euphoria, with the only negative thought being that Rangers couldn't possibly be as bad as that in the second half. But they were, and Celtic, apart from one moment, simply tore them apart. Billy McPHAIL got in on the act, heading home a Collins cross, and then for one brief moment Rangers came back with a good headed goal by Billy Simpson. This goal was not entirely unconnected with an injury to Bobby Evans caused by a couple of bad tackles on him from Maxie Murray and Sammy Baird.

It did not really matter. Rangers might have taken heart from that, but it was Celtic who reasserted themselves. McPHAIL volleyed a Mochan corner, but his shot was parried by Niven straight back to him and he was able to get there ahead of anyone else and to make it 4-1. The next was MOCHAN again, driving home a cross from Wilson first time, and soon after that came the goal of the game when McPHAIL earned his hat-trick by picking up a clearance from goalkeeper Dick Beattie, flicking the ball past the luckless John Valentine, and running half the length of the field to slip the ball past Niven.

6-1 really should have been enough, and Rangers fans were either throwing bottles, fighting with each other or going home when the seventh was scored. Billy McPhail was brought down in the box, referee Jack Mowat, ruthlessly impartial, did NOT listen to Rangers' pleas for mercy and awarded a penalty, and Willie FERNIE was given the job. It was appropriate that Fernie finished things off, for no one had contributed more than he did to the victory.

But there wasn't a single Celtic failure on the field, and the teamwork, discipline and cohesion were a thing to behold. It was Celtic at their best. In the stand that day were two grand old Celts, Jimmy McMenemy and Davie McLean, the last two survivors of Maley's great side of 1908. How they enjoyed themselves! Maley himself, now 90, was too old and frail to attend but listened to the game on the radio, as indeed did Jock Stein, who was now retired from the playing side of the game and recovering from an ankle operation. Celtic, however, sent a car to bring him to the victory celebration.

Celtic supporters walked on air for days afterwards, and it is a pity that so soon after this game, injuries, old age and sheer greed for transfer fees saw this great team broken up and replaced by a 'youth policy'. Nothing wrong with a 'youth policy' in itself, but it needed to be monitored and controlled a little better than this one was. As it happened, Celtic's next happy day would be 24 April 1965, and a Biblical 'seven years of famine' ensued in the interval.

Rangers were of course distraught and took a while to recover, but they got back into the habit of winning things more quickly than Celtic did. Not immediately, however. The Scottish League was won by Hearts that year, and although Hearts had a good team, wise analysts of the game pointed to this League Cup Final as the reason for Rangers' inability to sustain the pace.

But this game will always be remembered. It is a British record for a score in a national cup final, and naturally Celtic's biggest-ever score against Rangers. It is curious, too, the significance the number seven has on Celtic's history. The first league and cup double was achieved in 1907, the Scottish Cup was won in both 1927 and 1937, and 1967 has its own significance as well! It was of course the squad number of Jimmy Johnstone and Henrik Larsson – and that says a lot, but for those supporters old enough to remember this game, number seven will always be associated with it on that sunny day of 19 October 1957.

TWENTY FOUR

THE FOGGY DEW

Celtic 3 Rangers 2 aet   Glasgow Cup First-Round Replay
Celtic Park   21 November 1962

Celtic: Haffey, Young and Kennedy; Crerand, McNeill and O'Neill; Chalmers, Murdoch, Divers, Gallagher and Jeffrey

Rangers: Ritchie, Shearer and Caldow; McKinnon, Baillie and Baxter; Henderson, Greig, Miller, Brand and Wilson

Referee: Mr T. Wharton, Clarkston

IT is probably true that supporters of a younger generation cannot appreciate just how bad 1962 was. Basically Celtic were still working on a youth policy which they had consciously started in the wake of the 7-1 victory over Rangers in 1957. It should have paid dividends by now. The word always being employed was 'arrived'. The young Celtic team have 'arrived', they kept telling us. Maybe they 'arrived' on occasion, but if they did, they soon went away again.

A major blow was struck to the youth policy when Jock Stein was allowed to depart to become manager of Dunfermline in 1960. From then on, there was no one to guard and guide, to protect and encourage the youngsters. The manager was Jimmy McGrory, a venerable and much-loved figure, but he was manager in name only. The real power was wielded by chairman Bob Kelly, a powerful and influential man with a great love for the club – but with no real knowledge of the dynamics of actually playing football. Still less did he show any ability in man-management.

In these circumstances, it was hardly surprising that Rangers won most things. They had the experienced Scot Symon as manager, a man who had already done well with East Fife and Preston North End before he went to Ibrox in 1954, and he was also given money to buy men like Jim Baxter from Raith Rovers, for example. There was a culture of wealth, prosperity and success at Ibrox. At Celtic Park it was one of underachievement and increasingly a feeling that Celtic weren't meant to win against Rangers. A couple of months ago, at Celtic Park in September, for example, Celtic had all the possession against Rangers and couldn't score – and then Pat Crerand missed a penalty, and Rangers won 1-0!

And yet there were some good straws in the wind as well. Crerand and McNeill had both played excellently in the game in which Scotland beat England 2-0 at Hampden in April, and other players were beginning to appear as well, not least the 18-year-old Bobby Murdoch, who certainly looked as if he had something going for him. Others like Chalmers, Hughes and Divers all had good days, but were never consistent.

A feature of the Celtic team as well in 1962 was that they were unlucky. One may argue that a team makes its own luck, but there are times when you need a bit of luck – a ball to go in instead of out after it hits the post, for example – and that was never forthcoming for Celtic in 1962. They might have qualified for the Scottish League Cup quarter-finals at Tannadice Park that year, for example, but they were denied a goal that had clearly crossed the line, and in addition hit the woodwork on countless occasions – and bounced out!

The club also made some unbelievable miscalculations. They signed a player from England called Bobby Craig. He was a man of some ability, it has to be said, but he arrived at Glasgow Central Station at 4.30pm in the afternoon, was bundled into a taxi and played for Celtic that night in a European Inter-Cities Fairs Cup tie against Valencia! Not surprisingly, that idea was no great success.

League form was woeful and inconsistent. 6-1 v Airdrie, 7-0 v St Mirren – and then they lost 0-1 to Queen of the South at Parkhead! In the Glasgow Cup they had been drawn to play Rangers at Ibrox in October and fought back to equalise twice, but it was no great game. It meant, however, that a replay was needed and Wednesday, 21 November was the date agreed. The kick-off was 2.30pm because, although Celtic Park had excellent floodlights, the police were very keen that the game should finish in daylight if possible in case of crowd trouble. Such precautions were justified, for Celtic supporters had a bad reputation for hooliganism in those days – and to a large extent it was caused by frustration at poor team performances.

The day of the game saw Glasgow looking like Dickensian London with fog and frost. The sun tried weakly to come out, but without any great success. This was before all the Clean Air Acts had begun to kick in, and the air was filthy and horrible with much sound of claxons and fog horns on the Clyde. The pitch was hard, and it must have been very tempting for Mr Wharton to say 'no game' and wait for another day, but after a lunchtime inspection he sanctioned play.

For Celtic, Bobby Craig, the recent signing from Blackburn Rovers, was ill, and the team was a very young one indeed. Ian Young at right-back and Bobby Jeffrey on the left wing had only made their debuts recently, Bobby Murdoch was in his first season and Willie O'Neill had made his debut in the unfortunate circumstances of the Scottish Cup Final of 1961 and had played only a handful of games since. Rangers were more experienced, and it was widely expected that they would be too good for the young Celts.

But inexperience is not always a bad thing. There was certainly loads of enthusiasm in the Celtic ranks, and of course the frozen pitch (it was hard but not unplayable) is always a leveller in circumstances like those. The crowd was 24,000, a poor crowd perhaps for Celtic v Rangers, but not today, which was a working day for most people, and road conditions were such that it would have been very difficult for anyone from outside Glasgow to get there. Motivation may well have been lacking as well, especially when there was a real possibility of the game being off. 1962 was long before mobile phones and computers for anyone to get any accurate and reliable information.

It was the fog that presented the biggest problem. Although the Parkhead lights were deployed, figures at the other end of the ground tended to be just shadows, a problem made more acute by the distance between the touchline and the terracing at both ends of the ground. Most sensible spectators, realising that, made their way to the Jungle to get a better view, and what they saw was worth seeing.

The most notable feature of this game was the speed of the Celtic players. Jim Baxter, great player though he was, was not the quickest and the game passed him by now and again. Rangers' twin centre-halves of Doug Baillie (Doug's son Lex would play for Celtic in future years) and Ron McKinnon were not the speediest either and they clearly struggled in a first half in which Celtic were very much on top. Charlie Gallagher, in the 30th minute, was charging in on goal when he was upended by Doug Baillie. It would have been a red card if the game had been played in the 21st century, but this was 1962 and a free kick outside the box was all you got. Pat CRERAND, however, took it and scored, getting the aid of a deflection, but it was a pile driver which might have gone in anyway. Hopes of a half-time lead, however, were dashed when Willie Henderson scored for Rangers. It was a good goal, but hardly justified on the run of play.

The second half saw more Celtic dominance, but not enough to win the game, until John Divers, a talented but sometimes moody and inconsistent player, made ground on the right and sent in a low cross which Bobby MURDOCH completed. That was in the 55th minute and things looked good for Celtic, for they were well on top, but then the Celtic paranoia complex got a great boost when Ralph Brand scored from a blatantly offside position, and that was not just the opinion of Celtic supporters, but also of respected journalists like Cyril Horne of the *Glasgow Herald* and Gair Henderson of the *Evening Times*. No one was prepared to make excuses about the fog for that one.

Melancholy now settled on the Celtic support. Once again, it was beginning to look as if Celtic were to be robbed of a victory over Rangers that they deserved. Yet Celtic kept pressing and Rangers goalkeeper Billy Ritchie kept his side in the tie with several good saves until Mr Wharton blew for the end of 90 minutes, and signalled the start of extra time.

It was the same pattern in extra time. John Divers, who was playing one of his best-ever games for the club, hit the bar in the first half of extra time, but then with only four minutes to go Divers again got the better of Doug Baillie and slipped the ball through for Bobby MURDOCH to finish things off. It was a famous victory and much enjoyed by the Celtic Park faithful, who would not listen to any counter arguments that it was 'just' the Glasgow Cup!

But we had to enjoy it when we could. Such was the inconsistency of the club in 1962 that we lost 0-2 to Partick Thistle at Parkhead on the Saturday after, and the next time we met Rangers was New Year's Day 1963 when we lost 0-4. Then 1963 was worse than 1962, and we shudder at the recollection of it.

TWENTY FIVE

CELTIC SINGING
IN THE RAIN

Celtic 3 Rangers 1　　　　　　　　**Scottish League**

Celtic Park　　　　　　　　**5 September 1964**

Celtic: Fallon, Young and Gemmell; Brogan, Cushley and Kennedy; Johnstone, Divers, Chalmers, Gallagher and Hughes

Rangers: Ritchie, Hynd and Provan; Greig, McKinnon and Baxter; Henderson, McLean, Forrest, Brand and Wilson

Referee: Mr H. Phillips, Wishaw

THE year 1964 was a remarkable, improving but still disappointing, year for Celtic. Celtic had played Rangers five times in 1963/64 and had lost five times. Each game had followed the same depressing pattern of Celtic on top at the start with plenty of missed chances and possibly a refereeing error, then an unlucky break in the sense of a soft goal or another refereeing error, followed by a collapse in the second half leading to the belief that somehow or other, Celtic were not allowed to beat Rangers.

Form against other teams and in Europe had been acceptable – they had even reached the semi-final of the European Cup Winners' Cup – but it was obvious that if Celtic were ever to get any kind of success, they had to break the Rangers complex. It was not that Rangers were in any way invincible, as their record in Europe had proved. Whenever they came up against a good European team like Tottenham Hotspur or Real Madrid, their lack of quality was ruthlessly exposed. It was up to Celtic to provide that sort of opposition from within Scotland.

Jimmy McGrory's side had got off to a good start, winning their difficult League Cup section of Hearts, Partick Thistle and Kilmarnock with a degree of ease. The sting, however, came in the tail. With the section well won and nothing, apparently, at stake, Celtic travelled to Ayrshire to take on Willie Waddell's Kilmarnock, who were in a bitter and vindictive mood. It was a terrible game with Billy McNeill and Bobby Murdoch badly injured, and at one point both captains (Jim Kennedy in the case of Celtic acting as captain for McNeill who had been carried off injured) were called together and warned that the game might be abandoned if everyone did not calm down! And the section had already been decided!

All this meant that Celtic had problems for the game against Rangers. For McNeill there was a capable and competent centre-half called John Cushley, and John Divers, talented but often indolent and apparently half-hearted, came in for Bobby Murdoch. John Clark was also out and replaced by young Jim Brogan who had only played a handful of games for the club, and Bobby Lennox was also missing from the line-up.

Against that, Rangers were more or less at full strength in their key positions. Their main man was Jim Baxter. Baxter's problem was that he was not a team man. Superbly talented and even inspirational, he had to get to run the show or else he became moody and unresponsive. In particular, if he got off to a bad start, he often found it difficult to raise his game. Celtic today at long last 'wised up' to this. Baxter's contribution was minimal, his concentration not helped by the well-publicised presence in the stand of Billy Wright, the manager of Arsenal, a club who were rumoured to be on the point of tabling a huge bid for Baxter. Following this game, no bid ever came, but the great Billy Wright, captain of Wolverhampton Wanderers and England in the 1950s, must have been impressed by Celtic.

He would also have noticed that it was raining. Steady, prolonged, relentless Glasgow rain. Never heavy enough to put the game in any danger, but still a factor in the game and one that would have an effect on some players, in particular Celtic's mercurial and unpredictable John Hughes. 'Yogi Bear', as he was called after a TV series of a few years previously, was a great 'bad weather' player. He was very good on hard, frosty pitches, and here, on a heavy pitch, he was just as good. Today he was virtually unstoppable.

Only three minutes had gone when, with Celtic playing towards the wet and bedraggled Rangers supporters on the uncovered terracing, Hughes beat Roger Hynd more or less at the halfway line, ran the length of the Rangers half and crashed an unsaveable shot past Billy Ritchie. It was marvellous stuff and the Celtic fans celebrated – but no one had noticed that referee Hugh Phillips had blown for a foul as Hughes beat Hynd.

This was a bad blow, and worse was to come. A few minutes later, Jimmy Johnstone beat a few men, dashed into the penalty area, and was downed by Davie Provan, Rangers' somewhat agricultural full-back. A penalty it had to be, and up stepped Charlie Gallagher to do the needful as the fans in the distant Celtic end held their breath. Gallagher hit Billy Ritchie's right-hand post (Ritchie may or may not have got a hand to it) and the ball bounced way out to the right-hand side of the park. It was a bad miss, and the Celtic end lapsed into anger and then introverted silence. We had been here before. Were we about to blow it all again?

It certainly began to look like that, for Rangers now came more and more into the game with Willie Henderson on the right wing beginning to look as if he might cause a few problems, and Davie Wilson similarly on the left. This would be Rangers' best spell of the game, and the tackles were beginning to fly in thick and fast as well, with a few players being spoken to by Mr Phillips, and a few close things at either end. We had the sight, for example, of Jimmy Johnstone in the back of the Rangers net, but, sadly, he had missed the ball and failed to take it in with him!

But as half-time approached, Celtic took the lead and a fine goal it was as well. Jimmy Johnstone got the better of Dave Provan once again and sent over a fine cross for the diving head of Steve CHALMERS to score a brilliant and significant goal. It was good to see Stevie score, for he had been the victim of some dreadful abuse in the past from those who claimed to be supporters of the club, but that goal was a great one of the honest, hard-working and gentlemanly Chalmers.

Half-time arrived with Celtic still 1-0 up in spite of a particularly hairy moment when Ian Young cleared off the line with John Fallon beaten, and how nice it was to be part of a rocking, happy Celtic end while the other end started throwing bottles! In the past it had too often been the other way round. The memory remains of the glint as the bottle came out of the terracing, then Glasgow's finest dived in and brought out some pitiful specimen!

That this was to be Celtic's day was proved early in the second half when, a minute after Rangers hit the bar, Celtic went further ahead. It was a curious goal as well. A cross from Johnstone was pushed onto his own crossbar by Billy Ritchie and rebounded to John Hughes, who headed it on to CHALMERS again to finish the job as the Celtic end erupted. Minutes after that, John HUGHES charged forward again, but his shot was a weak one. Not that it mattered, for on the very wet ground the ball slipped between Billy Ritchie's legs. The *Evening Times* talks about a 'cemetery silence' at the far end, but it was bedlam under the roof of the Jungle and the Celtic end as total strangers grabbed and hugged each other in a collective delirium which had not been seen at Celtic Park for a long time.

All the old songs were trotted out again – rebel songs, songs about Charlie Tully and Jimmy McGrory, and the grand old team to play for, as Celtic now in total command reduced the arrogant Jim Baxter to a sort of catatonic impotence, and as often happened, looking uninterested in helping his team-mates, even though he was the acting captain (one of Scot Symon's stranger decisions!). Rangers did have one moment of glory when Davie Wilson, one of their few successes, pulled one back in the 81st minute, and of course the pessimistic among us feared a Rangers revival, but there was no chance of that as Brogan, Cushley and Kennedy mopped up any possible danger.

The full-time whistle brought great rejoicing and deserved praise for the Celtic side. This game did show that Rangers could be beaten, but consistent success for Celtic was still a long way off. Maybe this performance swelled a few heads disproportionately, but on the following Wednesday Celtic managed to lose to East Fife in the League Cup quarter-final (fortunately only the first leg) and by Christmas the club was once again in crisis. The

League Cup Final had been lost to Rangers (once again Celtic were the better team, but lost agonisingly), the team were out of Europe and had lost to teams like St Johnstone, Dundee and Dunfermline in the league. It was indeed the worst crisis of them all, but fortunately Mr Kelly at last made the right decision in January and appointed the right man for the job in Jock Stein.

TWENTY SIX

NO MORE MR NICE GUY

Celtic 2 Rangers 1   **Scottish League Cup Final**

Hampden Park   **23 October 1965**

Celtic: Simpson, Young and Gemmell; Murdoch, McNeill and Clark; Johnstone, Gallagher, McBride, Lennox and Hughes

Rangers: Ritchie, Johansen and Provan; Wood, McKinnon and Greig; Henderson, Willoughby, Forrest, Wilson and Johnston

Referee: Mr H. Phillips, Wishaw

THIS was possibly the most significant Celtic v Rangers game of them all. This was the game that swung the balance of power, more or less irreversibly, from Rangers to Celtic for the next ten years and more, and this was the game that guaranteed Celtic a permanent place at the top of Scottish football, when for a few years in the early 1960s they had slipped dangerously close to insignificance.

The reasons for all this were complex. The game must be seen in the context of the last few years of the early 60s when Celtic teams came out to play Rangers with an almost visible and tangible look about them that they were expecting to lose. No matter how well they had played up till then, there was almost an immutable law of heaven that Celtic had to lose to Rangers. Since the glorious 7-1 game of 1957, children had grown up knowing nothing else and were almost schooled and programmed into accepting it.

The difference now was Jock Stein. The Scottish Cup had been annexed in April 1965, but, other than in a Glasgow Cup tie at the end of the 1964/65 season, Stein's Celtic had still not yet beaten Rangers. When the clubs met at Ibrox a month previously Celtic had lost 1-2 – a narrow defeat, at least partly to be explained by an injury to Billy McNeill, but a defeat nevertheless, and in the context of the Old Firm that meant everything. It followed then that a defeat here today might mean that paradise had not in fact arrived in April, and that the long dismal tunnel of defeats to Rangers was to continue.

Celtic had only reached the final on the Monday before when they beat Hibs 4-0 in a semi-final replay. It had been a commanding performance – but could this be carried on until the Saturday when it really counted? Assistant manager Sean Fallon wrote a piece in Wednesday's *Scottish Daily Express* (an influential and normally very pro-Rangers newspaper in 1965) to the effect that Celtic were going to win on Saturday. Very matter of fact, and for this he was much ridiculed by Rangers fans, but it did give the impression to Celtic fans that the club believed it was possible, and that the glorious celebrations of last April could be replicated, and this time with a victory in a cup final against Rangers.

The precedents were hardly encouraging. Last year at this time, the Scottish League Cup Final had seen Celtic well on top, but the 'death wish' took over in the missing of vital chances and the lapses of concentration in defence, and there were the vivid memories, still fresh in the mind, of the Scottish Cup replayed final of 1963 when 50,000 turned their backs on Celtic in protest at a spineless and spiritless surrender to the arrogant Rangers.

Today attracted a massive crowd of 107,609 (still a record for the Scottish League Cup Final) to see this game, which had clearly caught the imagination of both sets of supporters and quite a few of the neutrals as well. The game was by no means the best there has ever been between the two of them – for example, there wasn't a single good goal in the 90 minutes, and very few defence-splitting passes – but what the crowd saw was a different Celtic, a Celtic who were prepared to lower their much-vaunted standards of behaviour (so cherished by chairman Bob Kelly) in pursuit of victory. In short, Celtic descended to the same level as Rangers, and the game, though devoid of the finer touches of football, nevertheless gave some great entertainment, and lacked nothing in passion.

The first sight of the new Celtic was the foul by Ian Young on Willie Johnston. This was a clear indication that there was to be 'no more Mr Nice Guy' from Celtic. Both players were booked by referee Hugh Phillips, generally regarded as one of the best around, Young for the foul and Johnston for retaliation. Young, apparently, has regretted that tackle for the rest of his life; Johnston, on the

NO MORE MR NICE GUY

other hand, went on to collect what is claimed to be a world record for the amount of times that he got himself sent off!

There would be three more bookings in the game – Bobby Murdoch and Jimmy Johnstone of Celtic and Ron McKinnon of Rangers. Five bookings in a game in 1965 was considered a lot, but possibly by modern standards the game was not quite as dirty as the banner headlines 'Orgy of crudeness' and the 'X Certificate Cup Final' implied. But certainly few prisoners were taken.

Celtic's two goals came from the penalty spot at the Celtic end of the ground. One was when Ron McKinnon of Rangers, in a moment that he himself could never understand, handled a harmless ball in the box, and the other was when Rangers' Davie Provan (no relation to the Celtic Davie Provan of the 1980s) brought down Jimmy Johnstone. He claimed there was no contact, but Mr Phillips said there was, and that was that, even though Rangers chairman John Lawrence allowed himself to be quoted as saying that what he wanted to say about that decision could not be printed! An odd quote that, come to think of it.

Anyhow, all this meant that twice the lumbering figure of John HUGHES had to come up to the mark. John, that quixotic, moody, temperamental, idiosyncratic, individualistic sort of player, the subject of many a discussion and argument on the terracings and the supporters' buses, must have felt that destiny was calling him on those two occasions. He had already in this campaign scored a marvellous goal at Dens Park, Dundee on the day that we qualified, and today he did not let us down. Billy Ritchie got a hand to one of them, but both went in, and Celtic now reached half-time 2-0 up. The Celtic end cheered, but there was anxiety as well, for 45 long minutes remained.

They were not an easy 45 minutes to watch. There was little in the way of good attacking play by either side, but Celtic had the edge in midfield. Such times as Rangers came close, the Celtic defence dealt with it competently and well, and we began to breathe just a little more easily as the minutes ticked away. Bobby Murdoch was immense and men like Charlie Gallagher and Joe McBride proved their versatility by acting as emergency midfielders and even defenders when required. Behind them all stood Ronnie

Simpson who had twice won an English Cup winners' medal in 1952 and 1955 with Newcastle United. By no means a tall man, he nevertheless radiated confidence and reassurance. It was also apparent that Rangers forwards, Alec Willoughby and Jim Forrest, had their limitations when up against a good defence.

But then within the last ten minutes disaster struck when Ronnie Simpson, Ian Young and John Greig all went up for the same ball, and the ball went in off the face of Ian Young! Now the heat was turned up as Rangers redoubled their efforts, and we became very introverted and worried on the terracing. McNeill had had a great game but was now showing signs of tiring and beginning to lose the plot. But how comforting it was to see Ronnie Simpson talk quietly to him, banging one fist into the palm of his other hand, and generally taking control of the situation!

The full-time whistle came, the cup was presented and Celtic set off on their half-lap of honour to show the beautiful three-handled trophy to their own fans. It did not go down well among the thickos at the Mount Florida end and some managed to get on to the pitch. No real damage was done, although trainer Neil Mochan and Ian Young were manhandled, and the real heroes of it all were the Celtic supporters who did not retaliate. Breathtakingly, some newspapers managed to say that it was Celtic to blame for it all because of their 'provocative' lap of honour (cheerfully ignoring all the times that Rangers had held a lap of honour!) and the upshot was that laps of honour were banned for several years, something that punished Celtic almost exclusively!

That was by way of a sideshow. The bottom line was that Celtic had won the League Cup and had shown to the world that they were no longer going to lie down to Rangers as they had done so often, so abjectly and so abysmally in the past. The anonymous writer of *The Times* in an excellently restrained and thoughtful piece of writing puts things very well when he sums it all up perspicaciously by saying, 'They [Celtic] are moving into a new era of success.' No one knew just how successful we were going to be, but everyone agrees that things might have been different if we had not beaten Rangers in this final, which was low on skill but high on significance for the future.

TWENTY SEVEN

THE TURN OF THE TIDE

Celtic 5 Rangers 1	Scottish League
Celtic Park	3 January 1966

Celtic: Simpson, Craig and Gemmell; Murdoch, Cushley and Clark; Johnstone, Gallagher, McBride, Chalmers and Hughes

Rangers: Ritchie, Johansen and Provan; Greig, McKinnon and Hynd; Wilson, Setterington, Forrest, McLean and Johnston

Referee: Mr T. Wharton, Clarkston

OFTEN the Celtic v Dunfermline Scottish Cup Final of 1965 is referred to as the 'turn of the tide' day when Celtic changed from under-performing to virtual world beaters. Others will point to the Scottish League Cup Final of October 1965. A strong case, however, can be made out for this game to be given such a title, on the grounds that it was such a comprehensive victory. It did not, of course, in itself win the league for Celtic that season. Far from it. A few 'sair dunts' were to come, but it certainly played its part in the eventual success.

This was, of course, Jock Stein's first full season as Celtic manager, and things were upbeat at Celtic Park. The *Celtic View*, the first newspaper of its kind in the world, brought all sorts of glad tidings to the support from plans for the demolition and replacement of the old Jungle (which looked like an elongated cowshed and had massive holes in the roof), to young Brazilians getting a trial for Celtic, to the weekly assessment of the footballing world by Jock Stein himself. The Scottish League Cup had been won in October, crowds began to come back, and for the first time in a long time you could honestly say that Celtic were involved in a league race.

Up to Hogmanay 1965, there was nothing between Celtic and Rangers in the league. Celtic had lost to Rangers at Ibrox in September, and that was significant, but Celtic had finished 1965 strongly, notably by beating the strong-running Dunfermline at

East End Park, and then a spectacular demolition of Morton on Christmas Day, followed by a hard-fought win on New Year's Day against Clyde at Shawfield. Celtic had lost one game (to Rangers) and had also drawn disappointingly with Partick Thistle at the beginning of November. Rangers were doing well also, and things were nicely set up for the derby game on Monday 3 January. Both teams were now level on points but Celtic had a game in hand.

The weather was frosty, and there was a certain doubt about whether the game would go ahead at the appointed kick-off time of 2pm. Those of us who were admitted early saw the two unmistakeable bulks of referee Tom (called 'Tiny' because he wasn't!) Wharton and Celtic manager Jock Stein walking round the park in animated conversation, the obvious topic being whether the game would go ahead. Stein was obviously very keen for the game to be played. Centre circles and both goalmouths were prodded and poked. The two men had tremendous respect for each other, but no great affection or cordiality. Nevertheless, they shook hands and the game was on. Two interesting points about this was that there did not seem to be any representative from Rangers present, and the other thing was that it was a close thing, for Partick Thistle v Clyde was called off at the last minute that day.

Celtic were without the injured McNeill (he had been out for some time) but had the capable John Cushley in his place and were otherwise at full strength. Even as the game started, there were signs that the fog was beginning to come down, and this would be a factor in the second half. It was Rangers, playing towards the Celtic end, who opened the scoring within the first two minutes. John Greig shot, the ball bounced off John Cushley and came to Davie Wilson, who put Rangers one ahead. It was an early hammer blow, but the key word was 'early', for Celtic had time to do something about it. But for the rest of the first half, although Celtic were clearly the better team, it was also obvious that Rangers were defending well, with Ron McKinnon, their centre-half, in particular having a great game. It was also obvious that the pitch was only marginally playable, and one or two players on each side were seen to skid alarmingly.

Celtic's players were wearing 'sandshoes' as they were then called. Modern nomenclature is 'trainers', and it was obvious from an early stage that Celtic were keeping their feet a little better than Rangers, who were wearing more conventional footwear. Celtic were also a great deal more nimble and fast, big John Hughes in particular, one of the best 'bad weather' football players of that age.

Half-time saw the Celtic end concerned, not about the way that their team were playing, nor their commitment to the cause, but whether it was going to be one of those games when Celtic 'did everything but score'. Fog was now a major factor with Ronnie Simpson's yellow jersey in the distant goal becoming less and less visible. Not that it really mattered, mind you, for all the action took place at the end closest to the Celtic supporters and what we saw was a real treat.

We had felt, before the goals started to go in, that we had been here before. All over them but couldn't score! This had indeed, of course, been the case so many times in the recent past (one recalled with horror New Year's Day 1964), but not this time. Five minutes into the second half, Celtic equalised through CHALMERS. Tommy Gemmell started it all by sending in a cross from the left. The ball was cleverly dummied by Joe McBride, and Stevie was there to do the needful.

Level terms, but only in the scoreline. The actual play on the field bore no comparison at all, as Celtic charged forward relentlessly, and Rangers becoming 'prodigal of fouls'. Three Rangers players would be booked – Provan, Johansen and Setterington (a young lad clearly out of his depth at this level of football).

It was the 69th minute before Celtic went ahead and it was CHALMERS again with a glancing header from a Charlie Gallagher corner kick. Gallagher was of course famous for taking the corner kick in the Scottish Cup Final against Dunfermline, but this one was equally significant, and then it was GALLAGHER himself who hammered home the third after a fine run and cross from John Hughes. The fourth came from Bobby MURDOCH, who crashed home a great shot from just outside the box. But old film of the game will show how the referee Mr Wharton had a part of play here. He got in the way of the pass from Gallagher to Murdoch, but simply opened his legs to let the ball run through, and the Rangers defence were bamboozled by it all.

The Celtic end was now in ecstasies at all this, as goal followed goal. We had a great view of them all going in, but there was still the lingering fear that the game might yet be abandoned, for on the rare occasions that Rangers went on the attack there was little that we could see. This meant, of course, that the Rangers supporters at the far end did not see the goals going in. One of them told me later that all they could make out was the noise from the distant Celtic end. A few Rangers fans, of the more mentally challenged variety, lobbed some bottles on to the field – a singularly pointless exercise at Celtic Park where the distance between the bottom of the terracing and the touchline was quite considerable, and all that the bottles did was endanger the lives of their own supporters. (A case of 'friendly fire', perhaps, a common phrase in 1966 and later years, for the Americans in Vietnam managed to kill a lot of their own people!)

However, any fears that the game might have to be abandoned dissipated when, in quick succession, Stevie CHALMERS scored the fifth goal, and then Mr Wharton blew the final whistle. Rightly did Celtic enjoy the cheers of their fans at the end. To their credit, Rangers themselves did not make any complaint about the conditions and admitted that Celtic were, on that day, by far the better side.

One was particularly happy for Steve Chalmers, a man who had had to endure an incredible amount of abuse from so-called supporters in the bad days. The same was true to a lesser extent of the other goalscorers, Charlie Gallagher and Bobby Murdoch, both of whom had had to work hard to earn their credentials, but the man of the match was undeniably John Hughes, a man whose form was normally unpredictable and haywire, but who, one hoped, could now settle down to some consistent form under Jock Stein. On his day, 'Yogi' was a world beater!

In point of fact, this would turn out to be a very interesting league race, for Celtic, their eye off the ball to a certain extent because of European commitments (including a barely credible involvement with the prickly Soviet Union and their red-tape flying arrangements!), lost games at Pittodrie, Tynecastle and Annfield (the home of Stirling Albion) before coming good at the end. They probably did owe a lot to this particular victory in the fog and the frost at Celtic Park.

TWENTY EIGHT

A DAMNED CLOSE-RUN THING

Celtic 1 Rangers 0   **Scottish League Cup Final**

Hampden Park   **29 October 1966**

Celtic: Simpson, Gemmell, O'Neill, Murdoch, McNeill, Clark, Johnstone, Lennox, McBride, Auld, Hughes (Chalmers)

Rangers: Martin, Johansen, Provan, Greig, McKinnon, D. Smith, Henderson, Watson, McLean, A. Smith, Johnston

Referee: Mr T. Wharton, Clarkston

A CROWD of 94,532 turned up to see this League Cup Final, some 10,000 fewer than a year previously. Why this was, no one could explain, but as Celtic and Rangers had also contested the 1966 Scottish Cup Final, possibly this, the third Hampden final between the two of them in a year, lost a few fans to 'turnstile fatigue'. You would not have thought that, though, for the entertainment and tension levels in this game were very high indeed. Celtic won this game, but it was mighty close.

Rangers had been very worried in summer 1966. They had seen the rise of the new, Stein-driven Celtic lift the Scottish League and felt that they had to do something about it. Using their substantial wealth, they bought two Smiths, Alex from Dunfermline and Dave from Aberdeen. Neither of them was cheap by 1966 standards, and it showed the lengths to which they were prepared to go to try to get the better of the new Celtic.

The transfers, however, did not have any great immediate success. Rangers lost twice to Celtic, once in the Glasgow Cup and once in the Scottish League, and now the Old Firm teams found themselves confronting each other in the League Cup Final for the third successive year.

Celtic had started the season with a bang. They were as yet undefeated in any competition, and they had played tremendous football to demolish teams in their way. They had a tremendous camaraderie about them, born on their lengthy tour of the USA in the summer, and they were simply very good to watch. The wiles of Johnstone, the speed of Lennox, the craft of Auld, the power of Murdoch and the sheer class of McNeill were great incentives for anyone to turn out and see them. Today would reveal another aspect of them – their ability to defend when they were up against a team that were at least their equals on the day.

Rangers, on the other hand, probably lacked the class of Celtic, but they were still a fit, determined outfit with loads of good players like John Greig and Willie Johnston. Possibly they suffered a little from an obsession as far as Kaj Johansen was concerned. Kaj had scored the goal which settled the 1966 Scottish Cup Final with a fine, but possibly fortuitous, strike. Stein knew that, and also knew how to exploit this. Kaj would never be able to resist the temptation to try again, and this could leave a hole at the back.

The week before this game was intense, for the first trophy of the season meant a huge amount to both sides. Stein gave an off-hand interview saying that he hoped Celtic would retain the League Cup, but it wouldn't matter all that much if they didn't, trying to give the impression that it wasn't all that important, for there were other trophies to be concerned about as well. One wonders how many people he deceived by this. Most sensible supporters realised that this was all part of what is now called 'mind games'. He was in fact as obsessed with winning the League Cup as anyone else.

The weather was not as sunny as we sometimes got for League Cup finals, but it was mild and pleasant enough, and the crowd was well behaved, watching a final that newspapers praised for its high quality. The Celtic end was the better end to watch this game from, not only because it was the 'winning' end, but because most of the action in each half happened at that end. Celtic, playing towards their own supporters in the first half, started the stronger team, and certainly had the bulk of the play in the early stages without really threatening. The tackling was also quite robust but fair by both sides, and it was enthralling stuff. The referee was Tom Wharton. He was an imposing figure and well known for his inability to suffer fools gladly.

Celtic deservedly went ahead in the 20th minute and it was a great goal, which became known as the 'three-card trick' goal. It started with Bertie Auld, who from about halfway inside the Rangers half, slightly to the left, sent over a high ball to Joe McBride standing on the right, just about level with the 18-yard line. Joe rose and headed the ball down to the inrushing Bobby LENNOX. It could hardly have been better placed, for Bobby did not even have to pause or break stride to run in and score. It all happened so quickly, and it had all the hallmarks of a goal that had been worked on in training. It was a tremendous goal, and was greeted with delirium on the terracing behind.

There was then a certain criticism of Celtic both from their own fans behind the goal and from the press afterwards to the effect that they did not then go for the jugular as it were, and put Rangers right out of the game. There were two ways of answering that – one was that it was surely better to keep a lid on things, as it were, and to play in a controlled way, and the other is that they didn't really have a lot of choice in the matter anyway, for this was a hard-working and by no means talentless Rangers side who fought back magnificently. It has long been the author's contention that 1966/67 actually saw one of the better Rangers sides in their history, but it was hidden because Celtic were better!

Celtic weren't necessarily a great deal better that day, however, as the battle raged. Rangers actually had the ball in the net from a Bobby Watson shot, but Mr Wharton disallowed it for a reason not immediately apparent to either set of supporters. Apparently there was a foul on Ronnie Simpson. A newspaper picture on the Monday provided another possible reason, for a Rangers player was in an offside position as Watson's shot went in.

Half-time came, and Celtic were still 1-0 up, but the Celtic end was nervous and apprehensive. The saving grace, however, was that Celtic's defence stood up well to the barrage, with Ronnie Simpson in goal having one of his best-ever games for the club. Not only was he saving well, but he was also very obviously in command of his penalty area. Those of us who recalled the last ten minutes of last year's League Cup Final remembered with pride and gratitude how he took control from a flustered McNeill. This year he was in control from the start.

Only once was Simpson beaten, and that was when he was caught out of position and the ball came to Alex Smith who miskicked his shot, but the ball was still trickling towards the goal line and would have gone in. But salvation came with the sudden appearance out of nowhere of left-back Willie O'Neill to put the ball round the post for a corner kick, earning himself a pat on the head from Ronnie Simpson. Willie is destined to be remembered for this clearance for ever, because he lost his place in the team after New Year. But this was his day, and credit must also be paid to him for the way that he handled the ever-dangerous Willie Henderson, who might have won the game for Rangers.

On another occasion, Simpson had a great save from John Greig, and the fact that it was John Greig perhaps says a great deal about the Rangers forwards, George McLean in particular who squandered some chances by shooting over the bar, one in particular from about the six-yard line, and generally looking somewhat lethargic, moody and uninterested. He would not last long at Ibrox after this.

Mr Wharton too played his part in this drama. At one point, within a minute of each other, both teams had reasonable claims for a penalty kick. One got the impression that Mr Wharton rather enjoyed himself by annoying 45,000 fans at one end and then sprinting up the park and annoying the other set of 45,000 fans. He may have been unpopular – but he was impartial! In fact, he had rather a good game and remained one of Scotland's most respected referees.

Slowly, towards the end of the game, the Celtic end became more and more animated as if sensing that Rangers had realised that they had shot their bolt and that they were not going to get past the magnificent defending of McNeill and Simpson. They were aided occasionally by unlikely characters like Jimmy Johnstone, who would suddenly appear in his own penalty box and dribble his side out of potential trouble to give his defenders some relief. But relief was certainly the word when Mr Wharton pointed to the Main Stand to indicate that Celtic had won the League Cup for the fourth time.

It was a curious reversal of roles. One thought of previous games – the New Year's Day game of 1964, the League Cup Final of 1964/65 and even this year's Scottish Cup Final of 1966. In each of them, Celtic had been the better side but could not score. This was exactly the case here, except the other way round. Victory, however, was sweet because it was not all luck. There was also the component of mature, sensible, controlled defending, something that we felt had not always been the case in the past, and might yet stand us in good stead in Europe!

TWENTY NINE

'... AND WHAT HAPPENED TO THE FUGITIVE?'

Celtic 3 Rangers 1	Scottish League Cup
Celtic Park	30 August 1967

Celtic: Simpson, Craig, Gemmell, Murdoch, McNeill, Clark, Johnstone, Wallace, Chalmers, Auld, Lennox

Rangers: Sorensen, Johansen, Provan, Greig, Jardine, McKinnon, Henderson, Penman, Ferguson, D. Smith, Johnston

Referee: Mr T. Wharton, Clarkston

WEDNESDAY, 30 August 1967 was a remarkable night, in that an Old Firm game had to share the stage, as it were, with a soap opera. This was the night on which the long-running American serial on STV called *The Fugitive* involving David Janssen was to come to its climax, and we would find out whether he had, after all, killed his wife. It was good drama, and as there were only really two channels in 1967 and one was limited in what one could watch, this drama gripped the nation.

Except, of course, for the millions who were interested in the Celtic v Rangers match at Parkhead. It was the penultimate game of the Scottish League Cup section, and Celtic held a one-point advantage. A victory, therefore, for Celtic would win the section. A draw retained Celtic's advantage, but a defeat would give Rangers the whip hand. It was enthralling stuff, for the other two teams in the section were Aberdeen and Dundee United, neither of whom would anyone describe as pushovers.

The other factor, of course, was that this was 1967. The summer had been spent basking in the glories of Lisbon. Arguably, and with the considerable benefit of hindsight, Stein made a mistake in not adding ᵗo the squad. Celtic would be punished for such complacency when the European Cup started again, but at the moment it was hard to argue against the contention that this superb team did not really need any strengthening.

There is a myth going around that Stein never fielded the Lisbon Lions again after Lisbon. This is not true. He was reluctant to let any other team claim that they had beaten the team who won in Lisbon (they were not called the Lions until sometime later), and he often made a slight tinkering with the team. Tonight, however, was important enough for him to play his best team available, and when Steve Chalmers passed a late fitness test it was the European Cup winners who took the field.

The crowd was an all-ticket 75,000 and Parkhead was a marvellous sight and the usual cauldron of noise for this Old Firm game. It started at 8pm (as was the custom in those days and much appreciated by those who had come some distance to see the game) and Celtic were playing towards their own supporters in the first half. The referee was, as often for Old Firm games, the mighty bulk of Tom Wharton, a man who would play a decisive part in this torrid encounter. He made one or two mistakes, but he also made sure that the game never really got totally out of hand, as might have been the case with a lesser referee.

Mr Wharton first encountered the wrath of the Celtic fans in the eighth minute when he allowed a goal by Willie Henderson to stand when Celtic thought he was offside. YouTube replays would tend to indicate that Henderson did indeed run on to the ball and that the goal was legal, but it was a marginal decision. What made things awkward was the action or non-action of the stand-side linesman who neither raised his flag to indicate offside, nor did he run up the touchline to the centre line to indicate a goal, as was the convention. The man was, clearly, in some doubt, as Celtic players ran to him to appeal while others asked the referee to go and talk to him. But Mr Wharton refused to go and the game restarted. 1-0 for Rangers.

Celtic had more cause for complaint about Mr Wharton later on in the first half when Bobby Lennox scored what looked like a valid equaliser, but it was called offside because Bertie Auld had been in the wrong place a few seconds earlier. This one did indeed definitely look to be the wrong decision, and Celtic felt ill done by. The Celtic end seethed and all sorts of things were said about Mr Wharton's parentage, with aprons, flutes and handshakes mentioned as well.

In the meantime the frantic action continued up to and after half-time, with players being booked and several times Mr Wharton indicating in no uncertain fashion that early baths might yet be the order of the day. Tommy Gemmell of Celtic, and John Greig and Alex Ferguson of Rangers were booked, and at one point a Neanderthal creature came out of the Rangers end, grabbed a corner flag and may well have attacked a Celtic player with it, but for the prompt action of Davie Provan of Rangers who grabbed him, ushered him off and even, most unusually, was given a reluctant round of applause from the Celtic fans for so doing!

But Rangers were still hanging on to their one-goal lead. Possibly they made a mistake in not going for another goal, being quite happy to fall back and allow Celtic most of the play. Celtic, clearly now the better team, were sadly unable to break through the Rangers defence. But all the action came in the last 13 minutes, and it all began with a penalty to Rangers! The trouble was that Celtic had too many men up front, particularly Tommy Gemmell, and Rangers made a quick breakaway. Willie Henderson was clearly brought down by John Clark inside the penalty box, and Celtic made no great protest when Mr Wharton pointed to the spot. Our hearts behind that Celtic goal sank as up stepped Kaj Johansen to take it!

Ah, Kaj Johansen! Kaj had been the scorer of the only goal in the 1966 Scottish Cup Final and it 'was praised not without cause, but without end' by the Rangers fans. It was, after all, the last time that they had won anything, but the adulation of Kaj (who was a decent human being, it must be said) had several side effects. One was that he was kept in the team longer than he ought to have been (even featuring in an embarrassing song which went 'Singing Kaj, yai, yippee, the Pope's a hippy'!), and the other was that he could never resist the temptation to try it again, something that left quite a few gaps at the back. Bobby Lennox in particular scored quite a few goals that way.

There would have been no coming back for Celtic if Johansen had scored, but Kaj hit the bar, then wrongly tried to kick the ball again before Ronnie Simpson or anyone else had touched it. Mr Wharton correctly awarded an indirect free kick for Celtic. With Celtic Park now animated and joyful, it was as if someone had pressed a button and the rejuvenated Celtic now charged forward to score three times before the end of the game, running through a disorientated and disorganised Rangers defence at will.

A corner kick was forced, goalkeeper Sorensen missed it altogether and three Celts vied with each other to score. It was Willie WALLACE who did the needful. A draw would, of course, have suited Celtic, but this team, aware that Rangers were now on their knees, kept pressing forward and Bobby MURDOCH picked up a pass from Wallace after some good work from Lennox, and crashed home the goal which put Celtic ahead, then just at the very end of the game, with the shattered Rangers end already half empty, Bobby LENNOX scored another to make the score 3-1. The full-time whistle came almost immediately after that, and Celtic had recorded one of their best-ever victories over Rangers, amazing in the sudden transformation of it all. It was really quite astonishing. But then again, that was why Celtic were the champions of Europe.

Rangers would, a couple of months later, sack their long-term manager Scot Symon, who had been with them since 1954. It caused a few people to wonder, for Rangers were at that time top of the Scottish League! But one of the reasons was certainly this particular night, which probably hurt them more than their other grizzly horrors of 1967 at Berwick and Nuremberg. For Celtic, if 1967 had not been so jam-packed with goodies, this would have been their best triumph. It certainly was a great game to see.

Celtic had now qualified for the quarter-finals of the League Cup, a trophy that they would duly go on to win. Things were not so good on the European or world fronts that autumn, and this is perhaps why some new blood in the summer might not have been a bad idea. But no one said that as we made our way back to the buses and trains that night.

And *The Fugitive?* Well, sadly there were no facilities for recording TV programmes in 1967, but those who did not go to the football that night were able to tell everyone that Dr Richard Kimble was indeed innocent of his wife's murder, and that a one-armed man did it. Then they would turn and ask what happened at Parkhead. In some ways it was difficult to work out which of the two stories was the more intriguing! They certainly both enthralled the nation.

THIRTY

FOUR GOALS AND
ONE TREBLE

Celtic 4 Rangers 0   **Scottish Cup Final**
Hampden Park   **26 April 1969**

Celtic: Fallon, Craig and Gemmell; Murdoch, McNeill and Brogan;
Connelly, Chalmers, Wallace, Lennox and Auld

Rangers: Martin, Johansen and Mathieson; Greig, McKinnon and
Smith; Henderson, Penman, Ferguson, Johnston and Persson

Referee: Mr J. Callaghan, Glasgow

RARELY had Glasgow been in such a ferment as it was in the
weeks leading up to this Scottish Cup Final. Celtic had won the
Scottish League on the Tuesday night and the Scottish League
Cup earlier in the month, but had, to the intense disappointment
of their fans, gone out of Europe to AC Milan in March after a
bad mistake by Billy McNeill at Celtic Park. Yet they had won
the tournament two years earlier, and that was the thing that
hurt Rangers most of all. Rangers for their part had won nothing
in Scotland since 1966, but were still in Europe and due to play
Newcastle United in the Fairs Cities Cup semi-final. Every Old
Firm fixture means a lot to both sides, but this one more than
most. A Celtic win meant a treble and a barren season for Rangers;
a Rangers win meant that they were back among the honours.

It was difficult not to contrast this year with 1963. Then, it
was Celtic who were intimidated by Rangers and approached the
Scottish Cup Final like a man going to the dentist's, expecting
defeat and duly getting it in the replay after a respectable
performance in the first game, but now Jock Stein dominated the
scene, having the intellectual capacity to win the all-important
psychological battle, the tactical awareness to win football matches
and the physical bulk to make it appear that he meant what he said.
As against that, Rangers had some good players, but a manager

called David White, who had done well with Clyde and would do likewise with Dundee, but was simply out of his depth in this harsh and unforgiving environment.

Side plots abounded. Both teams had now won the Scottish Cup 19 times, and this would be the decider, as it were. Rangers had a Stein of their own, Colin, but he was suspended. A ridiculous attempt was made to break the suspension and allow Stein to play in the Scottish Cup Final on the grounds that it was a 'showpiece occasion'. A director of Greenock Morton was behind this idea, the *Scottish Daily Express* saw a way of boosting sagging circulation figures among their more gullible readers, and Rangers themselves went along with it for a while before it collapsed in deserved ridicule. Meanwhile, Jimmy Johnstone of Celtic was similarly suspended. A dignified but eloquent silence emanated from Celtic Park.

And then Rangers made a vainglorious public pronouncement about a victory parade at Ibrox on the Saturday night a few hours after the cup final. It was an attempt to boost their support and to give the impression that this was the day that it was all going to turn. Once again, Celtic failed to rise to it all and continued their preparations, as the 134,000 tickets all vanished to eager punters.

In addition to the suspension of Jimmy Johnstone, Celtic would be without John Hughes, his ankle injury that had bothered him for some time failing to heal up in time. But three weeks before the Scottish Cup Final, Celtic had beaten Hibs 6-2 in the League Cup Final in an absolutely devastating display of football, and it was difficult to imagine any team on earth living with Celtic on that form. But AC Milan had, and Rangers fans held on to that ray of hope. But Rangers were not AC Milan, even though their fans on the trains going to Mount Florida station sang songs about the Italian champions! These ditties sat ill with the other songs with their perverted interpretation of Irish history! Not to mention the gentleman whom they did not like – but who lived in – er – Italy! Rome, mind you, not Milan!

Celtic's tactics were simple. The two makeshift wingers, Connelly and Auld (both of whom were a great deal better in other positions), were told not to stray more than ten yards from the touchline. This would have the effect of keeping the Rangers full-backs on the wings and leave more room for the speedy Lennox, Wallace and Chalmers to run through the ponderous Greig and McKinnon in the middle. In addition, both sides were very aware that Rangers had won the Scottish Cup in 1966 through a Kaj Johansen strike. It was, of course, a fluke, but Johansen was never likely to be able to resist the pressure from his team-mates and the Mount Florida end to try it again. Celtic were encouraged to give him a little space and, as it were, to 'encourage' him to have another go, leaving some space at the back. This tactic had worked in the past and it was likely to work again.

Rangers, on the other hand, were told to 'watch McNeill' at corner kicks. Billy too had won games by heading in corners – the Scottish Cup Final of 1965, the Vojvodina European Cup tie of 1967 and the World Club Championship against Racing Club of Argentina sprang to mind – and he would certainly try it. Alex Ferguson, in the team for the suspended Colin Stein, was detailed to mark McNeill because he was quite good with his elbow, and the two full-backs were detailed, as per normal practice, to take a post each.

Unaccountably, Rangers failed to take these two elementary precautions. Such derelictions of duty can, one supposes, be put down to 'nerves'. Rangers fans were less charitable. Celtic, having won the toss, decided to attack the end where their own fans were. Billy McNEILL rose like a bird in splendid isolation to head home a Bobby Lennox corner kick in the second minute. Ferguson did nothing to stop him, and Johansen was nowhere in sight at the post, and Celtic were one up with the psychological battle already well won. Ferguson would have many better days in football than this one – he allowed himself to become involved in some of the subsequent rough stuff, as well – and Johansen never again regained his heroic status of 1966.

The game now turned rather nasty as Rangers, stung by the early reverse and already aware that they had been suckered, poured everything forward in an unstructured, disorganised and aggressive way, with several challenges on goalkeeper Fallon looking, even to the neutral press and radio commentators, to be rather brutal. Fortunately, John, ever courageous in the cause of his beloved Celtic, had the protection of men like Gemmell and Murdoch to look after him, and these two were not easily shoved about. Jim Brogan was the only man of the 22 to be booked. In that respect, Jim was very unlucky, for many others might have joined him. Indeed, this was well before the days of red cards, but some players might well, justifiably, have been invited to take the 'long walk'.

It was, however, a spectacle devoid of any great football, and the approach of half-time looked welcome for both sides, Celtic glad to be on top and Rangers relieved to be only one behind … as they thought. But then the two minutes before half-time altered the picture. Orjan Persson, who frankly looked out of it, lost a ball to George Connelly who found Lennox. LENNOX simply charged in and scored, slipping the ball wide of Norrie Martin in the Rangers goal. That was good enough, but then, to the further consternation of the boys in blue at the far end, John Greig, still reeling from the last blow, was slow on a goal kick from Martin and in nipped George CONNELLY from reserve-team football and the mines of Fife to score a third. Some Celtic fans were even hoping for a fourth before half-time, but 3-0 it was.

Jock Stein's job now was to calm them down. Three weeks ago in the League Cup Final against Hibs, the score had been 3-0 at half-time. 'Aye, it'll no' be 3-0 at half-time today' said those who claimed to know their football! Glory be, it was! The second half saw Celtic keeping control, refusing to rise to provocation, and simply playing sensible football. Anything can happen in football, of course, we all know that, but about halfway through the second half, as arrests were happening on a regular basis at the Mount Florida end, Steve CHALMERS picked up a ball half-way inside the Rangers half, ran on and scored. This triggered a pitch invasion with the mentally challenged trying to get the game abandoned or maybe just wanting home, but the Glasgow Police simply pushed them back onto their terracing and, sadistically, made them watch the rest of the game.

Full time came with Celtic well on top. Rangers did try, but simply did not have it. Alex Ferguson did not play for Rangers again, and it was maybe round about now that he began to wonder whether he might be a better manager than a player. But for Celtic, it was their second-ever treble, and there were those who felt that the football played in 1969 was even better than that played in 1967.

So Celtic's hegemony continued, and how we enjoyed that summer of 1969!

THIRTY ONE

TOUGH BUT TRIUMPHANT

Celtic 3 Rangers 1 **Scottish Cup Quarter-Final**
Celtic Park **21 February 1970**

Celtic: Williams, Craig, Gemmell, Murdoch, McNeill, Brogan, Johnstone, Lennox, Wallace, Hay, Hughes (Hood)

Rangers: Neef, Johansen, Mathieson, Greig, McKinnon, Smith, Conn (Henderson), Penman, Stein, MacDonald, Johnston

Referee: Mr T. Wharton, Newton Mearns

IT was 1970 that Celtic might have repeated 1967. Still going strong in Europe and about to play Fiorentina in the quarter-final of the European Cup, Celtic were also comfortably placed at the top of the Scottish League, had already won the Scottish League Cup, and today was the day that would tell us which of the Old Firm would remain in the Scottish Cup. Celtic had already defeated Dunfermline Athletic and Dundee United in this competition, while Rangers made rather too much of their, admittedly spectacular, defeat of Forfar Athletic.

Rangers were not having things anything like as well as Celtic were, and late in 1969 in the wake of a European exit they had sacked David White and appointed Ibrox legend Willie Waddell as manager. Waddell had been a highly successful manager of Kilmarnock, but in recent years he had been writing for the *Scottish Daily Express*, a position which he had used to attack and undermine his predecessor David White in a particularly unsubtle way. But now he had the job he had always craved, and results began to improve, although the Old Firm game at Parkhead on 3 January had proved little – a dull, cagey 0-0 draw on a frosty pitch – and was possibly one of the least interesting Old Firm games of them all.

Frost and snow looked as if they might prove a problem in this Scottish Cup tie as well, for the weather was hard in the week leading up to this game, obliging Celtic to move to the Ayrshire coast at Seamill Hydro for their training. But then on the Friday, the weather broke as a westerly airstream brought rain, and loads of it. The result was that the pitch changed overnight from an ice rink to a quagmire, but it was perfectly playable. It was indeed a typical Glasgow derby, played in traditional Glasgow weather.

The build-up tended to focus on Rangers and asked the question whether, with Waddell now at the helm, Rangers could win back some sort of supremacy from Celtic. Jock Stein, on the other hand, was deliberately low-key about this game, trying to imply that the really important game on the horizon was the forthcoming clash with Fiorentina in the European Cup rather than Rangers in the Scottish Cup. That was for public consumption. What he said and did with his players in private at Seamill Hydro was a different matter altogether.

Alcohol was normally allowed at football matches in 1970, but for Old Firm games, including this one, it was now banned. So too were banners and flags. Neither of these two bans were totally successful, however, for there was evidence of both in the 70,000 crowd which packed Parkhead. Sean Connery (James Bond) called himself a Celtic supporter in those days (he would change his mind in later years) and he was seen in the stand along with his wife Diane Cilento, but he was not the main focus of attention today.

The teams came out together as normal in Old Firm games (in other games at that time, they came out separately) and it was immediately obvious that the pitch was going to cut up very badly from the stud marks on the turf as they walked out. Stein had decided to play John Hughes (always a good player on heavy ground), and he also included young Davie Hay who normally played at right-back, albeit an attacking full-back, but today he played Jim Craig in that position and included Hay in the midfield. This would be a sensible and even inspirational move.

Within five minutes, controversy was in the air. First Celtic, attacking the Rangers end goal, had a Lennox shot cleared off the line by Willie Mathieson, but it looked to some journalists and neutrals that the ball may have been over the line. However, given the muddy conditions, it was difficult to say, but then immediately after that the game erupted and bad feeling would now persist throughout the whole game. Jim Craig had the misfortune to score an own goal as the wet ball spun off his foot. That was bad enough but then he was 'congratulated' by Willie Johnston and Colin Stein for so doing. Not unnaturally, he reacted to that. McNeill complained bitterly and lengthily to the referee about it and was given a long talking to.

So Rangers were 1-0 up, the crowd was in a ferment, and the players were all angry. Only five minutes gone, and the next 85 would show some of the worst of Scottish football in terms of tackles and elbowing, but it would be a game from which Celtic emerged triumphant. Mr Wharton was a key figure in all this. He possibly made a rod for his own back by not taking stronger action against the two Rangers players who 'congratulated' Jim Craig, but he then went on to have a good game, not being afraid on several occasions to use his considerable bulk to break up potential clashes between players. One would have imagined that Mr Wharton, with his middle-class background, would have been a Queen's Park supporter. He was certainly not pro-Celtic, nor pro-Rangers that day, and with a weaker referee, this game might have seen real serious trouble.

Celtic equalised just before half-time. Jimmy Johnstone and Davie Hay teamed up to send over a long ball looking for John Hughes. Hughes missed it but the ball came to Bobby LENNOX, who managed to squeeze the ball past Neef from the tightest of angles to make the score 1-1. Half-time brought some relief to the exhausted players and indeed spectators, but it was seen as the players made their way down the tunnel that vendettas were continuing.

Soon after the interval, we had a major 'handbags' moment after Neef saved from Lennox. A melee developed, caused to a certain extent by players being unable to stop themselves on the wet turf, everyone started pushing each other around, a few fists were seen, but Mr Wharton managed to impose some sort of order, and wisely took no action other than stern words to all concerned. A case could, nevertheless, have been made for several on both sides to get 'the long walk'.

The football then resumed for a spell, but then just on the hour mark the game erupted once again. The referee had to take action when Alex MacDonald went in hard on goalkeeper Evan Williams and was then confronted by Jim Brogan. MacDonald was rightly sent off, but some of the Rangers supporters felt that Brogan should go as well. A few illegal bottles and cans appeared on the track and some pathetic specimens of humanity appeared on the track as well, presumably fancying a riot, or perhaps trying to avoid the bottles and coins thrown by their own supporters.

Order having been restored, Celtic now had the extra man. There was now a welcome concentration on trying to score goals, as Jock Stein was clearly seen telling his men to calm down and all would be well. Ten v 11 men should be significant on a day and a pitch like this. But the bookings continued. Willie Mathieson tripped up Jimmy Johnstone, and both captains ended up in the book as well – Billy McNeill for arguing excessively.

But as the game approached its closing stages, it was clear that Celtic were gaining the ascendancy. Rangers would have been very happy with a draw and an Ibrox replay, but Celtic, who feared fixture congestion given their European commitments, went for a win, and with five minutes to go those who thought that David HAY was a class player were proved correct as he hammered the heavy ball home from 25 yards to give Neef no chance.

Parkhead erupted at all this, and one sensed that Rangers knew they were beaten. Apart from anything else, they were exhausted and had indeed been outplayed by Celtic, for whom Bobby Murdoch had been outstanding in midfield. Bobby was not a man to be pushed about, but he also had enough sense not to get involved in anything silly and he concentrated on the football. Another man who was targeted was Jimmy Johnstone. In his younger day, Jimmy might have retaliated (as he did famously on New Year's Day 1965), but today he ignored it all, and it was somehow fitting that with the Rangers now reeling and their supporters disappearing it was Jimmy JOHNSTONE who ran through and scored the third goal to remove any possible doubt about the outcome.

And so Celtic were into the semi-final of the Scottish Cup, while Rangers' season more or less ended there and then. The match, however, had some repercussions with some players being summoned to SFA headquarters, Glasgow Police headquarters and even Glasgow Corporation to be told that their behaviour was a disgrace. Politicians got involved as well, but the general reprimand was as successful as past or future attempts to stop trouble at Old Firm games! Celtic now moved on, duly won the Scottish League about a month later to no one's surprise, but their cup adventures at Hampden and Milan in 1970 were a lot less successful. The season did not end well for Celtic.

THIRTY TWO

ANOTHER DOUBLE

Celtic 2 Rangers 1   **Scottish Cup Final Replay**
Hampden Park   **12 May 1971**

Celtic: Williams, Craig, Brogan, Connelly, McNeill, Hay, Johnstone, Hood (Wallace), Macari, Callaghan, Lennox

Rangers: McCloy, Denny, Mathieson, Greig, McKinnon, Jackson, Henderson, Penman (D. Johnstone), Stein, MacDonald, Johnston

Referee: Mr T. Wharton, Newton Mearns

THERE were 103,332 at Hampden this beautiful Wednesday night to see the Scottish Cup Final Replay. The winning score seemed narrow, but in fact it was a convincing win for Celtic, so much so that Jock Stein could not resist the jibe to a BBC reporter to the effect that 'this is a good result for Rangers'!

The year 1971 was defined, almost before it started, by the Ibrox Disaster which happened on 2 January. There were 66 Rangers supporters killed on Stairway 13 in a dreadful crush. No words could express the horror, but it was a moment that managed, temporarily, to bring both factions together. But life had to go on and football had to continue, if for no other reason than it was needed to prevent people dwelling on the horror. To their credit, Celtic and Celtic supporters shared in the grief and the first home game after the disaster (a 2-1 win over Hibs) saw a very impressively kept one minute's silence.

In the wake of the disaster, Rangers' league campaign collapsed, and Celtic won the league with a degree of ease. Their only challenge came from Aberdeen, a club revived by manager Eddie Turnbull and a somewhat fortuitous capture of the Scottish Cup in 1970. But Rangers, who had won the Scottish League Cup this season by beating Celtic, had a good run in the Scottish Cup and reached the final after beating Hibs in a replayed semi-final.

Celtic's season had been a rebuilding one. The European Cup Final defeat of 1970 hung heavily over Celtic Park. (It was difficult to accept that Celtic were only the second-best team in Europe!) Stein himself, after appearing to go through a bad phase, had rallied and a new team was now beginning to develop out of the old – men like Clark, Chalmers and Auld being marginalised and new players like Macari, Hay and Connelly emerging more and more. Stein even appeared to enjoy stringing the media along by hinting that he was going to Manchester United – a continuing theme in the newspapers, particularly on quiet days when there was no other story – but he eventually killed that one by denying it at a crucial time in the championship race, the day before Celtic played Aberdeen at Pittodrie, and Celtic duly won the league! A considerable amount of egg was detected on the faces of many pompous journalists for a long time after that!

What was considerably less acceptable from the press was the campaign to persuade Rangers to win the Scottish Cup, particularly when they kept saying that there were 66 reasons why they should do so, often beside a picture of the buckled Stairway 13 of 2 January. Frankly, this was in bad taste and even embarrassed Rangers themselves. Nor can it really have been of any great comfort to the bereaved families. But it nevertheless sold newspapers and had the effect of galvanising the Rangers support, who certainly outnumbered Celtic fans on both cup final occasions in May.

The first game was played on Saturday, 8 May. A week before, Stein had grabbed the headlines by playing all his Lisbon Lions in the last league game of the season against Clyde. It was great publicity, and there was even a touch of subliminal propaganda by having the players come out of the now half-demolished old stand walking down planks of wood. The old was thus being, symbolically, replaced by the new.

Over 120,000 appeared for the first Scottish Cup Final at Hampden. The Rangers end looked seriously overcrowded (so much for all the cant about 'the safety of spectators is paramount'!) and there was also serious crowd disorder there at the half-time interval. What it was all about, we cannot guess, but neurotic fears about another disaster must have been a factor.

The game itself was even, with possibly Rangers having the balance of the chances, but yet it was Bobby Lennox who scored first for Celtic. Indeed, Celtic looked the likely winners until Derek Johnstone popped up from what may have been an offside position to level the score late in the game. It was a disappointment, but possibly Rangers deserved another chance. And in any case, as the ever-present cynics pointed out, the replay on Wednesday was hardly likely to be a financial disaster, was it?

Over the weekend, there was more than a little concern expressed about the size of the crowd that might attend on Wednesday night. There was no time to make it an all-ticket game, and although the crowd would be slightly down on Saturday for obvious logistic reasons, it would still be huge. (In the event, it was 103,332.) With all this in mind, both BBC and STV tabled bids to show the replay live on TV, offering a considerable amount of money to do so, and even being prepared to negotiate a 'first half from the studio and second half live' sort of deal. These offers were supported by the police, by politicians and by the general public, but with breathtaking arrogance the SFA turned them down saying it would 'deter the fans from attending'! But that was the whole point, was it not?

Nevertheless, it had to be admitted that Hampden Park on that lovely spring evening of Wednesday, 12 May presented a wonderful spectacle, and this time there was an improvement in the behaviour, even though at both ends there were disturbing signs of overcrowding in some parts. The balance had possibly now swung to Celtic in view of injuries to Rangers players including Alex Millar who had played on Saturday with a broken jaw, and Rangers had been forced to bring in a youngster called Jim Denny at right-back. Jock Stein had not been happy with Celtic's attacking performance on Saturday, and Willie Wallace was dropped for the replay, his place being taken by young Lou Macari.

The score was only 2-1 but it was in fact one of Celtic's best-ever displays against Rangers as they won the Scottish Cup for the 21st time. It was generally regarded as Jimmy Johnstone at his best, and there was no point in trying any zonal marking on him, for he popped up all over the place, wreaking havoc as he did so. In addition, it was now apparent that in George Connelly Celtic had unearthed a world-class defender/midfield player (for he was equally at home in both areas). Stein's instructions had been for Celtic to attack down the left as much as possible where the inexperienced Rangers full-back was, but in fact it was a first half in which Celtic were all over them.

Billy McNeill, of all people, should have opened the scoring but shot wide after good work from Jimmy Johnstone, but the opening goal was only delayed until the 24th minute. It came from a corner on the left taken by Bobby Lennox which missed a few people on the near post before coming to Lou MACARI. Playing in his first-ever cup tie for the club (let alone his first cup final) Lou prodded the ball home. The Celtic end was still in ecstasy a minute or two later when Jimmy Johnstone was running in on goal and was wrestled to the ground by Ron McKinnon. In later years a red card would have been shown, but in 1971 a penalty was enough, and Mr Wharton, now on the point of retirement, pointed to the spot. Harry HOOD did the needful, and further explosions of joy followed from the Celtic end. The first half finished the way it had been all the way, though with Celtic well on top, Jimmy Johnstone providing loads of entertainment, and such efforts as Rangers could provide down the wings being well contained by the two full-backs Jim Craig and Jim Brogan.

In the second half, after quarter of an hour, Rangers pulled one back. Frankly, it was the only way they were likely to score – an own goal with Jim Craig, in trying to clear, slicing the ball into his own goal and clearly not relishing the 'congratulations' bestowed on him by Willie Mathieson of Rangers. But Jim and Celtic would have the last laugh.

Rangers now pressed but it was the hysterical pressure that was not likely to produce anything against such a resolute and competent defence as Celtic had. Celtic for their part kept a tight grip of the midfield, fed Jimmy Johnstone as often as they could, and remained in control. Greig of Rangers and Brogan of Celtic were booked for tackles that Mr Wharton deemed to be a trifle too robust, but the game was never dirty. Only once did Rangers come anywhere near close, and that was almost at the death when a shot from Colin Stein of Rangers hit goalkeeper Evan Williams on the chest and the ball ran clear. But Mr Wharton signalled the end of the Scottish Cup Final (and his own career) with the score still Celtic 2 Rangers 1 as 'You'll never walk alone' resounded from the Celtic end.

It was the third time that Stein had won a league and cup double, and he was clearly proud of what he had achieved. Almost seamlessly, a new Celtic had developed out of the carnage of last season's Milan fiasco, and summer 1971 would be spent by Celtic fans talking about their new team. If you include Willie Wallace, who came on as a substitute for the tiring Harry Hood, only five Lisbon Lions were in that 1971 Scottish Cup-winning side. Stein, about whom the press had used phrases like 'resignation', 'move to Manchester United' and 'struggling at the top', had now quietened them, and how the Celtic fans enjoyed his triumph!

THIRTY THREE

LIVE TV MAKES AN APPEARANCE

Celtic 1 Rangers 0   **Scottish Cup Final**
Hampden Park   **7 May 1977**

Celtic: Latchford, McGrain, Lynch, Stanton, McDonald, Aitken, Dalglish, Edvaldsson, Craig, Conn, Wilson

Rangers: Kennedy, Jardine, Greig, Forsyth, Jackson, Watson (Robertson), McLean, Hamilton, Parlane, MacDonald, Johnston

Referee: Mr R. Valentine, Dundee

THE attendance of 54,252 was not the least important of the topics of conversation about this Scottish Cup Final. By any standards the turnout was poor, and it contrasted starkly with the Scottish Cup Final of 1973 between the same teams when the attendance was more than double that. There were several reasons for this. One was that it was simply an awful day, another was that Rangers' attendances had dipped alarmingly during this season (Celtic's had too, but not so much), yet another was that football attendances in 1977 were generally poor and rapidly diminishing, but the main reason was that the game was, controversially, live on terrestrial television.

Only two Scottish Cup finals had previously been on television – Celtic v Clyde in 1955 and Falkirk v Kilmarnock in 1957. Since then it had been a closed book. Even on occasions when a six-figure crowd had pledged to turn up by buying tickets, the SFA said 'No'. The reasons were specious and seemed to owe a lot to the Calvinistic desire to prevent people from being happy – a very Scottish quirk – and there was the additional humiliation that they would not let us watch the English Cup Final either, even though the rest of the UK enjoyed that privilege. But in 1977 things had changed. The Scottish Cup was sponsored, the sponsors insisted on live TV coverage of the final and money talked very loudly indeed, drowning out those who talked about 'principles' and 'integrity'. BBC and Archie MacPherson were there, and so were we all, even those of us who didn't go to Hampden on that awful day.

Hampden in 1977 was (and would remain for another two decades) a disgrace. Inadequate catering, insanitary toilets, no cover at the Celtic end, puddles of rainwater where you queued up for the rusty turnstiles – were all good reasons why many of us decided that there was no place like home on 7 May.

Celtic were the clear favourites. They had won the league a few weeks back, and it looked now as if another good team was being built up after an indifferent 1975 and an awful 1976. Jock Stein had had a year off after a nasty road accident, but had now returned, his acumen and sheer football knowledge being observed in the players that he bought. Joe Craig came from Partick Thistle, Pat Stanton, apparently 'finished' and out of favour at Hibs, came to Celtic Park to play the best football of his life and then, spectacularly, Alfie Conn came from Tottenham Hotspur.

The problem about Alfie was that he had once played for Rangers. But was that a problem? Not really. Jock had consulted Danny McGrain and Kenny Dalglish and the three of them thought that there would be no problem with Alfie at Celtic Park. And neither there was. On his first game at Parkhead he was given a hero's reception and the crowd sang 'He used to be a H** but he's all right now, Alfie, Alfie Conn!'

Rangers, on the other hand, were in a mess. It is not often that albatrosses hang round the necks of dinosaurs, but the mixed metaphor is appropriate here. The team played badly, and after a friendly game in England in which their fans rioted (not for the first time), they suddenly announced that they would now sign Roman Catholics. They had been under pressure on this issue from informed opinion for some time, and they didn't immediately go out and buy a player of that persuasion, but oh how it upset their supporters! They stayed away.

Celtic had reached the final by beating Airdrie, Ayr United, Queen of the South and Dundee in an undistinguished passage, and were without Ronnie Glavin who had injured himself when playing for Scotland – to the intense anger of Jock Stein. Stein also decided to play Edvaldsson in the forward line instead of the young Tommy Burns, while Johnny Doyle was also rested in favour of the talented but inconsistent Paul Wilson.

Stein made sure that the tracksuit jackets worn by the players in the warm-up had 'league champions' on them, and several times in his pre-match interview mentioned 'league champions' as well. He knew how to win the propaganda battle, being charming to the press and public as distinct from the brusque and boorish Jock Wallace who did not come across on television as well as Stein did.

The morning newspapers tended to go for a Celtic victory on the grounds that Celtic had more flair players than Rangers did. McGrain and Dalglish were the ones mentioned, and it was also felt that the double centre-half pairing of Roddie McDonald and Pat Stanton, with a little help from the young Roy Aitken, might be enough to contain whatever Rangers could throw at them.

The weather remained wet, cold and unpleasant, and the atmosphere with empty spaces on the huge terracing was a million miles away from what one would have expected in a Scottish Cup Final. Celtic started playing towards the Rangers supporters, but the first phase of the game showed little for commentator Archie MacPherson to get excited about, hard though he tried. Defences were clearly on top. One or two tackles were possibly a little more enthusiastic than one would have hoped for, but referee Bob Valentine wisely allowed a little for the wet ground and the general tension of the occasion.

It was in the 20th minute when it all happened. A corner kick from Conn found McDonald, whose attempt was only partially cleared by goalkeeper Stewart Kennedy. The ball came to Johannes Edvaldsson whose shot was stopped on the line by Derek Johnstone. Ah, but how? Well, if you support Rangers, it was his knee, and if you are a lover of the green and white, it was his hand. TV coverage remains inconclusive some 40 years later, but Mr Valentine thought it was a penalty, and he was the only one that mattered. His decision earned him the nickname 'Bob Vatican' from the boys in blue!

Celtic now had a problem. The regular penalty taker, Ronnie Glavin, was out of the side, so would it be captain Dalglish? No, Andy LYNCH stepped up to the mark. A few weeks before, the luckless Andy had managed to score two own goals in a game against Motherwell, but today he calmly faced the baying Rangers supporters and fired the ball home to the keeper's left.

Celtic were thus in the lead. A long time to go, but Celtic now only had to retain the ball and the cup would be theirs for the 25th time. Tackles were fierce and hard, flair and silky football were distinctly absent, but half-time was reached with Celtic still 1-0 ahead.

The lack of good football was equally marked in the second half. It soon became apparent that, although no football game was over until the referee's whistle, Rangers simply lacked the ability to force a win. Any goal that came would have to be through a mistake in the Celtic defence or a lucky break, and that did not look like happening with Pat Stanton in charge of the defence. Edvaldsson totally nullified the potential aerial threat of Derek Johnstone, and Celtic's midfield won far more battles than it lost.

Indeed, it was Celtic who had the better chances, two that really should have been put away. One was when Joe Craig was clean through and put the ball past the post, and the other Paul Wilson miskicked with the goal at his mercy. Against that, the only time when Celtic hearts missed a beat was right at the death when Rangers' young substitute Chris Robertson hit the junction of the bar and the post.

The final whistle saw great delight on the wet east terracing and in Celtic households. There was no trouble inside the ground (as there would be three years later in 1980) but there was a great deal of disorder in the streets around the ground, with 137 arrests made. 1977 was a bad year for football hooliganism but a good one for Jock Stein and his revived Celtic. And yet, the seeds of destruction were already sown. No one could have imagined as Kenny Dalglish received the Scottish Cup (he actually lost his medal which had fallen into an umbrella as he was showing some disabled supporters the Scottish Cup) that he was already contemplating departure, something that would destroy Celtic's

1977/78 season more or less before it started and lead indirectly to the downfall of Jock Stein who couldn't cope with it all.

But that was next year. For the moment, there was the Scottish League and the Scottish Cup to savour. Celtic had now won the trophy 25 times. It was by no means one of their more spectacular cup finals, but it was to be enjoyed nevertheless. Celtic and Rangers had now crossed swords in ten cup finals. Celtic had won in 1899, 1904, 1969, 1971 and now 1977, whereas Rangers had been successful in 1893, 1928, 1963, 1966 and 1973. 1977 brought a very satisfying double to Celtic supporters.

THIRTY FOUR

TEN MEN WON THE LEAGUE

> **Celtic 4 Rangers 2** **Scottish League Premier Division**
> **Celtic Park** **21 May 1979**
>
> *Celtic:* Latchford, McGrain, Lynch, Aitken, McAdam, Edvaldsson, Provan, Conroy (Lennox), McCluskey, MacLeod, Doyle
>
> *Rangers:* McCloy, Jardine, Dawson, Johnstone, Jackson, MacDonald, McLean (Miller), Russell, Parlane, Smith, Cooper
>
> *Referee:* Mr E. Pringle, Edinburgh

THE legend of the ten men who won the league is a famous one in the annals of our great club, and one could argue that this game is, possibly, the third most famous in our history, behind Lisbon and the 7-1. For sheer drama, this game cannot really be bettered, but it is also a game that had so much of a background to it that it cannot really be considered in isolation. There were so many other factors, as well as it being a thrilling game of football.

In the first place, this era was really a rather poor one in Celtic's history. Celtic, and the game in Scotland in general, were really at a very low ebb with poor attendances and the game struggling to retain the interest of the Scottish population. The year before, 1978, had seen the Argentina fiasco, football's equivalent to the Darien Scheme of the 1690s, when Scotland made a complete international fool of themselves after having built everyone up to high expectations. So complete was the rout that many people asked themselves if they wanted to see a football match again. Attendances in Scotland in the 1978/79 season were low, and stayed low.

In Celtic's case, there was another factor as the club tried to retain some credibility. In summer 1977, Celtic had made the astonishing mistake of selling Kenny Dalglish to Liverpool without making adequate provisions to replace him. The impression grew that the directors were only interested in money, not football, and Jock Stein, whose part in the Dalglish departure remains mysterious and a serious blot on his record, departed after an incredibly awful and depressing 1977/78 season. New manager Billy McNeill was still struggling to cope with this cloud of despair throughout the 1978/79 season.

And there was the weather. Autumn 1978 saw Celtic play football that struggled to reach the mediocre, but it must be stressed that this was true of other teams as well, and at the New Year no team had as yet taken a grip of the league. Then bad weather came down, more or less wiping out football (certainly as far as Celtic were concerned) during the months of January and February. This was long before the days of under-soil heating, and a hard frost meant that no football could be played. The result was that when March arrived, Celtic still had 18 league games left to play. It was almost as if the league season was starting now, and that what had gone before in late 1978 did not really matter.

Yet another factor which influenced this particular game was industrial relations. This game on 21 May was played to the background of strikes on the railways, the buses and even on television – all of which played a significant part in supporters' ability or otherwise to attend or to watch this game. It was, after all, the end of the 'winter of discontent' – with some seriously ill-thought-out trade union activity that played its part in defeating their own sympathetic Labour Government and introducing, a few weeks previously, the Conservative Government of Margaret Thatcher.

The winter lay-off may actually have helped Celtic in that it allowed McNeill's two excellent recruits – Davie Provan from Kilmarnock and Murdo MacLeod from Dumbarton – time to bed in with the rest of the team, and for McNeill to analyse his resources. Generally speaking, the team began to win games, although there was still the occasional lapse at grounds like Easter Road and Tannadice Park. The form was not always totally convincing, but points began to be acquired, sometimes painfully – one recalls two games against St Mirren, one home and one away, both of them won by the odd goal but with the loudest cheer being for the referee's final whistle.

The bad winter meant that the season would go on well into May. Indeed, at the end of April six league games remained, two of which were against Rangers. The first of these was at Hampden, because Ibrox was out of commission for repairs, and Rangers' 1-0 victory there in a poor game led some of their supporters to believe, prematurely, that they were going to win the league.

But wiser Celtic supporters realised that there was still a great deal of football to be played, and that the important thing was to win the games against Partick Thistle, St Mirren and Hearts before worrying about the final game of the season against Rangers at Celtic Park on Monday, 21 May. Celtic duly did win these games, not without a little anxiety. The St Mirren game, incidentally, was played at Ibrox because Love Street was out of commission. But did we not say that Ibrox itself was out of commission for repairs? Conspiracy theorists worried about that one, but could come up with no real answer other than sheer incompetence! In the meantime, Rangers had drawn the Scottish Cup Final twice against Hibs in a couple of really rather poor games, which indicated not only exhaustion but also a serious lack of quality.

All this was as nothing compared to the events at Celtic Park on 21 May. Basically, a win for Celtic won the league. Any other result favoured Rangers, who still had another game to play. The crowd was 52,000, slightly less than the tickets sold for the original date of 6 January, but that was due to bus and rail problems and the fact that it was a Monday night. No TV, no radio as a result of labour problems with STV, and general uselessness with the BBC. No computer updates, no Teletext in 1979, so if you weren't at the game, you had to wait until the BBC News deigned to tell you who had won, in my case the dulcet tones of Angela Rippon!

Rangers were marginally the better team in the first half and went in at half-time 1-0 up. The second half saw more frustration for Celtic, and Johnny Doyle could not contain his emotion when he aimed a kick at a prone Rangers player whom he suspected, not without cause, of faking an injury to waste time. Early bath for Doyle, and only ten men left to win the league.

Fortunately, one of the ten was Roy AITKEN. Not for the first nor the last time in his life, Roy took the game by the scruff of the neck, realising that Celtic now had nothing to lose, and about halfway through the second half he equalised for Celtic after picking up a pass from Provan. That was not in itself much use to Celtic, but it gave everyone a boost, and at this point McNeill decided to bring on (in place of the adequate but uninspiring Mike Conroy), his ex-team-mate and the only remaining Lisbon Lion, Bobby Lennox, now rearing the end of his lengthy career, but still one of the fastest men around.

The second goal would have been enough to win the league for Celtic, and it came from a superb shot by George McCLUSKEY. That was in the 82nd minute, but in the 84th the rocking Celtic Park was brought back down to earth when Rangers equalised in the wake of a corner kick; 2-2, but now everything was thrown into the game, and the fact that one of the sides had only ten men was hardly noticed.

Five minutes from time came a personal nightmare for Rangers' Colin Jackson. He really couldn't do anything about it when a cross from George McCluskey was parried by goalkeeper Peter McCloy into his path and he simply could not get out of the way of it and diverted the ball into his own net. Clichés like 'Parkhead erupted' did not quite cover what the terracings and the Jungle were like after this as heaving and surging humanity jumped on each other, kissing and cuddling anything in sight.

But five minutes still remained. Celtic wisely did not fall back to defend – that might have been fatal given that Rangers had the extra man – but kept surging forward, keeping hold of the ball trying not to let it go out of play, reckoning that if they kept the ball in the Rangers half, Rangers could not possibly equalise. This was long before the days of boards being raised to show how many minutes were left, and no one knew how long Mr Pringle (who had had a good game) would allow for the Doyle sending-off and the sundry bookings that he had made. Everyone looked at him beseeching him to blow for time, and then the ball came to Murdo MacLEOD.

Murdo, rather than hold on to the ball and risk losing it, decided to try for goal, reckoning that he was shooting towards his own supporters who would take their time to return the ball and use up what time was left. So he shot – right into the top corner of the net with McCloy nowhere near it. In some ways it was a trademark Murdo MacLeod goal, but never was there a more significant one.

Once more Celtic Park erupted, and then did so again immediately after the restart when Mr Pringle signalled full time. The league had been won in breathtaking fashion, and Celtic players and supporters celebrated endlessly, many of them prepared to admit that they appeared at their work the following morning without having been to bed. My own personal memory was that of my dog charging about a public park on a beautiful Tuesday morning while his owner waited for the newsagent to open!

THIRTY FIVE

A GREAT WIN, BUT...

Celtic 1 Rangers 0 aet   **Scottish Cup Final**
Hampden Park   **10 May 1980**

Celtic: Latchford, Sneddon, McGrain, Aitken, Conroy, MacLeod, Provan, Doyle (Lennox), McCluskey, Burns, McGarvey

Rangers: McCloy, Jardine, Dawson, Stevens, Jackson, Forsyth (Miller), Cooper, Russell, Johnstone, Smith, MacDonald (McLean)

Referee: Mr G. Smith, Edinburgh

IT is a shame that everyone will refer to 1980 as the 'riot' cup final. Like 1909, the occasion of another riot, the year 1980 seems permanently to be stained with this title as far as the Scottish Cup is concerned. The riot was serious enough, and no one would want to minimise the causes or effects, but it would be a pity if one forgot the football that was played in what was generally reckoned to be one of the better Scottish Cup finals between the two old rivals. And at least the players behaved – most of the time, at least!

Celtic approached this cup final in a bit of a mess, and it was by no means a confident support which made its way to Hampden Park this bright sunny May day. The supporters and the players themselves were in a state of shock after the way in which they had thrown away the Scottish League in the general direction of Aberdeen. At the beginning of April, having defeated Rangers 1-0 at Celtic Park on Wednesday, 2 April, they then lost twice to Aberdeen at Celtic Park and compounded the felony by blowing up badly in the city of Dundee. Losing to Dundee United was bad enough, but then on 19 April at Dens Park, in one of the worst Celtic performances many of us could remember for many years, the team lost 1-5 to a Dundee side that was heading for relegation – and that was after Celtic had scored first!

It was a spectacularly awful piece of self-destruction. The only possible excuse was a dry, bumpy pitch, but it was so bad that it hinted at a certain amount of disharmony behind the scenes.

What caused it all, we cannot tell, but it might well have been Celtic's age-old enemy of complacency. Another possibility was the somewhat insular Celtic belief that as long as they beat Rangers nothing else matters. The win on 2 April (narrow but decisive) over Rangers may have taken Celtic's eye off the ball and prevented them from seeing Aberdeen as a major threat. However that may be, Aberdeen could not believe their luck and, taking advantage of Celtic's new lack of self-belief and general vulnerability, beat Celtic 3-1 on 23 April before 48,000 incredulous spectators, some of them so traumatised by recent events that they could hardly even boo or shout their displeasure. It was a shockingly unprofessional performance.

All this had followed a 2-0 win at Parkhead over Real Madrid in the European Cup quarter-final first leg, and then the heartbreak of seeing the lead disappear at the Bernabeu. Indeed, with the exception of the signing of Frank McGarvey, which at least said something about the ambition of the club, spring 1980 was a dreadful time, and the approach of the Scottish Cup Final against Rangers was not helped by the news that Roddy MacDonald and Tom McAdam, both central defenders were suspended, and that Mike Conroy, a fringe player for most of the season and not really a central defender, would have to partner Roy Aitken in the centre of the defence.

The saving grace was that Rangers were themselves struggling. They had clearly not yet recovered from the 'Ten Men Won The League' night of May 1979, and Celtic had beaten them twice that season and drawn twice. They had not been in any way impressive in their Scottish Cup games, although they had done well to beat Aberdeen in the semi-final, and they had finished up fifth in the Premier League to the disappointment of their fans who sometimes gave the impression that they were now looking for something else to do on a Saturday afternoon.

Celtic had reached the final by beating Raith Rovers unimpressively 2-1, St Mirren 3-2 in a tense replay at Love Street, Morton 2-0 in the quarter-final at Parkhead, and a poor Hibs side 5-0 (even with George Best in their ranks) in the semi-final at Hampden. On 3 May Aberdeen clinched the league at Easter

Road – a painful experience for us, however deserved it might have been by the eager and talented play of Alex Ferguson's Dons, and 10 May was the Scottish Cup Final, something that represented the only chance of a trophy for either set of Old Firm fans after what had been a disappointing season for both of them. The centre of power seemed to have travelled to the north-east.

The Scottish Cup Final itself was actually a good game of football on a nice sunny day, with both teams having chances to win the game before the end of 90 minutes. Derek Johnstone of Rangers failed once or twice to capitalise on the good work of Davie Cooper, and Frank McGarvey came close for Celtic on several occasions. It would be fair to say that although Rangers possibly had the better chances, Celtic played the better, more controlled football, a factor that became more evident the longer the game went on. Celtic's makeshift central defence of Aitken and Conroy performed heroics throughout the match, and the game went to extra time without either side having scored a goal.

Celtic were definitely the better team in extra time, and it was a shame that the game had to be settled by a rather unsatisfactory sort of goal. It came in the second half of extra time in the aftermath of a Celtic corner on the right-hand side at the Mount Florida end of the ground. The ball was only partially cleared (twice) and it came to Danny McGrain. Danny, never the greatest finisher in the world, shot for goal, and the ball was going harmlessly past the post when George McCLUSKEY stuck out his foot, more in hope than in anticipation, and diverted the ball past Peter McCloy. It all happened in front of the Rangers fans, and it seemed to take a long time for it to register at both ends of the ground that a goal had been scored.

The jumping about at the Celtic end caused a mini-sandstorm from the dust – the Scottish word 'stoor' is a brilliant description – and there was still dust about a few minutes later when, with the ball safely in the arms of goalkeeper Peter Latchford, referee George Smith (who had done an excellent job in controlling the game) signalled that Celtic had won the Scottish Cup for the 26th time. It was one of Celtic's better cup finals, in spite of the narrow scoreline, and all the more welcome to the fans after such a catastrophic last month of the league season.

It would have been nice to end the story there and move on, but unfortunately we can't and we must talk about the distressing events afterwards. Although there is no point in saying that one crowd was better than the other – they were equally culpable – we can say that it was the Rangers crowd who started it. Some Celtic supporters had come on first but merely to congratulate their team. It was a foolish, but basically benevolent, invasion. One could not say that about the Rangers invasion, which was starkly hostile and aggressive.

The arrests and injuries were equally shocking, but at least four other factors must take a share in the blame. The police were nowhere to be seen until the battle was raging. With more police on duty in the right place, neither invasion would have occurred. The media and the TV commentator are also to blame for encouraging and highlighting things. Both Archie MacPherson of the BBC and Alex Cameron of STV could be heard saying things like 'Here comes another charge' and giving the impression that they were enjoying themselves or fancied promotion to the job of war correspondent. And finally, alcohol was definitely a factor – but how could the SFA wring their hypocritical hands in despair at that, when a well-known Scottish brewery firm was sponsoring the Scottish Cup?

We can also, of course, blame the educational system – a clear and obvious failure this day in spite of comprehensive education having been around for ten years. There were also the politicians who had done little to improve life for the educational under-achievers, and of course the parents who did not control their children. It being a very sensitive topic in this context, no one dared mention churches and religion, but they had also done little to minimise sectarian divisions.

The debate went on for months and years, and there were some good points – like alcohol being banned from football grounds, and the move towards all-seated stadia was given a further impetus – but 10 May 1980 was a day that was shrouded in infamy, as the whole world on their TVs saw the unacceptable face of Scottish society. It was a day that should have been a triumph for Celtic and nothing else, but as it was Celtic had to share their moment of glory with everyone asking everyone else 'What is wrong with Scottish society?'

It is important, however, to see the matter in perspective. The stone throwers were very much a minority. Most supporters of both teams watched the game, and then went home, the Celtic ones having had the extra bonus of seeing their team with the Scottish Cup as well.

THIRTY SIX

I'M SINGING IN THE RAIN

Celtic 2 Rangers 1   **Scottish League Cup Final**
Hampden Park   **4 December 1982**

Celtic: Bonner, McGrain, Sinclair, Aitken, McAdam, MacLeod, Provan, McStay (Reid), McGarvey, Burns, Nicholas

Rangers: Stewart, McKinnon, Redford, McClelland, Patterson, Bett, Cooper, Prytz (Dawson), Johnstone, Russell (MacDonald), Smith

Referee: Mr K. Hope

THIS was a very successful League Cup Final for Celtic, but also, for their supporters, one of the wettest! Hampden Park was in the early 1980s a major disaster area with sporadic and fitful attempts at redevelopment, and today the grand old lady of a stadium was not only showing her age, she was undergoing a major operation at the same time. Yet the Scottish League insisted on the League Cup Final going ahead with half the ground out of action and on this ridiculous date of 4 December, when a postponement to the spring would surely have been a far better option. Not for the first or last time, we wondered about the sanity of those who ran Scottish football.

Hampden was a strange sight. The old stand to our left, the opposition at the other end of the field (it would be an exaggeration to say that they were snug and comfortable under their roof, but they were certainly drier than we were), nothing at all to our right apart from a few bulldozers, men in yellow oilskin jackets and tabards, and advertisements for a firm called Telejector which has failed to survive, while we, in large numbers, paid our money to stand in the rain! It must go down as the strangest-ever national cup final, and it would be hard to imagine it happening anywhere other than in Scotland!

The Scottish League Cup had been a trophy that Celtic had fallen badly out of love with in recent years. Following the five-in-a-row successes of the late 60s, there had been a succession of losing finals, some unlucky, some careless, some self-inflicted, all of them awful to live through, with only 1974/75, admittedly a very good occasion, to cheer us up in this competition. Since 1978 we had even failed to reach the final, and Danny McGrain was the only member of our team who had previously won a League Cup medal.

However, 1982 had been a good year. League champions in the summer, the team had started well. Admittedly there had been the usual naïve European exit, but in November there had been good wins over St Mirren, Motherwell and Hibs in the league as well as a hard-fought League Cup semi-final success over two legs against Dundee United. Rangers, on the other hand, were struggling. Their fans were far from happy.

The week of the final, Rangers had brought back on loan Gordon Smith from Brighton, and were, astonishingly, allowed to play him in the League Cup Final. Celtic fans may have complained about that, but it was apparently legal. In any case, was it wise for Rangers to put a loanee in a final for his first game? And why, in the middle of the season, were Brighton so compliant in letting him go? Might it possibly have anything to do with the fact that Smith was struggling to hold on to a first-team place at Brighton? 'Desperation' was a word that frequently came to one's lips in discussing this move.

Much of the Celtic talk in the lead up to the final centred on the precocious talents of Charlie Nicholas. Frequently compared to two other Charlies of different eras, Tully of the 1950s and Napier of the 1930s, not to mention even more favourable comparisons to Pele, Puskas and even Patsy Gallacher, Nicholas was 'something'. The snag was that he was too good, in a way. In a way that did little to dispel the widespread belief that the Scottish media is irredeemably anti-Celtic, the newspapers all lined up behind the idea that Charlie was going to England very soon. Sadly, this campaign affected the less-than-totally streetwise Nicholas himself and, more significantly, it did little to discourage the Celtic directorate, money-grubbing and grasping as always, from cashing in.

But that was for the future. Today we saw what was, in effect, the last hurrah of Charlie Nicholas in his brief Celtic career. 1983 would not be so nice for either Celtic or Nicholas, but today, in spite of the rain, we enjoyed him. The game kicked off at 3pm more or less already in the dark and with Celtic playing towards their own supporters in the King's Park end of the ground. We thus had an excellent view of both goals that Celtic scored, although those of us who wore glasses could have done with windscreen wipers!

Early on, it was apparent that although both teams were 'up for it', Celtic were that little bit smarter to the ball. Our creative players, Provan, MacLeod and Burns, were all enjoying themselves in the conditions. Hampden's surface, for all the rain that had descended upon it in the last 24 hours, was actually quite lush and conducive to the good football that Celtic played, with Davie Provan in particular looking as if he could do something for Celtic.

The first goal came in the wake of a throw-in to Rangers, level with the penalty box on the Celtic right. Rangers failed to clear the ball upfield and somehow Davie Provan emerged with the ball, ran across the field, prodded it on to Charlie NICHOLAS who saw an opportunity and fired home with his left foot from the edge of the box. It was a fine opportunistic goal, and worthy of the talents of both Provan and Nicholas. The rain-soaked Celts in the 57,000 crowd cheered this goal, but the rain still would not stop.

That was about halfway through the first half. Ten minutes later it was 2-0, and this time it was Murdo MacLEOD who scored. A Davie Provan corner kick came back to Davie, he sent an inviting ball across the penalty area, which Tom McAdam headed towards the Rangers goal. It was imperfectly cleared to the edge of the box and MacLeod positively lashed the ball home. Cue once again delirium on the terracing! The following day on a TV programme Ian McColl, ex-Rangers of the 1950s who had never come to terms with the 7-1 defeat, claimed incongruously that that goal was a foul on the grounds that a Celtic player had 'swivelled his hips' when the Rangers defender had tried to clear the ball. It was a bizarre piece of sour grapes, that one!

Rangers had barely laid a glove on Celtic all the first half, and certainly did not get a shot on target until after the second goal had gone in. Even then it was a weak one, well gobbled up by Pat Bonner, and half-time came with Rangers, to all intents and purposes, out of it, and some Celtic supporters, wet, bedraggled but happy, wondering whether we could even get a repeat of the

7-1 score of 25 years ago. But to their credit, Rangers fought back. They got a lucky break in the award of a free kick outside the penalty area, when Tom McAdam tackled Gordon Smith. The free kick seemed a little harsh, but the referee Kenny Hope, who otherwise had an excellent game, was adamant. Jim Bett took it, beat the Celtic wall and scored as the ball just edged it at the post. This was now Rangers' moment. Could they now seize the initiative and get back to level terms? As it was, they were now definitely back in the game, something that could not have been predicted at half-time.

But this was a mature Celtic side. Well marshalled by the experienced McGrain, they tackled well but fairly and the midfield of Burns, MacLeod and the young and very impressive Paul McStay took command. (Sadly, McStay sustained a knee injury and had to be withdrawn and replaced by Mark Reid.) Rangers huffed and puffed, but failed to get 'quality ball' into the penalty area. Whenever they did get the ball into the box it was easily dealt with by the Celtic defence. Indeed, the closest the second half came to yielding another goal came at the other end of the ground when Rangers' Donnie McKinnon had to hook the ball clear after some inspired play from Davie Provan.

The full-time whistle came with Celtic well on top, and, although we all suffered a few qualms now and again on the East terracing, there had been very few clear-cut opportunities for Rangers. Danny McGrain picked up the trophy, Celtic's ninth Scottish League Cup, and the occasion was much celebrated by players whose first-ever major trophy this was – Mark Reid, Graham Sinclair and a few others. It was much deserved.

For the supporters, it was a sight for sore eyes to see the trophy draped with green and white once again after eight years, and being lifted by Danny McGrain that grim December day of relentless rain. One item that hardly anybody noticed in this game was that not a single player got booked. Tackles were fierce but fair, and the referee had a good game. Even on the terracings and after the game, there was not a hint of trouble.

So we enjoyed Christmas that year. Just as well, for 1983 was not going to be nearly as good.

THIRTY SEVEN

McSTAY'S TELEVISION SPECTACULAR

Rangers 1 Celtic 2	Scottish Premier League
Ibrox Stadium	20 March 1988

Rangers: Woods, Nisbet, Bartram, Roberts, Wilkins, Gough, D. Ferguson, I. Ferguson, McCoist, Durrant, Walters

Celtic: Bonner, Morris, Whyte, Aitken, Baillie, Burns, Stark, McStay, McAvennie, Walker, Miller (Rogan)

Referee: Mr R. Valentine, Dundee

THE year 1988 was tremendous for Celtic. It was of course the centenary season. Pedants may argue whether the club was founded in 1887 (the year of the decision to start a football club) or in 1888 (when the club played its first game) but in either case the 1987/88 season would cover both contentions. History called upon Celtic to make this a special season for their supporters – and they did.

As winter gave way to spring in 1988, it was clear that Celtic were doing well. They hadn't lost since October, and there was a consistency about the team that impressed – as well as a tendency to score late and decisive goals. They were still in the Scottish Cup as well, and things were looking good, and, as they geared themselves for this game against Rangers at Ibrox, Celtic were four points ahead (only two points for a victory in 1988) with a game in hand. A draw would therefore suit Celtic, but a win would give Celtic a possibly insuperable advantage in the league race.

And this game was to be televised on STV. 1988 was before the rise of Sky TV. Nowadays almost every Celtic game is on TV on some channel or another, but in 1988 a live TV game was a treat and much looked forward to not only by the supporters of the participants but also by the general public at large. Live televising of Scottish football had only been agreed in 1986, and at this stage only a handful of games per season were allowed. BBC had chosen Celtic v Hibs in the Scottish Cup a month ago – a dull, disappointing 0-0 draw – but STV seemed to have pulled out a plum in this one.

Rangers were displeasing their fans. True, they had won the League Cup in October, beating Aberdeen in a penalty shoot-out, but since then they had failed to hit the heights. They had not yet beaten Celtic this season, having twice lost at Celtic Park, and the previous game at Ibrox had been a disgraceful 2-2 draw with red cards and various players charged with public disorder offences! A month ago, to general delight, they had gone out of the Scottish Cup at Dunfermline in a game which saw John Brown being sent off.

One says 'to general delight' because Rangers were not popular. The paranoid of the Celtic support are convinced that the world of Scottish football is against Celtic. This is not always necessarily true, and certainly in 1988 neutral opinion would tend to side with Celtic, who were seen as the better football team, as distinct from the bullying and hard-man tactics of Rangers. The game at Ibrox this Sunday afternoon was much looked forward to, and the balance of the country supported Celtic.

Those Celtic supporters who went to the game would probably have been compelled reluctantly to admit that, in terms of stadia, Ibrox was a great deal better than Celtic Park or indeed any other ground. Rangers had built Ibrox into an all-seater stadium in the early 80s (possibly at the expense of team building, for the early 1980s had been a time of gross underachievement by the Ibrox men) and if Ibrox was not the best stadium in Great Britain, it was certainly one of them. Celtic Park was still all-standing (apart from the Main Stand) with even some of the directors, in an astonishing piece of self-delusion, claiming that the supporters preferred it that way!

The game was a thriller and would have been difficult to call at half-time when it was goalless. There had been a few chances at both ends, but nothing really clear-cut, and 0-0 was generally agreed to be a fair reflection on the run of play, with possibly Rangers just having the edge. Celtic were probably the happier of the two teams because a draw would certainly have suited them. They were, after all, the team who were heading the league. It was also clear that both teams had one outstanding midfield player – Ray Wilkins of Rangers and Paul McStay of Celtic.

Wilkins was a good player and one of a type. Rangers' team had by now departed far from the traditional Rangers teams of men born within a small radius of Glasgow. Such had been the desire to dominate Scotland that no expense had been spared to bring English and foreign players to Scotland. In addition, Scotland was a particular attraction to English players, for English teams were banned from Europe following the disgraceful events at the 1985 European Cup Final at the Heysel Stadium where hooliganism by Liverpool fans had led indirectly to the deaths of 39 fans. Graeme Souness had tapped into this supply of English talent as Rangers relentlessly raised the ante in Scottish football.

To their credit, Rangers had not shrunk from signing a high-profile black player in Mark Walters, although the ultimate departure from the Rangers traditions of the past, namely the signing of a Roman Catholic player, had not yet been made ... but it would soon. In the meantime the cultural trend that was evident was the loosening of the idea that Rangers represented Scotland. Traditionally, their supporters had sung Scottish songs like 'the Wells o' Wearie' and 'Loch Lomond' (admittedly with a few changes in the lyrics about what they were going to do to the 'Fenians' and the 'Papists') but now fewer and fewer Scottish Saltire flags were seen at Ibrox and more and more the Union Jacks of Great Britain.

When the teams came out for the second half, it was not long before discerning spectators noticed that Celtic, now attacking the Broomloan Road stand where their spectators sat, were winning more of the midfield battle with Tommy Burns and Billy Stark showing their mettle. McNeill had also brought on Anton Rogan to play the 'Tommy Gemmell' role of an attacking full-back in place of the less effective Joe Miller. Yet Rangers came the closest when a fierce Ray Wilkins drive was touched by Pat Bonner onto the top of the bar before bouncing back into his arms.

Just about halfway through the second half, Celtic went ahead. It was a move begun and ended by Paul McStay. McStay sent a cross from the right which found the head of Anton Rogan who headed it back into the penalty box. The ball was then half-cleared, bounced about in the penalty box for a spell before Paul McSTAY with a left-foot drive crashed the ball home to put Celtic one up.

But Rangers fought back. Seven minutes later, they won a free kick on the right and it was headed out by Lex Baillie, but only as far as the Danish full-back Jan Bartram, who levelled the score with the aid of a slight deflection. Bartram's love affair with Souness and Rangers was not destined to last long – he departed in summer 1988 using words like 'beast', 'hooligan' and even 'bastard' in the context of his manager – but here he had put Rangers on level terms.

But Celtic had the last word, as they deserved to on the run of play in the second half. After a series of corner kicks all threatening to produce a goal, Celtic at last made one count. Tommy Burns took a corner on the right and found the head of Anton Rogan, who headed strongly for goal, but the misdirected header would have gone past if it hadn't rebounded off the chest of Andy WALKER, who knew little or nothing about it.

It was now 2-1 for Celtic, and that was enough to win the game. Rangers now felt that the game was up, and if anything Celtic looked like increasing their lead once or twice, before Bob Valentine blew for full time. It had been a good game of football, well enjoyed by the crowd and the TV audience. Three men had been booked – Frank McAvennie and Derek Whyte of Celtic and Scott Nisbet of Rangers, but it had been a very clean game, and the Glasgow Police were proud to announce that there had been 'only' 36 arrests – and most of them for drunkenness rather than violence.

Manager McNeill had every reason to feel proud of his team that night. They were now six points ahead, and nine points from the last eight games would ensure that Celtic would be the champions. It was not necessarily a foregone conclusion, for there were difficult away trips to Aberdeen, Hearts and Hibs, but Celtic did not look as if they were going to drop many points now. A win at Ibrox was significant, and indeed quite rare. Celtic were also in the semi-final of the Scottish Cup and were due to play Hearts. Things were looking good, and the end of the season would see Celtic triumphant in both the Scottish League and the Scottish Cup. They never really looked back from this game at Ibrox.

THIRTY EIGHT

JOE HAS THE LAST LAUGH

Celtic 1 Rangers 0	Scottish Cup Final
Hampden Park	20 May 1989

Celtic: Bonner, Morris, Rogan, Aitken, McCarthy, Whyte, Grant, McStay, Miller, McGhee, Burns

Rangers: Woods, Stevens, Munro (Souness), Gough, Sterland (Cooper), Butcher, Drinkell, Ferguson, McCoist, Brown, Walters

Referee: Mr R. Valentine, Dundee

IT would be fair to say that season 1988/89 had not been one of Celtic's better seasons. In fact, it was one of their worst, and performances were all the more depressing after the heady success of last season, the centenary year. A slight improvement in the latter part of the season saw them finish third behind Aberdeen and Rangers, but there was nothing to be happy about in their league performances. Europe and the League Cup had been brief and awful, but there was still the Scottish Cup, Celtic's favourite tournament, and they had reached the final to play Rangers.

But it had been a Rangers complex that had haunted them all season. At the end of August, Celtic, last year's double winners of the Scottish League and the Scottish Cup, went to Ibrox and lost 1-5 in one of the most significant results in Scottish football history. The defeat in itself was bad enough, but it need not have been fatal, as long as they recovered and fought back. This Celtic failed to do so and they kept on losing more and more games – out of the League Cup the following Wednesday night, out of Europe by November and nowhere in the league. It is no exaggeration to say that the slippery slope which led to March 1994 started on that horrible day at Ibrox.

Rangers, on the other hand, went from strength to strength with no one left to oppose them. True, Aberdeen did put up some sort of a fight, and Celtic did beat them at Celtic Park in November, but it was a profoundly depressing time for Scottish football, and this would continue more or less all through the 1990s, until Celtic at last rallied.

So what had caused all this? The previous season, 1987/88, Celtic had been a great side and could have challenged most teams, even at a European level, but their folding at the sight of the resurgent Rangers was woeful. Manager Billy McNeill had made the fatal mistake of standing still. He had not bought in the summer to strengthen the squad, which in all truth had looked good enough, he also had bad luck in an injury to Paddy Bonner, but the big factor had been the loss of form of so many key players. And why had they lost form? Because they could not cope with that 1-5 hammering at Ibrox at the start of the season! There was a depressing lack of resilience or fighting back.

The Scottish League had been a lost cause well before Christmas, but in the Scottish Cup, Celtic beat Dumbarton and Clydebank, and the two Edinburgh teams. The game against Hearts was a tight and tough one, but Celtic won 2-1 at Celtic Park in spite of Frank McAvennie's whimsical and rather ill-timed desire to go back to West Ham. Frank's announcement split the support – some booed him, some cheered him. It was not the only talking point that day, however, for three men were sent off! Then Hibs were defeated with a degree of ease in the semi-final in a game played the day after the Hillsborough Disaster in a strange, unnatural atmosphere.

And so it was Rangers in the Scottish Cup Final on Saturday, 20 May. The ticket limit was set at 72,000, and tickets were not easily got for either end. The smart money was on Rangers, but then again one never knew with Celtic this season. At this stage, however, enter Maurice Johnston. Maurice had played for Celtic from 1984 to 1987, after which he had gone to Nantes in France. But now, apparently, he was suffering from homesickness and was wanting back to Scotland. The day before the Scottish Cup Final, in a very rare propaganda coup, Celtic paraded him with a Celtic scarf alongside Billy McNeill, and it was on this occasion that he made the famous remark to the effect that 'Celtic are the only team I ever wanted to play for'.

All seemed fine, and Celtic supporters on the eve of the Scottish Cup Final thus received a major boost. Admittedly, nothing had

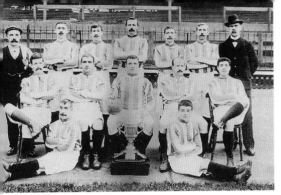

Celtic in 1899 – The Celtic team which beat Rangers in the Scottish Cup Final of 1899. Observe the green and white vertical stripes. The horizontal hoops were first used in 1903

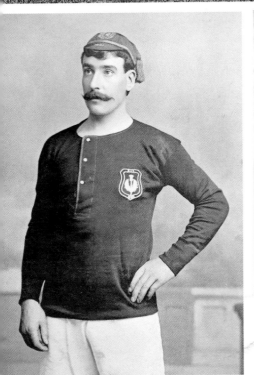

Dan McArthur, Celtic's great goalkeeper of the Victorian era

Jimmy Quinn – The Mighty Quinn, Celtic's hat-trick hero of the 1904 Scottish Cup Final

Young, Loney and Hay – Celtic's half-back line of the Edwardian era

*Patsy Gallacher –
Celtic's greatest ever
player and architect of
the 1925 Scottish Cup
semi-final victory*

*Old timers, Sean Fallon (Celtic), Willie Henderson
(Rangers) and Dixie Deans (Celtic)*

*George Niven of Rangers saves well in the 1957 Scottish League Cup Final, but
poor George would be beaten on seven occasions in this game*

Billy McNeill comes out with the Scottish League Cup after beating Rangers 2-1 on 23 October 1965. Also in the picture are Neil Mochan, John Clark, Bobby Lennox, John Hughes and Bob Rooney

Billy McNeill rises to head home the opening goal in the Scottish Cup Final of 1969 which Celtic would go on to win 4-0

Jock Stein and Jimmy McGrory after Celtic had won the Scottish Cup in 1969

Billy McNeill of Celtic and Ron McKinnon of Rangers walk off together after the game on 21 February 1970 at Celtic Park. But is that a football pitch or a swamp?

Jock Stein grabs Alfie Conn after the 1977 Scottish Cup Final victory. Andy Lynch, Paul Wilson and Kenny Dalglish are also in the picture

Malky Mackay disappears under his team-mates after scoring for Celtic in the Scottish Cup game at Celtic Park on 6 March 1997

Henrik Larsson in familiar pose after scoring

Darren O'Dea (not in picture) scores Celtic's first goal in the 2009 Scottish League Cup Final

Moussa Dembele slots home a penalty in the Scottish Cup semi-final of 2018

Leigh Griffiths shows his delight after Celtic have beaten Rangers 4-0 in the Scottish Cup semi-final of 15 April 2018

Rod Stewart is seen in the stand watching Celtic. He is not exactly unhappy with the 4-0 scoreline!

Rod now joins the Huddle!

James Forrest scores the third goal in the game that Celtic beat Rangers to win the Scottish League on 29 April 2018

Mikael Lustig seems to have committed a rather serious crime as he celebrates with his team-mates on 29 April 2018, but fortunately, he returned the policeman's hat!

as yet been signed, but these trivial details could soon be sorted out and Mojo was apparently back raring to play for Celtic next season. Just a pity that he couldn't play in the Scottish Cup Final tomorrow! Well, we all know that it didn't quite work out like that, but the point was that Celtic had at last won a propaganda battle against Rangers. Football being a game that is played in the mind as well as on the field, it was little surprise that Celtic got the better of them on the field as well that day.

This was probably the hottest Scottish Cup Final in terms of temperature that there had ever been. Normally Hampden got a shower of rain or two, and there was seldom a game passed without something of a breeze, but not today. It was a perfect advertisement for summer football, and the Celtic fans basked in the sun while Rangers fans were cooler in their shelter. Many bare torsos were visible at the Celtic end.

Celtic started off playing towards the Rangers fans in the Mount Florida enclosure, and the game was even for a long time. Indeed, one would have to say that the teams looked well matched. The crowd waited for the fireworks but, although both sides had a half chance or two, no one really had claimed any supremacy over the other until, with half-time approaching, the ball ran out of play for what looked like a Rangers throw-in about halfway inside the Celtic half.

Roy Aitken didn't think so, however, and as no clear decision came from either Mr Valentine or his linesman, Roy simply picked up the ball and threw it in. Rangers protested, but Mr Valentine simply allowed the game to flow. The ball came to Peter Grant who launched it towards Joe Miller, but it didn't get past Gough, and then the ball came to Gary Stevens who passed it back to the goalkeeper – except with not enough force and the ever-alert Joe MILLER nipped in and scored.

It was a strange goal. Gary Stevens tried unconvincingly to claim after the game that there was a clump of long grass there! But full marks to Miller, a man who had not always enjoyed the whole-hearted love and support of the Celtic fans, to put things as tactfully as possible. He was the hero of the hour today. Half-time came soon after this goal, and the Celtic fans were happy.

The second half was much about the same as the first except for the fact that the Celtic defence and midfield, buoyed up by that goal, were now first to most balls and played sensibly. Yellow cards were dished out, Celtic might have scored with a Tommy Burns header but so too could Rangers have scored, but for the intervention of Derek Whyte whose best game for the club this was. In desperation Rangers brought on Souness and Cooper, but that made no difference, for Celtic were playing confidently and were well on top. Almost at the death Rangers thought they had an equaliser, but the whistle had already gone for a foul on the goalkeeper. Minutes after that, Mr Valentine, whose last game this was before retirement, blew for full time and Celtic had won the Scottish Cup for the second year in succession and for the 29th time overall.

The Celtic fans deserved that one after such an awful season, and it did prevent Rangers from winning a treble, but Celtic fans would have been well advised to enjoy this triumph. The dark ages now descended, the likes of which had not been seen since the early 1960s, and another six long and horrible years would pass before another Scottish Cup (or indeed any other honour) was won. The next few years would see the occasional win over Rangers, but a singular failure to lift any silverware.

Rangers would indeed be held to account for what they did with their dodgy deals, but not for another 20 years. Celtic's downfall came from their failure to match Rangers or even to look as if they were vaguely interested in matching them. It was an awful time to be a Celtic supporter, and we had little to look upon with happiness other than this game. But in the fullness of time, the old board got their comeuppance, and Celtic supporters eventually got their football club back.

And Maurice Johnston? Well, history tells that he never did sign a deal for Celtic (some vague problems about income tax were mentioned) and then round about 12 July (ironically enough!) he signed for Rangers. He then wondered why all Celtic supporters hated him, but at least as far as this Scottish Cup Final was concerned, he had served his propaganda purpose!

THIRTY NINE

A RAY OF LIGHT

Celtic 1 Rangers 0	Scottish Cup
Celtic Park	25 February 1990

Celtic: Bonner, Morris, Wdowczyk, Galloway, Elliott, Whyte, Grant, McStay, Dziekanowski, Coyne (Walker), Miller

Rangers: Woods, Stevens, Munro, Ferguson, Spackman, Butcher, Steven, Walters (Vinnicombe, Dodds), McCoist, Johnston, Brown

Referee: Mr B. McGinlay, Balfron

I THINK that the rebel song 'The Manchester Martyrs' contains the line 'it was a dreadful year' in reference to 1867. 1990 was another such dreadful year. The causes were not difficult to work out. The main problem was Rangers, and Celtic's supine inability to challenge them, either on the field or in the broader business sense. Rangers had even been allowed to capture some of the moral high ground in their signing of Maurice Johnston, for they could now claim that they were a non-denominational club! They were allowed to strut their stuff all over Scotland, intimidating and terrorising everyone, and Celtic, who might have resisted, failed to do so. The Celtic board would in the fullness of time be held to account for this, but in the meantime life was hard.

A major blow was the loss of Roy Aitken. He had gone to Newcastle United ('out of the frying pan into the fire' as far as underachieving football clubs were concerned) claiming persecution by a Scottish journalist called Gerry McNee, but also, one feels, because of the way that some supporters, understandably frustrated and angry, tended to blame him for what was going wrong. There had been two high-profile signings – Paul Elliott, a good but injury-prone centre-half whose Celtic career took a long time to get going, and Dariusz Dziekanowski, a charismatic sort of character who promised a lot more than he actually delivered.

The team had departed Europe and the Scottish League Cup in the autumn in ludicrous circumstances in both cases, and league form was woeful. Since the New Year, the team had beaten only St Mirren in the league and Forfar Athletic (luckily) in the Scottish Cup, dismal draws were the order of the day, and to be honest, the team was going nowhere.

The pairing of Celtic with Rangers in the Scottish Cup caused a certain excitement, but no great optimism. There were even those who felt that a defeat here might indeed bring along a great deal more quickly the necessary changes at the top of the club. Everyone loved Billy McNeill and sympathised with him having to work in such circumstances, but even Billy's greatest admirers had to admit that he didn't always seem to be in total command of the situation. But, for the meantime and in view of the arrival of Rangers, a closing of ranks was detected.

Rangers had twice before been to Celtic Park that season. A 1-1 in August had been respectable, and the 0-1 defeat at the New Year had been unlucky, with Paul Elliott coming close near the end on at least two occasions with headers. So honours were almost even there, and it was also true that Rangers traditionally didn't do well at Celtic Park in the Scottish Cup. In the last Scottish Cup game that they had won at Celtic Park, Jimmy Quinn had been unfairly sent off! That was 1905!

Nevertheless, almost everyone fancied Rangers to win here. In spite of that, Celtic Park was full and the game was live on STV, with the commentator one Jock Brown who would play his own debatable part in Celtic history in years to come. The weather was damp and wet, typically Glasgow in February, and the pitch was heavy and tended to cut up.

The opening exchanges were high on drama and tension, and extremely high on the booing of the execrable and detestable Maurice Johnston, but the game was lacking in any great skill. It was a matter of relief to the Celtic fans that the first half hour was played without any loss. Indeed, it was clear that the Celtic players were 'up for it' and were, on this occasion, not going to lie down. Celtic players realised that a defeat today would have meant the end of the season and indeed the end of several Parkhead careers. Their determination was appreciated by the fans, who had not been slow to criticise in the past few weeks.

Paul McStay was the most accomplished player on the field. It was a tragedy that Paul's career coincided with Celtic at their worst, but today he had a good game in so far as it was possible for him to play any good football in that frenetic atmosphere on a heavy pitch. However, little appeared to be happening on the field, neither team having exerted any dominance, and half-time was approaching with both teams level.

One of the few good moves of the game produced the only goal. It started with Tommy Coyne running at the Rangers defence, passing to Dziekanowski and then Joe Miller, who then sent the ball across the penalty area and Tommy COYNE slid in on the wet surface to score. Rangers and their fans would claim unconvincingly that Coyne was offside, and in the excitement of it all no one seemed to notice an indiscretion by John Brown of Rangers who grabbed and pushed Coyne in the immediate aftermath of the goal. (They had both been team-mates at Dundee, as well!) The main thing was that it was a goal, scored at the psychologically vital moment of just before half-time. This meant that the Celtic team left the field with the cheers of their now revived and energised fans ringing in their ears.

This was Tommy Coyne's finest hour. He had joined the club from Dundee about a year ago for £500,000, but it would be fair to say that he had not impressed so far. Today, however, he was at last the Parkhead hero, and Tommy and his family relished the moment.

There were still, however, 45 minutes to go. The first half had been equally balanced, most people would agree, and the play in the second half went along the same lines. If this was Tommy Coyne's finest hour in a sadly underperforming Celtic career, the same could be said in the second half of Paul Elliott whose command of McCoist and Johnston was total. McCoist did not seem entirely fit, and Johnston seemed to disappear and shrink. Perhaps the booing and vitriol from the crowd got to him, perhaps he even got a twinge of conscience. Certainly that day he was made aware of the enormity of what he had done, and was probably the loneliest man in Glasgow, hated by his own people and despised by those whom he had sought to serve in his despicable desertion.

The longer the game went on, the more confidence began to grow in the Celtic ranks. Yet it was tense and uneasy as well, with the certain knowledge that any slip could lead to a goal and a replay at Ibrox, where we would surely perish. This was our only chance. The game continued at its furious pace. Referee Brian McGinlay who controlled the game well, it would have to be said, booked six players (four Celts and two Rangers), but the game, although tough, never got out of hand.

Slowly the minutes ticked away. Dziekanowski after a good Celtic move could have killed the game with a second goal, but shot straight at goalkeeper Woods, and then in the middle of all the tension, there was at least one funny moment. Maurice Johnston, his hair now dyed red (or maybe it was meant to be orange!) fouled Derek Whyte with a rather blatant push in the back. A supporter close to me jumped to his feet and shouted at Johnston for being a 'Catholic bastard' – a form of abuse not common at Celtic Park!

An inordinate amount of added-on time was allowed as Rangers pressed desperately but the Celtic defence was well up to the task, possibly more so than the pleading green-and-white supporters and the frantic McNeill. But full time came at last, and the joy was unconfined. There was then a revealing TV interview with Billy McNeill just inside the players' tunnel. Billy spoke well, but there was the sight of players coming off in the background. I thought I may have heard bad language (but maybe I misheard!) and I certainly heard the sound of some damage being done to the woodwork. Such butchery (sorry!) of the furniture clearly upset Mr McNeill who nevertheless pointed out that it just showed how upset Rangers were.

So it was at least one Monday morning in that dreadful year that we could go to our work and be happy. It would have been nice to see that form maintained, but no, it wasn't. League form lapsed to such an extent that it did not even deserve the word 'mediocre' and the Scottish Cup proved another painful experience. After defeating Dunfermline in a replay, and then Clydebank in the semi, Celtic faced Aberdeen in the final. Aberdeen had been the better side during the season, but Celtic raised their game in the final to take them to a penalty shoot-out. The predictable then happened. Yes, 1990 was a dreadful year.

FORTY

THE EIGHTSOME REEL

Celtic 2 Rangers 0	Scottish Cup Quarter-Final
Celtic Park	17 March 1991

Celtic: Bonner, Wdowczyk, Rogan, Grant, Elliott, Whyte, Miller, McStay, Coyne, Creaney, Collins

Rangers: Woods, Stevens, Munro (Cowan), Gough, Nisbet, Hurlock, Steven (Huistra), Ferguson, Hateley, Johnston, Walters

Referee: Mr A. Waddell, Edinburgh

THIS astonishing game at Celtic Park is remembered for the four players sent off, but it is a shame that this is how it is recalled, for there was some good football played here as well, and Celtic thoroughly deserved their 2-0 victory to put them into the semi-finals of the Scottish Cup. As for Rangers, the whole world was able to see on their TV screens just exactly what they were like.

Season 1990/91 had not been a great season for Celtic. The loss of the Scottish League Cup Final after extra time to Rangers in October had been hard to take, especially as Celtic had been on top for a good part of the game, but then things got a lot worse. November form was poor and December was disastrous, with successive losses to Dundee United, Dunfermline and St Johnstone, and then a 2-0 defeat at Ibrox immediately after the New Year meant that there could be no league challenge this year.

Fingers had been pointed at quite a few players and at manager Billy McNeill himself, with all sorts of stories being leaked about the lack of dressing-room harmony and players being unhappy, etc. It was clear that things were far from acceptable, but we all knew that the problem went a lot deeper than that. There had been no attempt to match Rangers in their spending, and the question was rightly asked how it was that a team like Celtic could not match what Rangers were doing. It was difficult to believe that whatever Rangers did, Celtic could not also do.

The answer, of course, lay in the boardroom where the directors, while helping themselves to bonuses, seemed unwilling to spend enough money on new players. They were obsessed, for example, with a new stadium, when what we all really wanted was a team on the park that was worthy of the name Celtic. As it was, Rangers were being allowed to do more or less what they wanted without any challenge from the other big team in Glasgow. Aberdeen were putting up a fight, but nothing came from Celtic.

As the days began to lengthen in January and February, however, the form of the team began to show a slight improvement. There was no obvious reason for it in terms of personnel, but there was a certain improvement in attitude, and there was still the Scottish Cup to be played for. Defeats of Forfar at Station Park and St Mirren at Celtic Park gave a glimmer of hope, and the pairing with Rangers at Celtic Park meant that this game was now win or bust for the season. A defeat here must surely mean the departure of Billy McNeill and quite a few of his players. It might also mean more radical changes in the club.

The game was moved to the Sunday for TV purposes, and as luck would have it, it was St Patrick's Day. Possibly the Saint himself was watching 'from his mansions above' as the old song (now rarely heard at Celtic Park, alas!) would have it. If so, he would have been delighted at what he saw. Certainly anyone connected with Celtic was happy, and Scottish neutral opinion had reason to feel that someone at last had stood up to Rangers, and Rangers did not like it!

Graeme Souness, the manager of Rangers, had upset the authorities several times recently and was obliged to watch the game from the directors' box, where he suffered a fair amount of abuse, even though gentlemanly Celtic director Jack McGinn more than once gestured to the Celtic fans to desist. Souness, to his credit, would apologise after the game for the behaviour of some of his players. He would not, in any case, stay much longer at Ibrox. Rangers also had Maurice Johnston in their side, and it was hardly surprising that he received pelters from those who once adored him. In the event, his contribution was peripheral.

Celtic opened the scoring as early as the sixth minute when Gerry CREANEY received a knock down from Tommy Coyne. It had come from a free kick taken by Dariusz Wdowczyk. Coyne outjumped Richard Gough and Creaney took his goal clinically well. It was no more than Celtic deserved, and half an hour later they went further ahead, once again from a Wdowczyk free kick. This time WDOWCZYK scored himself, although he did get the benefit of a wicked deflection. Nevertheless, if you have the courage to try a shot, you deserve all the luck that you get.

Thus Celtic went in at half-time two goals ahead. The general opinion was that Celtic deserved their lead, even though there was an element of luck about the second goal. It was also agreed that some of the tackles were getting a bit fierce, and that Mr Waddell from Edinburgh, although having a reasonable game so far, would have to work hard to avoid things getting out of hand as Rangers became ever more desperate to avoid a defeat and an exit from the Scottish Cup, a trophy they had not now won for ten years.

It was in the second half that the game really got silly, with the red cards dominating the news the following morning rather than the football played. The first red card was for Celtic's Peter Grant for breaking too early from the wall at a free kick. This sounds draconian, but in fact Mr Waddell was technically correct, for Grant had just previously been booked (for a foul on Maurice Johnston!) It was still harsh, but Peter's only fault was overenthusiasm while Mr Waddell might, to advantage, have ignored the trivial offence.

But off went the influential Grant, and now the Rangers supporters began to see a glimmer of hope. It is often said that at 2-0, the next goal is the important one, and in this case, if Rangers could only score once and Celtic were a man short, then Rangers were in with a chance. In the event, no further goals were scored, and it was the next *sending-off* that was crucial.

It was, in fact, Terry Hurlock of Rangers who got the long walk. He had had a few meaty tussles with Tommy Coyne throughout the game, and on this occasion Tommy got the better of him, and he lashed out with his elbow. This was about the hour mark in the game. He did not play often for Rangers after that.

Then we had Mark Walters. Much had been made of the racial abuse that he received from opposition fans when he first came to Scotland. It was deplorable, of course, but Walters was not above making capital out of it. However, no one could class him as any kind of innocent victim after his scything tackle on Tommy Coyne after two less successful attempts to put Tommy in a wheelchair. Mr Waddell was once again on the ball, and Walters joined Hurlock in the showers.

While all this had been going on, Celtic had been playing sensibly, passing the ball about to each other and refusing to rise to the bait. Centre-half Paul Elliott had been superb, playing on after a hard smack in the mouth with the ball (not, on this occasion, from a Rangers player!). But there was yet another sending-off after aggressive postures and use of arms after a clash between Anton Rogan of Celtic and Mark Hateley of Rangers. Rogan was rightly yellow-carded, but as Hateley had already seen yellow, red was the colour this time, and he also departed the scene, blowing kisses to the Celtic crowd!

By this time, any meaningful football had more or less stopped. Celtic, through Creaney, might have scored again, but it did not matter, for Rangers did not have enough players left on the park to inflict any damage. There was no need for anyone connected with Celtic to condemn Rangers for their misdemeanours, for Rangers' behaviour spoke for itself. They would be well punished for this, not least in the fact that they, yet again, missed out on their chance to win the Scottish Cup. In fact, Celtic had now put them out of the competition three years in a row.

For Celtic, however, it was possibly the only highlight in a miserable season. It was Motherwell who were our downfall this year, beating Celtic in a Scottish Cup semi-final replay to the general misery of all in green and white. It was hardly surprising that the ever-beloved Billy McNeill had to be handed his cards at the end of the season. A fanzine put it very well when it said that 'Billy was too much of a supporter to be a manager of this great club'.

But the dark, dark anguish of our soul still had several more years to run, and the decade of the 1990s, although in some ways the most interesting decade of our history, was also, with the exception of the 1940s, the worst of them all, and this is why games like this 2-0 defeat of Rangers had to be cherished along with the jokes about how at the next Rangers Dance, no one wanted to dance the Eightsome Reel, for they had already seen eight men reel at Celtic Park.

FORTY ONE

A MUCH-NEEDED VICTORY

Celtic 2 Rangers 0	Scottish Cup Quarter-Final
Celtic Park	6 March 1997

Celtic: Kerr, Annoni, McKinlay, McNamara, Mackay, Grant, Di Canio (Thom), McStay, Stubbs, O'Donnell (Hannah), Cadete

Rangers: Goram, Cleland (Durrant), Robertson, Petric, McLaren, Bjorklund, Moore, Ferguson, Bo Andersen (McCoist), Albertz (Van Vossen), Laudrup

Referee: Mr J. McCluskey, Stewarton

1997 had certainly seen some sort of improvement in Celtic since the truly awful days of the early 1990s. The Scottish Cup had been won in 1995, and 1996 was a really good season – except that nothing was won. Rangers simply seemed to have the technique of winning when they had to. In particular they had the ability to beat Celtic. Often it all depended on lucky goalkeeping, sheer bad luck or refereeing decisions that were later proved by TV to be wrong.

The point about that, of course, was that Celtic found themselves dependent on things like refereeing decisions. Refereeing decisions only really matter in a close game, and if Celtic had been far enough ahead, a referee could only have had limited power. It is very easy to assume a conspiracy, even when the facts don't really back one's case, but the real problem, as far as Celtic were concerned, was one of expectation. Celtic went into games against Rangers expecting to lose – and therefore did. Those of us old enough to recall the early 1960s saw this all coming back. Inferiority complexes are very difficult to rid oneself of, and Celtic had not beaten Rangers since an unimportant and irrelevant league game in May 1995. There had been several draws (and honourable ones) but Rangers had held the upper hand and had not tasted defeat.

However, Rangers were put to Celtic Park in the Scottish Cup draw (and all those of the 'I knew it! Rangers and Celtic getting kept apart for the final' persuasion were forced to eat humble pie yet again!) and the game, somewhat controversially to keep the TV company happy, was scheduled for a Thursday night. This did not suit everyone (to put it mildly), but it did have the benefit of allowing more people to see the game on TV than might otherwise have been the case.

Rangers had already won the Scottish League Cup that season and were ahead in the league, but Celtic were not entirely out of it and a good run could yet have landed the title to stop Rangers winning their ninth league in a row. But it was the Scottish Cup, historically Celtic's favourite trophy, which represented our most realistic chance of an honour this season.

Celtic were managed by Tommy Burns in 1997. Tommy's love for the club shone through, but it was also clear that he was under pressure to perform. It was often said of Billy McNeill that he was too much of a supporter to be a manager, and the same might have been said of Tommy. The team was a good one and capable of good football, with Jorge Cadete and Paolo Di Canio brilliant footballers, but not always showing the mental stability or stamina that is also required in a professional football player. There was also Paul McStay, deservedly called 'the maestro', now coming to the end of his career, and honest, hard-working Celts like Peter Grant, Phil O'Donnell, Jackie McNamara and Tosh McKinlay. They were no mean side – even though they often disappointed.

Against that, Rangers, with their foreign hirelings, had a relentless look about them. Possibly Celtic had the better players, but Rangers were more successful as a team. And yet, all that was really needed was for someone some time to have the physical and mental strength to stand up to Rangers. What the early 1990s had proved was that if Celtic did not stand up to them, no one else would either. Aberdeen, Motherwell, Kilmarnock and Dundee United could all have their moments, but they lacked staying power. It was therefore all the more incumbent on Celtic to do the job. Although a cup tie was always a one-off, what supporters really wanted from Celtic was consistency of performance.

Celtic began kicking towards the Lisbon Lions end of the ground. That part of the stadium was now complete, although the other end still had its temporary accommodation. Celtic immediately seized the game by the scruff of the net and attacked. There had already been several close things – including a dreadful miss from Phil O'Donnell – before Celtic won a corner on the left. It was taken by Di Canio, a more or less perfect corner which found the head of one-time bank clerk Malky MACKAY, one of Celtic's lesser-sung heroes, who bulleted the ball past Andy Goram. Goram had come out for the ball and missed. It was a great goal and the following morning the *Daily Record* had the headline that Rangers had been 'Malkied', the word 'malky' being the Glasgow gangland slang for a murder!

With Parkhead now on fire, the team kept pressing and some six or seven minutes later they went two ahead. A long ball from Tosh McKinlay reached the penalty box and was pursued by Jorge Cadete and Bjorklund of Rangers. Bjorklund bundled Cadete over, and Mr McCluskey correctly awarded a penalty. There have been more clear-cut penalties than that one, but there was contact and a penalty was the correct decision. Di CANIO then calmly and gently sent Goram the wrong way to put Celtic 2-0 up, as delirium reigned in the high stands of Celtic Park.

Celtic continued to press and a few minutes after the penalty was awarded, Mr McCluskey turned down a far better penalty claim than the one that Celtic got. This time it was Di Canio who was barged by Alan McLaren when the ball was some distance away, and TV replays showed clearly that Mr McCluskey got that one wrong. To be fair, Di Canio did go down rather theatrically – but he was an Italian and an actor at the best of times. He had the looks of an opera singer in the Milan Opera House and the temperament to go with it, but he was much loved by everyone at Celtic Park, and he really should have had another penalty that time.

Celtic did not now make the mistake of defending their lead. They kept pressing and pressing and by half-time Rangers were completely overrun and glad to hear the half-time whistle. Rangers had seldom been in the Celtic half, apart from very early on in the game when Brian Laudrup, possibly Rangers' only 'flair' player, came close. Rangers' apologists kept saying that if Gough and

Gascoigne had been playing, it might have been a different matter, but the truth was that no Rangers team (and very few European teams) could have lived with Celtic on that form.

The pace sagged a little in the second half, but the intensity didn't. Celtic now decided that consolidation was perhaps a good idea, not necessarily total concentration on defence, but more controlled and calm possession of the ball. Tackles became quite fierce and five men were booked – Ferguson, McLaren and Robertson of Rangers, and Stubbs and Annoni of Celtic – and Mr McCluskey talked severely to several others. Craig Moore was particularly lucky not to be shown a card of some colour or another, not least for the time that he wrestled substitute Andy Thom to the ground before Thom had even touched the ball!

And then we had Ally McCoist coming on as a substitute. Ally had talked himself into comparison with Jimmy McGrory by saying that he needed just one more Old Firm goal to equal McGrory's record (to be fair to Ally, he always respectfully called him 'Mr McGrory') but Ally, as he possibly realised himself, was no Jimmy McGrory, and any comparison was ludicrous. And when he skied one shot miles over the bar, he was told that by the Celtic fans.

But all the time Celtic were edging towards an historic victory. In truth, one began to feel that Rangers and their fans were beginning to agree, and although they made desperate attempts to rally and get the one goal that would have brought them back into the game, the Celtic defence of Alan Stubbs and, the hero of the night, Malky Mackay were well on top of them. The full-time whistle came with 'The Soldier's Song' in full flow, and Parkhead was a happy and relieved place that night. It was also the night that the Celtic players did a huddle in the centre circle at full time to celebrate what was a famous victory.

The afterglow lasted all weekend (Celtic had no game on the Saturday or the Sunday) and one had the happy sight of more smiling faces in Scotland than for a long time. Rangers could not now do a treble, and, more importantly, Celtic had shown that they had the ability to beat Rangers and that they could yet mount a challenge for the Scottish League.

And did they? Well, no, actually. The flush of victory had not yet died down before they collapsed pitifully at Kilmarnock, and then the defeat to Rangers at Parkhead was a total disgrace, with several players on each side clearly offering to settle matters with their fists, and Rangers doing a mock huddle – and wondering why everyone hated them so much! Then Celtic blew up in the Scottish Cup as well to Falkirk in a very wet Wednesday night replayed semi-final at Ibrox.

Celtic's travails were not yet over and in general 1997 must go down as a poor year, but the night of 6 March was an indication of what could have been.

FORTY TWO

A RARE HAPPY NEW YEAR

Celtic 2 Rangers 0   **Scottish League**
Celtic Park   **2 January 1998**

Celtic: Gould, Boyd, Annoni, McNamara, Rieper, Stubbs, Burley, Larsson, Brattbakk (Jackson), Lambert, Wieghorst

Rangers: Goram, McCall, Cleland, Gough, Porini, Albertz (Gascoigne), Thern, Ferguson, Negri, Gattusso (Durie), Laudrup

Referee: Mr H. Dallas, Motherwell

IT had been a sad fact of life that New Year fixtures had seldom turned out well for Celtic in the last decade or so. There had been a couple of draws in 1995 and 1996, but Celtic's last New Year victory was exactly ten years ago – and that was also the last time that we had gone on to win the league! It was clear that this particular fixture meant more than the normal Celtic v Rangers game.

This was, of course, the potential 'ten in a row' season. Rangers had won the Scottish League for the past nine years. This had equalled the achievement of the great Jock Stein team from 1965/66 until 1973/74, and if Rangers were allowed to win the title this season, it would be a major blow, for they would undeniably claim that they had a better team than the great Celtic team of 30 years ago. Frankly, the history of this club would not allow that!

It was, of course, very easy to explain why Celtic had got themselves in this position. Incompetent, even perhaps corrupt, management of the club, characterised by a lack of ambition was the order of the day in the early 1990s, and although things had taken a turn for the better when the old board fell in 1994, there had still been a failure to land the league. Celtic had been close enough in 1996 and 1997 but had not enjoyed their fair share of luck.

This season had been a funny one. The manager was Wim Jansen, whose only connection with the club had been that he

209

played for Feyenoord in the team that beat Celtic in the 1970 European Cup Final! But the team had been good enough to come close to beating Liverpool in Europe. They had had some awful games as well. Off to a very bad start with defeats to Hibs and Dunfermline, then a steadying of the ship as new recruit Henrik Larsson began to show his worth, then a bad November with a defeat at Ibrox, another one to Motherwell at home before a late header from Alan Stubbs rescued a point the first time that Rangers came to Parkhead. (This game ought to have been played on 1 September but had to be delayed because of the death – some said 'murder' or 'assassination' – of Diana, Princess of Wales and all the subsequent hysteria.)

But then Celtic had an important success at the end of November, when they captured the Scottish League Cup for the tenth time, beating Dundee United 3-0. Incredibly, it was the first time for a whole 15 years that the trophy had been won, but it was significant in that it showed that Celtic under Wim Jansen could win something. It was something tangible that we could boast about, and good results followed over Aberdeen, Hearts and Hibs with the board showing willingness to invest in the buying of Paul Lambert, a European Cup medal holder, from Borussia Dortmund.

But then things took a turn for the worse again on the last day of the year when Celtic, without Henrik Larsson, went down to St Johnstone at McDiarmid Park. This was a blow and it meant that Celtic went into their New Year fixture with Rangers some four points behind. The title race was complicated this year by the presence of Hearts (some Celtic fans were heard to say in a moment of weakness that they would even settle for Hearts winning the league this year in that it would at least stop the 'ten in a row' abomination), but it was clear that if Celtic lost to Rangers on 2 January it would be difficult to imagine Celtic pulling back seven points, even though there were still loads of games to be played.

It was thus hard to overestimate the importance of this game. The day was pleasant enough with no rain, although there was certainly a wind, and tickets had been sold very quickly. The Jock

Stein end had yet to be built, and there were still the temporary seats there. Celtic had Larsson back after his slight injury and it was hoped that he and the newly arrived Harald Brattbakk could make up a Scandinavian duo that could break down the Rangers defence. Paul Lambert, who had only been with the club a matter of weeks, was also included.

There were two provocative sideshows as well. Andy Goram wore a black armband when no one else did. This presumably had something to do with the death of a loyalist recently, and Paul Gascoigne mimed playing the flute to the Rangers fans. Both of these things were apparently harmless, but in the toxic atmosphere of Celtic Park might have been taken very badly indeed ... had not the crowd had other, more important, things to get bothered about.

The first half was fast and furious, but goalless. Several times Brattbakk was through on goal but shot straight at Goram, and there was the occasional chance at the other end as well, but as the teams retired at half-time the impression all around the ground was that the best of the action was still to come, and that things were on a knife-edge. It was also generally agreed that referee Hugh Dallas, already a controversial figure in Scotland, was having a good game, letting the game flow and resisting the desire to throw yellow cards all over the place. Only one man had been booked – McCall of Rangers – but several others on both sides might have been. Honours even at half-time and, of course, that was the sort of result that would have pleased Rangers.

Some players admitted later that the Celtic dressing room at half-time was animated, but it was mainly because of the frustration at not having been able to score. But now attacking the west end goal, behind which stood the temporary seats (some people called then 'bleachers') in the second half, Celtic upped several gears.

Henrik Larsson had been quiet in the first half. Perhaps he had not yet recovered from his injury or perhaps he was just too well marked by the Rangers defenders, but in the second half he became a little more active. Midfield men Burley and McNamara now took more of a grip of the game, with Paul Lambert showing everyone just why he had been so well rated in Germany. Celtic poured men forward but without success until round about 'Lisbon' time, i.e. the 67th minute. This was when a long clearance from Paul Lambert found Jackie McNamara who made space, and then with a lovely side flick found Craig BURLEY, who beat Goram from about ten yards.

The joy of the spectators had to be contained for a while, for 22 minutes remained, and in desperation Rangers brought on Paul Gascoigne. A detestable man in many ways, and really more to be pitied than laughed at, he was nevertheless capable of winning a football match and the Celtic defence would have to watch him, we reckoned. But this was not one of his better days, and his impact was minimal.

Looking at our watches as the minutes ticked by all too slowly, we reckoned that the worst that could happen to us was a draw, something that would possibly keep us in the race, but would not really help our cause. But we did not really look like conceding anything with Tom Boyd and Marc Rieper well on top of things and the ever-popular Enrico Annoni having one of his best-ever days for the club.

But in any case, the 85th minute killed the game. Celtic pressing hard, they appealed for a penalty kick when a Rangers defender had his arms all over a Celtic forward, then another Rangers defender tried to clear but the ball went only as far as Paul LAMBERT, who hammered home an amazing pile driver from 20 yards to put Celtic 2-0 up. This effectively won the game for Celtic, releasing delirium in the ground and in pubs and clubs all over Scotland, and indeed the rest of the world, where the game was being shown on Sky TV. Rangers had no answer and were well beaten as the game finished to the strains of 'The Fields of Athenry'.

The importance of this game cannot be stressed too much. It was the first time that Celtic had beaten Rangers for a while, and it showed the fans that there was no longer any need to be afraid of Rangers. The mystique of the invincibility of Rangers and of Andy Goram in particular had gone. This year the phrase 'Happy New Year' really meant something!

The race for the flag this year was an exciting one. It would go to the very last day and is a story in itself, with Hearts also staying in the race until a very late stage. For sheer sustained drama it would be difficult to parallel those last few weeks of the league season, but what is certain is that if it hadn't been for this game Celtic's challenge would not have happened.

FORTY THREE

' ... AND THE CRY WAS NO DEFENDERS!'

Celtic 6 Rangers 2　　　　**Scottish Premier League**
Celtic Park　　　　**27 August 2000**

Celtic: Gould, Valgaeren, Stubbs, Mahe, McNamara, Petrov, Lambert (Mjallby), Moravcik (Boyd), Petta, Larsson (Burchill), Sutton

Rangers: Klos, Rickson (Tugay), Konterman, Amoruso, Vidmar (Kanchelskis), Reyna, Ferguson, Van Bronckhorst, McCann (Lovenkrands), Dodds, Wallace

Referee: Mr S. Dougal, Burnside

THIS was the day that changed, if not quite everything, then certainly rather a lot. In the summer of the year 2000, after one or two questionable appointments, the Celtic board at last got a decision right and appointed Martin O'Neill, a man with a good track record, as Celtic manager. Not only that, but they also backed him up with money. Throughout the autumn of 2000, a regular stream of talent arrived at Celtic Park. They were not all necessarily here by the time of this game, but Chris Sutton certainly was, his love affair with Celtic beginning the moment he stepped in the door.

It was certain that things needed to change in the year 2000. Since 1998, when Celtic had won back the Scottish League, Rangers had been allowed to capture the high ground again while Celtic struggled. The loss of the one player of international class, Henrik Larsson, to a broken leg in autumn 1999 meant that no challenge was made to Rangers in the league, and then of course the disaster of Inverness Caledonian Thistle knocking Celtic out of the Scottish Cup. 'Patch and mend' thinking saw Kenny Dalglish take over the club for a short time, during which time we saw a Scottish League Cup win (over a poor Aberdeen side, arguably the worst in their history) and a press conference held in Baird's Bar. That was actually a nice and unusual touch and a laudable attempt to take football to the fans, but nothing could disguise the fact that Celtic were not really going anywhere at all.

O'Neill's appointment was hailed by all. The season started with two good away wins at Dundee United and Hearts, and two somewhat uninspiring home wins against Motherwell and Kilmarnock, but everyone knew that this game against Rangers at Celtic Park would be the game that would set the tone for the coming season. The annoying thing about all of Rangers' arrogance and swagger was that they weren't really very good by any European standard, and that all that was really required to dethrone them was a determined effort by Celtic. Yet Celtic, pre-O'Neill, had not looked very good either. Clearly Henrik Larsson was a great player, as indeed was Lubomir Moravcik, but some of the others were distinctly ordinary. It remained to be seen whether Celtic could come together as a team under Martin O'Neill.

The day was fine and sunny – it often is when Celtic beat Rangers – and the game was played with a Sunday lunchtime kick-off. There was a certain doubt about when the game actually kicked off, and public transport isn't necessarily all that good on a Sunday, so quite a few fans actually missed the start. They did indeed miss something special, for Celtic were at Rangers straight out of the traps, as they would say at Shawfield at the greyhounds.

The first 15 minutes showed Celtic at their best, with Bobby Petta earning his brief but spectacular moment in Celtic history as he absolutely roasted Fernando Rickson, who had the humiliation of being taken off and substituted well before half-time by his manager Dick Advocaat. The three goals scored in that first quarter of an hour were superb. The first came from a Petta corner which found the head of Chris SUTTON, but his header was parried, and then the ball looked as if it were going past the post before Sutton flicked it in. Rangers appealed unconvincingly for offside, but there were two men on the goal line!

We hardly had time to indulge in our normal introverted speculation of 'Have we scored too early?', 'Rangers still have 89 minutes to equalise', when Celtic scored again. Once more it came from Bobby Petta, who won a corner kick, although some thought it should have been a free kick for a foul on him. Not that it mattered, for the corner kick found the head of Stilyan PETROV, totally unmarked, and Celtic were 2-0 up and we had not yet reached the ten-minute mark! I think it must have been that goal which created 'and the cry was no defenders' joke (a parody of the 'No Surrender' song sung by those with a perverted view of Irish history) which permeated Scotland within 24 hours of the event. 'Splendid isolation' simply did not come into it to describe Petrov's position. Full marks to Petrov (who before this game had not totally convinced all Celtic supporters of his value), but the Rangers defence had to learn two basic principles of defending a corner – someone on each post, and mark every man who can score.

Someone who had without a shadow of a doubt convinced Celtic supporters of his value was Paul LAMBERT. An inspirational signing by Wim Jansen at the tail end of 1997, Paul was one of the few players ever to arrive at Celtic Park with a European Cup winner's medal already in his pocket, and he played a great part in the stopping of 'ten in a row'. Here he crashed home a tremendous drive to make it 3-0. Once again, it came from Bobby Petta, who slipped a good ball to Lubo Moravcik, who cleverly saw some space and passed the ball back to Paul Lambert. Paul charged in unmolested to make it three well before the 15-minute mark.

On this basis, even Arbroath's 36-0 record defeat of Aberdeen Bon Accord in 1885 looked as if it could be broken, but Rangers eventually stabilised to a certain extent, and managed for the moment to stop Celtic scoring any more, although one could hardly say that they were really threatening to reduce the leeway until they got a break just before half-time when Claudio Reyna's header squirmed over the line. No great film evidence exists to prove it otherwise, but goalkeeper Jonathan Gould's guilty look and the lack of any great protest from the Celtic players or fans tended to indicate that the referee was correct. Mr Dougal and the North Stand side linesman were also correct a minute later to rule a Rod Wallace goal out for offside. 3-2 at half-time would have been a travesty. 3-1 was the half-time scoreline.

So was there going to be a Rangers revival in the second half? The answer to that one came five minutes into the second half when Henrik LARSSON scored an iconic goal to make it 4-1. Henrik had been comparatively quiet in the first half (like Jimmy Quinn and Jimmy McGrory of old, he often had the compliment paid to him of two markers!) but in this case he simply ran past three Rangers defenders as if they didn't exist and lobbed Klos to score a goal that no one will ever tire of seeing on video.

Then Rangers earned a penalty, possibly a bit harshly awarded (but it was clumsy by Stefan Mahe), and Billy Dodds pulled it back to make it 4-2. There was always, I suppose, the possibility of a fightback, but any chance of that was killed stone-dead when Henrik LARSSON scored again, from yet another Petta free kick. It was a brilliant header, but once again 'the cry was no defenders'.

Home and hosed now, we felt at 5-2, but Barry Ferguson decided to provide us with some extra entertainment (not that we really needed it!) by getting himself sent off. Ironically the 'coup de grace' was a silly but harmless handball, but Barry had shown all the signs of suffering from the red mist for some time. The tackle that earned his yellow card a few minutes earlier was a real shocker. Apparently, Barry then went on to make a night of it as well, by getting himself involved in a street brawl, thoughtfully and lovingly told to us in detail by the press – but, sadly, the TV cameras weren't there!

Just on the full-time whistle, SUTTON, who had started this carnage, had the honour of finishing it when he was on the spot to finish off a Mahe cross. Mr Dougal blew his whistle soon after this, and the astonishing scoreline of 6-2 was registered, and enjoyed by millions throughout the world.

It is not often that one can say that a treble was won in August. Indeed, it is ludicrous, but nevertheless this particular game laid down a marker and showed the world who was boss. Celtic now went from strength to strength, and even when Rangers got their revenge in November (an inexplicable 5-1 result), they were already far behind in the league race and unable to capitalise. Celtic wavered a little after that, but were soon back in the groove, removed Rangers from the Scottish League Cup, beat them again at both Celtic Park and Ibrox, and won a thoroughly deserved treble to equal the great years of 1967 and 1969.

At long last, Celtic had found themselves a successful manager and players who did not doubt their own ability as far as Rangers were concerned. And the sustained success that Martin O'Neill brought to the club in the early years of the century all started here. The game has become known as the 'Demolition Derby'. It is well named.

FORTY FOUR

SLICK CELTIC

Celtic 3 Rangers 1   **Scottish League Cup Semi-Final**
Hampden Park   **7 February 2001**

Celtic: Gould, Boyd (Johnson), Mjallby, Vega, McNamara (Petta), Lambert, Lennon, Petrov, Thompson, Larsson (Moravcik), Sutton

Rangers: Klos, Malcolm, Wilson, Konterman, Tugay (Johnston), Numan, Reyna, Ferguson, Albertz, Flo, McCann (Mols)

Referee: Mr W. Young

THE turn of the century had brought a turn in the fortunes of Celtic. Although early 2000 had seen the infamous defeat to Inverness, it had also brought us some consolation in the Scottish League Cup, and then in the summer the board at long last made the right appointment for a manager in Martin O'Neill. Not only that, but they backed him financially, giving him money to buy the right players, notably Chris Sutton and Neil Lennon.

It had not all been plain sailing. The 6-2 'Demolition Derby' (as it came to be called) was cancelled out by an astonishing 1-5 defeat at Ibrox in November, and Europe had been another hard-luck story. Nevertheless, progress had been made in the Scottish League Cup, and by the turn of the year and the hated winter shutdown Celtic were clearly at the top of the league with some fine performances to their credit, notably 6-0 defeats of Aberdeen and Kilmarnock.

But February presented a stiff test. There were two games against Rangers, one on the Wednesday night of 7 February in the League Cup, before Rangers paid their second league visit of the season to Celtic Park on the Sunday. Both games were on terrestrial TV, and it was clear that one would affect the other. Celtic, in order to sustain their newly acquired credibility this season, really had to win at least one and preferably both.

On the Sunday before the League Cup semi-final, Celtic had a difficult looking trip to Tynecastle to take on Hearts. The game was played on the Sunday evening (a ridiculous time, as was now agreed by everyone) in intermittent snow flurries, but Henrik Larsson was in top gear and notched a hat-trick in a fine win. Apart from anything else, it built up a great deal of confidence for the two Rangers games.

In some ways this League Cup semi-final (the winners would play Kilmarnock in March) was the acid test for O'Neill's new Celtic. The bad days of being 'psyched out' by Rangers were not all that far away in the memory, and it was time now to reassert themselves. Rangers had a strong team, on paper at least, but had had a few bad results of late and were now well behind in the Scottish Premier League. Now was the time, surely, for Celtic to kill them off for the season. Certainly man for man, almost everyone agreed that Celtic had the better players, and the sheer goalscoring ability of Henrik Larsson had everyone enthused.

But the key character tonight in many ways would turn out to be referee Willie Young. He was in some ways a likeable character, he seemed to have been around for many years, he did not always seem to be totally fit and he certainly had a reputation for eccentric decisions. He was not particularly believed to have covert Rangers sympathies (as several others were) but his refereeing was, on occasion, quixotic and quirky. He would be so tonight.

In point of fact, the game was more or less decided within the first 20 minutes when Celtic went two ahead. Celtic began attacking the Mount Florida end, behind which congregated the Rangers fans, and were soon on the attack, winning a free kick on the right. It was taken by Alan Thompson and duly found a Celtic head, in this case centre-half Ramon Vega, who crashed the ball against the bar. The ball rebounded to Chris SUTTON who hit it hard and high into the net. It was not undeserved on the run of play in the early stages.

The Celtic end was now in a ferment of excitement, and they had further cause for jubilation some ten minutes later when they went further ahead. This time it was from an innocuous looking long ball which looked as if it could either be dealt with by the Rangers defender or the goalkeeper could come out and grab it.

But for Henrik LARSSON, no cause is ever deemed lost, and he chased the ball, nipped it away from the young Rangers defender Robert Malcolm, then lobbed goalkeeper Stefan Klos and was there on hand to prod the ball home on the line just in case it wasn't going in anyway. It was one of these goals which made one realise just how special a player Henrik Larsson was. He was a superb goalscorer, never more so than in his ability to make a goal out of nothing.

Less than a quarter of the game had gone and Celtic were already 2-0 up and looking as if they could score more or less at any time of their choosing. But enter Willie Young to make his mark upon the game. The game was heading towards half-time, and Rangers were on the attack trying to get back in the game, but not really looking like it, for Mjallby and Vega looked more than capable of dealing with anything that was thrown at them. But Scott Wilson got himself in the box and was tackled by Sutton. There was certainly some contact, but the word 'nudge' was possibly the most appropriate word to describe it. Nevertheless, Mr Young pointed to the spot, and Jorg Albertz did the job for Rangers, and his team were now back in it. Every TV and radio commentator was of the opinion that it was a 'soft' penalty, but the referee is the referee and if he says it is a penalty, then a penalty it is!

Half-time was thus spent in a more sober mood than might have been the case. Yet a rational analysis would tell us that there was no real cause for worry, for Celtic were by far the better team. Nevertheless, there is nothing rational about Celtic v Rangers games. The second half continued in the same vein as the first, with Celtic playing the better football but not yet able to convert their superiority into a decisive goal. But then with 20 minutes left, Celtic got a penalty. It was every bit as soft as the Rangers one. Larsson clashed with Wilson and seemed to lose his balance somehow. He was as surprised as anyone when Mr Young pointed again to the spot. Even the most bigoted of us agreed that this looked no more like a penalty than the Rangers one. Mr Young, in fact, was giving every impression of trying to even things up. He was trying to be all things to all men.

It did, however, settle the game in Celtic's favour as Henrik LARSSON took the penalty and scored to make it 3-1. Larsson was taken off shortly afterwards, to be preserved for Sunday's game, and the game now looked as if it were petering out. Indeed, some of the Rangers supporters thought so, as they headed homewards, or if they were watching it at home, listened with favour to their wives' questions about whether there was anything interesting on the other channel on the TV.

But there was still Claudio Reyna and supporting company to entertain us. Reyna had done quite a lot of fouling and had already been booked for a challenge on Paul Lambert. Indeed, he then fouled him again not long afterwards and was lucky to escape the long walk. But now with time running out, he tackled Bobby Petta in a rather vicious way, and before one knew where one was a mini-riot had developed among the players.

One had to feel sorry for Willie Young here. Words like 'handbags' are often used to describe these moments when everyone pushes and jostles one another, sometimes under the guise of trying to cool things down, but no one actually lands a punch on anyone. Willie waited until it was all calmed down, then rightly sent Reyna off for his second yellow card. That probably would have sufficed followed by a chat with the two captains to tell them to get a grip on things. But no, he went for a couple of scapegoats in Lubo Moravcik and Michael Mols (ironically both on as substitutes and both of them the mildest men one could imagine) and gave them red cards. Replaying the 'action' will show that both these men were indeed involved but did nothing more than about three other players on each side did. They were very unlucky indeed. But Mr Young, as we have seen, liked to balance things.

But the full-time whistle went not much later and Celtic were in the final of the Scottish League Cup, which they would duly win on 18 March. They also beat Rangers in the league match on Sunday, 11 February, and won the league by some distance. The Scottish Cup came later to make it a treble. But it was this game, as much as any other this season, which proved that Celtic were a class outfit and that, under Martin O'Neill, the corner had been turned. As for Rangers, their season went from bad to worse.

'The poor teddy berrs, they've got nae silverwerr, and there's no Mister Sheen, for there's nothing to clean ...'

THE REMARKABLE COMEBACK

Celtic 3 Rangers 2　　　　　**Scottish Premier League**
Celtic Park　　　　　　　　　　**27 April 2008**

Celtic: Boruc, Hinkel, Caldwell, McManus (O'Dea), Naylor, Nakamura, Hartley (Brown), Robson, McGeady, Vennegoor of Hesselink (Samaras), McDonald

Rangers: Alexander, Broadfoot, Dailly, Weir (Faye), Papac, Whittaker, Hemdani (Darcheville), Ferguson, Davis, Novo, Cousin

Referee: Mr C. Thomson

FOR a while, spring 2008 saw Celtic supporters in a serious state of depression. Nowhere in the League Cup (won by Rangers), out of Europe after a brave fight against Barcelona, out of the Scottish Cup to Aberdeen at Parkhead in a replay after having done the difficult bit at Pittodrie, and to cap it all, a 0-1 defeat to Rangers at Ibrox on 29 March seemed to have ruled us out of the Scottish Premier League as well. This impression gained further ground the following Saturday at Parkhead when we lost 0-1 to Motherwell, the thousands pouring out of the ground long before the final whistle telling its own tale (and that was after Motherwell had had a man sent off!).

It was a desolate picture, with manager Gordon Strachan not likely to see the season out and indeed most of us expecting the chopper to fall a great deal earlier than that. It was not that we had poor players or indeed a poor team, but there seemed to be a problem with Rangers, who had now beaten Celtic twice at Ibrox that season. But Rangers had not yet been to Celtic Park. The death of Phil O'Donnell at the turn of the year had postponed the first game scheduled for early in the new year and the other game was to be played in the split.

An incurable optimist told me that providing Celtic beat Rangers twice, won the rest of their games and Rangers dropped another four points (i.e. drew twice to some team other than Celtic), then Celtic could yet win the Scottish League for the third year in a row. Frankly, that did not look likely, but incredibly it happened. Celtic began a week later, while Rangers were involved in the Scottish Cup, by getting some revenge over Motherwell beating them 4-1 at Fir Park. Then on Wednesday, 16 April there followed the first visit of Rangers to Celtic Park. For a while it looked as if it were to be a draw, in spite of a great Nakamura goal, but just at the very end Jan Vennegoor of Hesselink got the winner to keep Celtic in the league race. Rangers, however, still held the initiative.

There followed a narrow, welcome, but rather unconvincing win over Aberdeen, the highlights for the fans being a goal by Georgios Samaras and the final whistle! This meant that Celtic in fact were top of the Scottish Premier League, even though Rangers had three games in hand.

Rangers would have difficulty fitting in these games in hand, for their next two midweeks would involve the UEFA Cup, but Sunday, 27 April was the day which might virtually win them the league, as long as they defeated Celtic at Celtic Park. A draw would suit Rangers as well, and quite a few of their supporters felt that they might be better to finish the league off as soon as possible because they were now in at least one cup final and were aspiring to enter another, and they might struggle with some of their more mundane league fixtures.

Such reasoning was specious and ill-supported by facts. Rangers would indeed get to the final of the Europa League, but they seemed to have the advantage that the game was played in Manchester. Their Scottish Cup Final opponents were to be Queen of the South, playing their first-ever Scottish Cup Final and hardly likely to be considered favourites. The 'Doonhamers' had beaten Aberdeen, the conquerors of Celtic, in the semi-final in a strange turn of events. Aberdeen's failure (involving a serious death wish about Hampden) lent itself to the aphorism that 'When the cat's away, the mice will play!' – Celtic being the cat and Rangers the mice. Or, to put it more succinctly, if Celtic don't stand up to Rangers, nobody else will.

Celtic were ahead in the league race by two points as the game kicked off. The weather was warm and sunny, and Parkhead, as always on such occasions, was a beautiful sight. It was Celtic, playing towards the Lisbon Lions end of the ground, who drew first blood, and it came from the boot of Scott McDonald, the Australian who sometimes struggled to do the job at Celtic Park. He had arrived from Motherwell, for whom he had scored the two goals on that awful day in May 2005 which came to be known as 'Black Sunday'. He made a good job of this one though. A long ball out of defence to Vennegoor of Hesselink reached McDONALD who ran on and kicked the ball past McGregor with a deft flick. Such goals are not always easy to take and far too often in the past we had been guilty of hammering the ball straight at the goalkeeper or trying to be too clever and dribbling round him. Just the simple 'kick it once in the penalty box and make sure it's a good one' was enough. Rangers tried to claim he was offside but the match officials disagreed.

Much of the criticism of Celtic that season had focussed on the central-defence pairing of Steve McManus and Gary Caldwell. The criticism intensified today when Rangers scored twice from corner kicks, which the Celtic defence did not deal with. The first was from Weir in the centre of the goal and the second was from Cousin before the ball even got to the goalmouth. Both goals were dreadful ones to lose, and everyone was heard to say things like 'that's why we won't win the league this year – we didn't deal with our problem on defence'. Half-time approached and Celtic, having been ahead early on, were now 1-2 down and clearly struggling.

But the cause was not yet lost and Scott McDONALD, whose best game this had been for some time in a green-and-white jersey, scored a brilliant equaliser as he picked up a ball from Aiden McGeady inside the box, turned and shot well past Alexander to send the team in on level terms at the interval, but with the Celtic fans more fired up than the Rangers ones.

The second half was hard fought, but Celtic gradually took command and earned a penalty in the 70th minute when McDonald, going for an extremely rare Old Firm hat-trick, was wrestled to the ground by Kirk Broadfoot. Broadfoot might even have been given a red card, but what really mattered was that Barry ROBSON (a player that I felt Celtic might have employed a lot more often) scored the penalty, his clenched-fist celebration showing just what it meant to Celtic and to himself. Broadfoot escaped the red card but Whittaker was less lucky when he chopped down Nakamura, a man who had had a rare poor game for Celtic. That was a bonus!

Not that it really mattered. The only thing of real concern was that Celtic were now five points ahead at the final whistle. They now had three games left and Rangers had six. Celtic had a better goal difference, so all that was needed now was for Rangers to draw twice, but Celtic could do nothing about it because they were now finished with Rangers. The first weekend in May, however, saw Rangers drop two of these points to a stubborn Hibs side who held them to a 0-0 draw on the Sunday, the day after Celtic had beaten Motherwell. Rangers then beat Dundee United in contentious circumstances on the Saturday of the next weekend but Celtic stayed in touch by beating Hibs.

It was now agreed that the final games would be on Thursday, 22 May, with Celtic at Dundee United and Rangers at Aberdeen and both on TV. Rangers, of course, still had two more league games to play, and in one of them, on Saturday, 17 May (three days after they had lost the UEFA Cup Final), they could only draw with Motherwell on a dry pitch at Fir Park. Although they then beat St Mirren on the Monday, this meant that, given the equality on points and Celtic's better goal difference, all that Celtic had to do was get a better (or an equally good) result at Tannadice than Rangers did at Pittodrie. The games both kicked off at the same time.

At half-time it was 0-0 in both games, but then a roar from the stands told Celtic that Aberdeen had gone ahead at Pittodrie. Almost immediately, Celtic scored with a corner kick headed home by Vennegoor of Hesselink, and Celtic had won the Scottish Premier League in remarkable fashion. Celtic and the world of football had lost Tommy Burns to leukaemia the week before, he had been buried on the Tuesday (to their great credit, Walter Smith and Ally McCoist of Rangers attended the funeral) and the league was won on the Thursday night. Leagues are, by definition, won over the whole 38 games in a season, but the game against Rangers on 27 April was possibly the most important one. It was really a remarkable turnaround.

FORTY SIX

AIDEN ON THE IDES

> **Celtic 2 Rangers 0 aet**   **Scottish League Cup Final**
> **Hampden Park**   **15 March 2009**
>
> *Celtic:* Boruc, Hinkel, Loovens, McManus, O'Dea (Wilson), Caldwell, Nakamura, Brown, Hartley (Samaras, Vennegoor of Hesselink) McGeady, McDonald
>
> *Rangers:* McGregor, Whittaker, Weir, Broadfoot, Papac, Davis, McCulloch (Dailly), Ferguson, Mendes, Miller (Novo), Lafferty (Boyd)
>
> *Referee:* Mr D. McDonald, Edinburgh

THE Ides of March (15 March) was the date on which Julius Caesar was assassinated in 44 BC, and there was not a great deal of doubt that in 2009 knives were being sharpened for Celtic manager Gordon Strachan. Last week, Celtic had exited the Scottish Cup at the quarter-final stage to St Mirren. St Mirren had often got the better of Celtic in the past in Scottish Cup ties, but this one was hard to take, especially as it came at the end of a run of league results that had seen a defeat at Aberdeen and then three dismal draws, all the time that Rangers had begun to pick up.

Celtic had only reached the Scottish League Cup Final after a dreadful game against Dundee United in which no goal had been scored in the regulation 90 minutes and 30 minutes extra time. The game went to a penalty shoot-out and Celtic won 11-10 on penalties. Great entertainment and drama at the end, but dreadful football.

It was not that Celtic did not have great players. They had Shunsuke Nakamura, and he was often worth the admission money on his own, and a personality goalkeeper in Artur Boruc, and these two tended to be beyond criticism, but a defence of Glenn Loovens, Stephen McManus and Gary Caldwell were frequently slated on websites by fans, and the forwards – Georgios Samaras, Scott McDonald and Jan Vennegoor of Hesselink – seemed to lack consistency in their goalscoring. All were capable of great goals, but there was a distinct paucity of hat-tricks, for example.

No one divided the support more than Aiden McGeady. He had played for a few years now, and there was clear talent there, but he didn't always produce it. He did have the particularly annoying habit of running across the field with the ball, refusing to pass or to shoot, and then eventually running into trouble. Some supporters found that hard to accept; others swore by him and the song 'He runs to the left, he runs to the right' (arms waving in the appropriate direction as they sang), 'Aiden McGeady, he makes the H*** look s****' resounded all around the Celtic end at Hampden that day.

Gordon Strachan at the helm aroused feelings of different kinds. Some loved him for his footballing knowledge; others were less convinced. In his days playing for Aberdeen, he had been far from the darling of Parkhead, and now he did on occasion seem to be far too flippant and impertinent to be manager of Celtic, frequently alienating the media by being cheeky and silly when asked ordinary questions. He might have done well to remember the maxim that 'Wit carried to excess results in buffoonery'. Yet he had been with Celtic for three years and had won the Scottish Premier League in each one, so he wasn't entirely bad. He had also done better in Europe than quite a few Celtic managers. Not this year, though! And that counted against him. Losing to Manchester United could have been coped with. Losing to Aalborg of Denmark and Villarreal of Spain was a different matter.

Rangers, on the other hand, were more consistent. They did not have many flair players, but they tended to be able to defeat the teams that they were expected to defeat, something that could not always be said about Celtic, and although Celtic had defeated them 1-0 at Ibrox between Christmas and New Year, they had recovered from that blow. At the moment, one could not have predicted with any degree of certainty who was going to win the Scottish Premier League, any more than anyone could predict the winners of this League Cup Final.

It was a fine spring day, still a little on the cold side, but with plenty of sunshine. Maybe surprisingly, Strachan left Georgios

Samaras and Vennegoor of Hesselink on the bench and started with McDonald and McGeady up front. They produced little for Celtic, but then again the same could be said about the Rangers forwards.

The 90 minutes came and went, and one still did not see clearly who was going to win. The football had been enthralling but unproductive. The pitch, which had come in for a great deal of criticism on the occasion of the semi-finals at the end of January, had been re-laid, but even the new pitch was cutting up badly and doing little to help the flow of the game. Both teams could claim that they had had chances, but there had been very few clear-cut opportunities. But then again, you can never relax in an Old Firm game, and there is always the possibility of a goal at either end. Yet there was also little doubt that both sets of players were tired, and had either team been able to nick a goal in the last few minutes of regulation time, it would have been difficult for the other team to fight back and equalise.

Both managers, Walter Smith and Gordon Strachan, were seen to be laying down the law to their players before extra time started. The point was being made here as well that a goal would probably be enough to do it. The game restarted and we settled down for a tense 30 minutes. Celtic were attacking the Mount Florida goal and within a minute were awarded a free kick on the left after Scott McDonald had been downed by Steven Whittaker. The commentators made the point that it was a 'tired' challenge.

Nakamura took the free kick. 'Naka' had not had a great game, but he was still Celtic's free-kick expert. This one, however, was just too far to the side for him to have a pop for goal, so his crafty Oriental brain decided he would go for the forest of heads and hope someone could head home. This was what happened, but it wasn't the head that the Rangers defence expected. It was that of Darren O'DEA, the centre-half who was not renowned for his goalscoring exploits. Apparently his last goal had been against Livingston more than two years before! But this was his day. He met the ball cleanly and headed past McGregor in the Rangers goal.

The delight at the far end of the ground was tempered by the regret that this had not happened at the end of the 90 minutes, for we were now aware that we had half an hour to hold out. But in an even game like this, being ahead is a great advantage when both sides are tired. After all, the winning team merely has to keep the ball out of the goal, and can kick the ball anywhere else it wants. But this was no desperate defending. It was rather a controlled piece of ball retention and thoughtful passing on the part of the often despised and reviled Glenn Loovens and Stephen McManus, not to mention the new hero Darren O'Dea.

Half-time of extra time came and went, with Celtic gradually taking control. Samaras and McDonald both missed reasonable attempts to win the tie. There was a moment of low comedy as well when Barry Ferguson and Neil Lennon picked an argument with each other (it would be these two, wouldn't it?), something that they had both been spoiling for, and the fact that Ferguson was playing in the game and Lennon wasn't didn't really seem to come into the equation!

Confidence was steadily growing at the Celtic end that we had weathered the storm (if storm is the appropriate word for such an anodyne Rangers team) and the 30 minutes had been reached when the game was settled. Three minutes of added-on time to allow for an injury to Georgios Samaras, but when one and a half of them had gone, Aiden McGeady broke down the left and was tripped by Kirk Broadfoot inside the penalty box. Referee Dougie McDonald (harshly, perhaps) flashed the red card, but Aiden McGEADY would not be denied his goal. He called for the ball and insisted on taking the penalty kick himself. It would not really have mattered, but he sank the penalty anyway. Barely time for the restart, and Dougie pointed to the pavilion. Celtic had won 2-0.

It was Celtic's 14th League Cup, and a very welcome one indeed. It was a shame that Celtic did not get the momentum from this triumph to win the Scottish Premier League as well, but sadly the attack still failed to function. Twice Celtic drew with Hearts and failed to deliver in the vital game at Ibrox on 9 May. Gordon Strachan would indeed leave the club at the end of the season. He would be replaced by Tony Mowbray. A horrific season now awaited Celtic, and more than two calendar years would pass before Celtic won another trophy. For Celtic, a two-year hiatus is unacceptable. But this was a good victory.

FORTY SEVEN

JOE PUTS CELTIC AHEAD

Celtic 1 Rangers 0 Scottish Premier League
Celtic Park 28 December 2011

Celtic: Forster, Mulgrew, Rogne, Matthews, Brown, Ledley, Kayal (Ki), Wanyama, Samaras, Forrest, Hooper (Stokes)

Rangers: McGregor, Broadfoot, Papac, Wallace (Healy), Bocanegra, Bartley, McCulloch (Edu), Davis, Aluko (Wylde), Jelavic, Lafferty

Referee: Mr W. Collum, Glasgow

THE calendar year of 2011 had been a difficult one for Celtic. It was Neil Lennon's second year in charge, and he had done well to reach this stage of the 2011/12 season only one point behind Rangers after some dreadful performances in the early part of the season. Season 2010/11 had seen an appalling surrender of the league title in an inexplicably awful performance at Inverness, and although the situation was rescued to a certain extent by the winning of the Scottish Cup, the supporters were still muttering.

The start of the 2011/12 season had seen us needing UEFA to suspend the Swiss club Sion before we got into the group stage of the UEFA Cup (not that it did us any good!), and we also managed to lose at home to St Johnstone. We also lost to Rangers at Ibrox and Hearts at Tynecastle in the autumn, before that remarkable day at Kilmarnock when we were three goals down (and Neil Lennon openly admitting that he thought he was getting the boot) before we fought back and earned a draw. Since then, however, the team had stabilised and Celtic had rallied, winning games, not necessarily with any degree of ease, but doing enough to narrow the points differential which had been 15 points at the start of November, and was now down to one.

But in any case, even if Celtic thought they had problems, they were as nothing compared to those of Rangers, whose difficulties lay not so much on the playing field itself as in the broader world of business. Putting it simply, they were going bust as all sorts of previous financial misdemeanours came back to haunt them. In particular their arrogant refusal to pay income tax was an insuperable problem because HMRC were not the sort of people that one argued with. Nevertheless, there was an assumption that Rangers, with their 'connections', would get off with it.

But they had no 'connections' any more. Funny handshakes, playing of invisible flutes and bogus appeals to patriotism and royalty were of little use in the face of such a nemesis that was coming their way. It would all come to a head on St Valentine's Day 2012 when they officially went into administration, but everyone knew that there would be no money available for any new players in the January transfer window. Already Celtic supporters were singing about having parties on the day that Rangers were going to die, etc. Surprisingly perhaps, supporters of other clubs joined in, and when the crunch came, not a single finger was lifted to help them. The hatred was total and frighteningly all-encompassing.

Their fixture immediately before this one had been a 1-2 defeat to St Mirren in Paisley on Christmas Eve, whereas Celtic had defeated Kilmarnock. Rangers complained about one decision in particular, where a ball had appeared to cross the line but no goal was given, but that was clutching at straws. St Mirren had won well, and many of the Rangers players, whose exorbitant wage demands had hardly helped the club's finances, began to have serious doubts about their futures.

Wednesday, 28 December 2011 was a day of high winds and bitter cold. There may have been some doubt about the game going ahead, but one of the great things about Celtic Park was that it tended to shelter players from the worst of the blast. Although one could not say that the wind was not a factor in the game – as evidenced by the amount of newspapers and chip papers on the field – nevertheless it did not ruin the game or anything like that. A remarkable amount of good football was played, with two Celtic men in particular being outstanding. One was right-back Adam Matthews, and the other was midfielder Victor Wanyama, sometimes called the 'Kenyan Fenian' by the fans.

The bitter wind blew from the east, and therefore Celtic faced it in the first half. Honours were possibly even at the end of the first 45. Rangers felt that they might have had the ball over the line before Fraser Forster clawed it back, but there was no great protest, and Georgios Samaras had the ball in the net, but was rightly called for offside. There were a few other chances at either end, but when half-time came and no goals were scored the general opinion was that this was fair.

The wind if anything relented a little in the second half, but was replaced with steadier rain. Celtic seemed to prefer these conditions (they now, of course, had the wind behind them) and the first five minutes saw them well on top. In the 52nd minute they forced a corner on the right. It was taken by Charlie Mulgrew and it found the head of Joe LEDLEY, who 'simply wanted it more than anyone else' and Celtic were ahead. Joe Ledley, a talented and hard-working Welshman, did not score many goals with his head, but this one was very effective, giving Celtic the lead both in the game and in the championship race. It also hammered another very large nail into the coffin of Rangers (old company).

From then on, the complexion of the game changed. Celtic were in charge and stayed in charge, with Gary Hooper very unlucky to be pulled up for offside, a decision by the North Stand linesman which did not go down well with the Celtic fans, and TV pictures would show that they were correct. Rangers faded from the game, in a way that surprised even Celtic fans, let alone their own supporters. It was as if they knew that in every way the game was up. At full time, dignified handshakes were exchanged by the two managers. On a previous occasion, things had been a lot less cordial!

The end of the game came to scenes of great joy. It had been an astonishing turn around to move into the new year two points ahead, and they never looked back after that. When Rangers went into administration in February, they were deducted ten points. One must beware, however, of thinking that Celtic only won the league because of these points. Celtic in fact won the league by 20 clear points, i.e. ten points plus the other ten 'administration' points. The league could have been won at Ibrox on 25 March, but Rangers won that game, and the league was in fact clinched at Kilmarnock on 7 April in a glorious 6-0 expression of football.

Yet things did not go well for Celtic in the two cups. That same Kilmarnock had beaten Celtic in the League Cup Final at Hampden three weeks before we clinched the league – an unlucky 1-0 defeat, but then again Celtic had the chances and didn't take them, and the Scottish Cup semi-final defeat against Hearts was even more unlucky, with Hearts awarded a penalty for handball, and then minutes later at the other end a similar offence was committed and Celtic didn't get a penalty. 2011/12 possibly wasn't Celtic's best-ever season, but it had its moments, not least this game at Celtic Park on 28 December.

Rangers? A further blow was dealt to them on the playing side of things when they went out of the Scottish Cup to Dundee United in early February, and then came the big blow on 14 February. The spectacle of players (who had previously made great play of kissing the jersey and saying they were Rangers through and through) trying to get away from the club now that the money had gone was quite something. 'Like rats deserting a sinking ship' was a strikingly appropriate simile in this respect. On 29 April they came to Parkhead for what was to be the last game between the two clubs in that incarnation of Rangers. They lost 0-3, but the football was secondary to the marvellous display of humorous banners and flags, including the Four Horsemen of the Apocalypse and mock gravestones with 'Rot in Hell' written on them.

Much of this was sheer triumphalism and gloating, but there was also the serious feeling as well that Nemesis, the Goddess in Greek Tragedy who punishes the wicked, albeit belatedly, had arrived at Ibrox to dispense justice to Rangers for their misdeeds over the past 140 years. Such misdeeds had included not only dodgy transfer deals and refusal to pay income tax of more recent years, but also the shockingly bad behaviour of their supporters in places like Barcelona in 1972 and Manchester in 1998, and worst of all their deliberate introduction of a form of religious apartheid in their recruitment, something which would be hard to parallel anywhere in world football.

Conventional wisdom had always asserted that Rangers, because of their wealth and drawing power, would be saved by their old pals. The trouble was they now had neither money nor friends. They had alienated clubs like Motherwell, Dundee United, Hibs and Aberdeen, and were voted out of the SPL and placed in the lowest tier of Scottish football. 'Vae Victis' (Woe to the Conquered)!

FORTY EIGHT

THE OLD AND
THE NEW ENEMY

Celtic 2 Rangers 0	Scottish League Cup Semi-Final
Hampden Park	1 February 2015

Celtic: Gordon, Lustig (Matthews), Denayer, Van Dijk, Izaguirre, Brown, Bitton, Commons, Johansen, Stokes (Forrest), Griffiths (Guidetti)

Rangers: Simonsen, Foster, McGregor, McCulloch, Wallace, Black, Aird (Daly), Law, Hutton, Smith, Miller (Clark)

Referee: Mr C. Thomson

THIS was, technically, a new venture for Celtic in that they were playing a club that had just come into being. The reality was, however, that this team in blue jerseys and their large support looked, to some of us at least, to be very like the old Rangers. But were they?

On St Valentine's Day 2012 Rangers went bust. This had been coming for some time, but the reasons were easy enough to understand. Basically, Rangers had been spending money that they didn't have, and had, for a very long time indeed, been refusing to pay tax. You can get off with a little from HMRC, but you can't fool them forever, and the upshot was that Rangers were in administration.

They started again in the Scottish League Second Division. Whether they were the same club or not was a matter of debate. Celtic supporters called them 'Newco' and 'Sevco', but they called themselves Rangers, and possibly for ease of reference it is better to call them that. In any case, for Celtic fans, a win over Rangers sounds a lot better than a win over a team called Sevco!

Those of the Rangers supporters who hoped that things would settle down at boardroom level were in for a disappointment. It was confusing to follow, but it certainly kept the BBC news programmes going for years, while the Celtic supporters continued to sing the praises of Craig Whyte, the man who had been in the middle of it all.

The new Rangers were in the process of working their way up through the divisions. They had won the Second Division in 2013, the First Division in 2014 and were now battling in the Championship, a Championship that contained both Hearts and Hibs as well, clubs whose supporters were also reaping the dubious benefits of financially improvident boards of directors! However, it was difficult to argue against the contention that the Championship was more interesting this year than the Premiership, for Celtic, without necessarily reminding anyone of the Lisbon Lions, were winning the Premiership rather comfortably.

Celtic were also still in Europe and preparing to play Inter Milan (now that DID remind one of the Lisbon Lions!), and the support at this point were prepared to trust the unknown Norwegian who had been called in to lead us the previous summer. Ronnie Deila was, at the moment, all right and how we enjoyed the 'Ronnie Roar' at the end of each game that we won, with Ronnie punching the air with his left hand three times.

I suppose, in a funny sort of a way, we missed Rangers. We enjoyed the contest between the two of them, and now they were not even in existence. Jokes abounded about how the young Celtic lady turned down a proposal of marriage from a young Rangers suitor on the grounds that 'You are not in my league'. Thus, when the League Cup semi-final draw was made and Celtic were paired against Rangers, much was the rejoicing, for it would be the first time that the two clubs had met since the end of the 2011/12 season, or, depending on your view of history, it was the first time they had EVER met.

Be that as it may, Hampden Park on 1 February was the place to be. But there was a problem about Hampden. The pitch was, frankly, and not exactly for the first time, a shocker. All sorts of excuses were poured out about the Commonwealth Games last summer, but those of us who watched the other semi-final on 31 January on TV between Aberdeen and Dundee United (a surprise win for the men from Tannadice) were appalled at the state of the pitch which cut up badly and had loads of 'bobbles' in it, all of which shocked the Radio and TV commentators as well as the crowd. Basically, Hampden had let itself down once again.

We possibly worried that the poor state of the pitch might be a leveller for the Celtic v Rangers game. In other circumstances, and had the teams been more evenly balanced, it might have been, but the general opinion was that this Celtic team and this Rangers team were still poles apart. But it was still an Old Firm game (did that term apply any longer?) and Rangers were certainly up for it.

The weather for the first day in February was splendid. It was still a little cold, but the sun was out and Hampden, a place that Celtic had not been at for a while, looked nice. The Rangers fans, to their credit, had not deserted their club (the players and the directors who led them into all this had long gone, including now Ally McCoist) and they were now managed (temporarily) by a character called Kenny McDowall, who had once been a coach at Celtic, but had done 'a Maurice Johnston' and gone to Ibrox a few years back. Not that many people really noticed him though!

Whether this was the old Rangers or not, their fans certainly thought so, and all the old offensive songs about the famine and being up to the knees in Fenian blood were given a good airing by the more intellectually challenged of the Rangers support. But they had very little to cheer them up on the field, for almost from the start they were outplayed.

Celtic started playing upfield towards the Mount Florida end. It was thus a shame that we scored twice in the first half and not at all in the second half. We didn't get as good a look at the goals going in as we would have liked, but we saw enough, and in any case we enjoyed them on TV and YouTube when we got home!

The first came after about ten minutes when Stefan Johansen, who was having a good season, sent over a lovely ball which Leigh GRIFFITHS headed home. Griff being Griff, he ran to the Rangers fans and invited them to share his happiness, a gesture which earned him a yellow card from the rather too officious Craig Thomson. Celtic remained well on top and it was no great surprise when, about 20 minutes later, Kris COMMONS drove home another. Kris Commons had been in the middle of a contract dispute with the club, but soon after this he announced that the dispute had been settled.

There was no way back now for Rangers, for Celtic had a particularly good centre-half pairing in Jason Denayer and Virgil Van Dijk, and in any case Rangers hardly got over the halfway line for the rest of the game, with Scott Brown absolutely immense in midfield. There was a certain amount of fight, it would have to be said, in them – a total of five men were yellow-carded, Lustig, Brown and of course Griffiths for Celtic, and Foster and Hutton of Rangers (Mr Thomson clearly enjoying himself today!) – but aggression is not enough if it is not accompanied by skill, and skill was in short supply, even if the pitch had been suitable, which it manifestly wasn't.

A certain disappointment was felt at the Celtic end that Celtic did not go for the jugular and really inflict a hammering on Rangers. Celtic certainly could have done so, for Rangers' 11 men consisted of honest journeymen, good Championship men, perhaps, but nothing really more than that. Had Celtic decided to go for it, the 7-1 score might have been equalled, but how were Rangers going to get their consolation goal?

Possibly Celtic decided that enough was enough at two. There was also perhaps another dynamic at work here. Celtic would soon be playing Inter Milan in the Europa League. One of Celtic's chronic weaknesses in Europe had been their inability to defend by passing the ball around to each other. They seemed to be practising this skill today. The second half was, actually, a bit of a bore, for Celtic were just so far ahead. The game finished with a whimper, and Celtic were in the Scottish League Cup Final in March to play Dundee United.

Celtic thus won 2-0, and won the Scottish League Cup Final (on a re-laid Hampden pitch) in March. They also won the Scottish League that season, winning it at the beginning of May when, having defeated Dundee spectacularly on a Friday night, they were confirmed as champions when Aberdeen failed to beat Dundee United on the Saturday. The Scottish Cup was not so nice this year, for Celtic lost to Inverness Caledonian Thistle in a horrible semi-final which could only in part be excused by poor refereeing decisions. It had been a good first season for Ronnie Deila, nevertheless.

Rangers disappeared from the Scottish Cup to Raith Rovers a week later, and earned a play-off spot in the Championship. But, although they beat Hibs, they lost out to Motherwell and thus failed to join the Premiership. Thus 'Old Firm' league games would not happen for at least another year.

FORTY NINE

NEMESIS KEEPS VISITING

Celtic 4 Rangers 0	**Scottish Cup Semi-Final**
Hampden Park	**15 April 2018**

Celtic: Gordon, Lustig, Ajer, Boyata, Tierney, Brown, Ntcham, Forrest (Roberts), Rogic (Sinclair), McGregor, Dembele (Griffiths)

Rangers: Foderingham, Tavernier, McCrorie, Martin, John, Docherty, Halliday (Windass), Candeias (Bruno Alves), Dorrans (Holt), Murphy, Morelos

Referee: Mr R. Madden, Glasgow

THIS semi-final was a really rather remarkable occasion, the one-sidedness of the game and the total humiliation of the other team being something that was rather hard to parallel in recent Scottish history and certainly in the history of the two teams. There had been times in the history of the Old Firm when one team was noticeably and visibly better than the other, but never ever to such an extent as 2018 was. If ever Nemesis was in action in football, this was surely it, as Rangers paid the extreme penalty for financial mismanagement.

In this year's Scottish Cup, Celtic had defeated Brechin City, Partick Thistle and Greenock Morton (the Morton game on the weekend of the 'beast from the east', the worst few days of weather that central Scotland had seen for some time) en route to the semi-final. When the semi-final draw was made and Celtic were paired with Rangers, Rangers' caretaker manager Graeme Murty, a man totally out of his depth, told the press that his players were all upbeat about it, and had cheered loudly when they heard about the draw. Confidence was rising at Ibrox.

But the confidence took a knock on 11 March. In a sense this particular semi-final was won, not on 15 April, but more than a month earlier at Ibrox on 11 March, when Rangers were ahead against Celtic, a hyper-enthusiastic linesman who also happened to be a Conservative MP (No kidding! You couldn't make that up!)

managed single-handedly to get Jozo Simunovic sent off – but in spite of all that, Celtic still won 3-2! This had followed an intense spell of brainwashing, self-delusion and wishful thinking down Ibrox way, with phrases like 'the turn of the tide' and 'the fightback begins now' being trotted out for the benefit of the gullible.

The real body blow to Rangers in this one was that they really should have won. Celtic did not do particularly well but they did enough to win through, showing all the character in the world to do so. Rangers at home against ten men should have got at least a draw, one would have thought, but they blew up and the Rangers TV commentary of the game and Alfredo Morelos's miss became national jokes.

Celtic's reaction to being drawn against Rangers in the semi-final of the Scottish Cup was possibly relief, for Rangers were the easiest of the three possibilities, the other two being Aberdeen and Motherwell. These two played their semi-final on the day before the Celtic v Rangers game, and Aberdeen managed yet again (as they did with monotonous regularity) to blow up at Hampden and to condemn their torn-faced, unhappy, moaning fans to another miserable three or four-hour journey up the road again. Motherwell, however, looked slick.

So Motherwell awaited the winners of the Old Firm (if one could still call them that) semi-final. The weather was bright, as was befitting mid-April, but there was still a hint of coolness to tell everyone that winter had not yet gone. The referee was Bobby Madden, a man widely believed to have strong Rangers credentials, something that has never been denied, but on this occasion he had a good game, keeping a lid on things when necessary, awarding Celtic two penalties and sending a Rangers player off. Yes, he found it hard to deny his Rangers bias, but maybe he was as fed up of them as the rest of the supporters were. If anything, we even felt he was too hard on them today. Maybe he was a Celtic man after all? Or even a genuine neutral?

And then, of course, there was Andy Halliday. Andy managed to do a lot of talking and he told everyone that he was living the dream because he was a 'big Rangers fan' (what incidentally is a small Rangers fan?) and that he was confident of success in this game. He was substituted before half-time!

The game started with Celtic playing towards the Rangers supporters at the Mount Florida end, and almost immediately Moussa Dembele hit the post. Everyone said it was 'a wake-up call' for Rangers, but if that was the case, they didn't really heed it, for about halfway through the first half Tom ROGIC scored for Celtic. It was a classic Celtic move. Brown to Lustig, a long ball up to Dembele who had sprung the Rangers offside trap. He then slipped the ball back to Forrest, Forrest to Rogic who went one way then another before slipping the ball past Foderingham in the Rangers goal.

It was a marvellous piece of football, and how Rogic enjoyed scoring against Rangers! It proved (if we did not know it before) that the likeable Australian had the temperament for the big occasion. He had scored against Rangers at Ibrox a month ago, and now he had done it again. He had also, of course, scored the goal that had won the Scottish Cup against Aberdeen last May. He was a player who was not always guaranteed a place in the starting 11, and many of the supporters often felt that he was not a 90-minute player, and that he was a better substitute. But there was now no doubt that he could take a goal!

The goal came at a time when, although Celtic were the better team, some of the Rangers camp were beginning to feel that something could yet happen for them today, for they were certainly not out of it. The Rogic goal was a severe blow to their feelings of optimism, and one began to get the feeling that the Rangers players were now, even at this early stage, resigned to their fate.

Tom then miskicked a far easier chance than the one he had scored. Not that it mattered all that much, for before half-time Celtic were two ahead. This time the movement came down the left, and it was Kieran Tierney who was the instigator. The ball into the box was only partially cleared and the ball came to Callum McGREGOR, who, with all the composure in the world, hammered home to put Celtic two up before half-time. We then had the Andy Halliday tantrum. If only Andy had realised it, Mr Murty was doing him a favour by taking him off!

Half-time came and went, and, although there was some token defiance in the chanting from the other end, every member of the blue persuasion knew in their heart of hearts that the game was up. Although Rangers managed to create a chance or two in the second half, Craig Gordon was up to the task, and there was one crazy moment when Mikael Lustig sclaffed a clearance which hit his own bar, the ball rebounded to Alfredo Morelos who shot straight at Craig Gordon! It was as if Rangers were not meant to score!

When this happened, Celtic were already 3-0 up, Moussa DEMBELE having scored a penalty kick after he himself had been pulled back by Ross McCrorie as he ran in on goal. By the letter of the law, young McCrorie had to be sent off, and some of us were even generous enough to say that this was just too draconian. It was not as if we needed a break today! But the law is the law and Bobby Madden is Bobby Madden, and Ross McCrorie got the red card. Moussa took a delightful curling penalty, the goalkeeper having been sent the wrong way.

A fourth goal also came from the penalty spot. Patrick Roberts had replaced James Forrest, and he was bundled to the ground by Rangers substitute Jason Holt as he ran in on goal. Some of the Celtic fans behind that goal wanted another red card to be shown as well, but that would have been a bit too greedy. As it happened, it was Olivier NTCHAM who took the penalty kick and scored.

And so, Celtic were in to the Scottish Cup Final to face Motherwell. The victory was almost embarrassingly easy, but it was still a source of great celebration to Celtic. Not so to Rangers, of course, and two of their players apparently indulged in fisticuffs with each other in the tunnel. Graeme Murty did not last long after that, but he hadn't expected to in any case, and it was soon after this game that we began to hear stories about the imminent arrival of Mr Gerrard from Liverpool. It would be an appointment rich in irony. Gerrard had a daughter called Lourdes (and – incredibly, that seemed to still matter to some Rangers fans) but there was also the undeniable fact that Gerrard had never won a league title in his life. He had once made a bad mistake to throw away the league for Liverpool. And who was his manager at that point? One Brendan Rodgers!

FIFTY

SEVEN IN A ROW

Celtic 5 Rangers 0 **Scottish League Premier Division**
Celtic Park **29 April 2018**

Celtic: Gordon, Lustig (Hendry), Boyata, Ajer, Tierney, Ntcham, Brown, Forrest, Rogic (Sinclair), McGregor, Edouard (Griffiths)

Rangers: Alnwick, Tavernier, McCrorie, Martin, Halliday, Holt, Dorrans (Docherty), Candeias, Windass (Morelos), Murphy, Cummings

Referee: Mr C. Thomson

SELDOM, if ever, was there such a fuss about a fixture. There can be little doubt that the SPFL had made a rather large rod for its own back by having a 'split' – a piece of nonsense whereby the team finishing seventh can actually have more points than the team finishing sixth! It also means that fixtures cannot be arranged until such time as it becomes obvious who is in the top six of the division and who is in the bottom. The SPFL usually makes an even larger rod for its own back by being dilatory in issuing the fixtures. Instead of having a Plan A and a Plan B which can be instantly issued whenever the last round of the pre-split fixtures is completed, they wait until they see who it involves and THEN discuss kick-off times and TV contracts, etc.

This is, of course, no way to treat fans, but when did the SPFL consider their interests? However, this year the problem was the Celtic v Rangers fixture. We knew it had to be played at Celtic Park, but when? Much was the talk about whether Celtic should be given the chance to play Rangers to win the league in front of their own fans. All sorts of politicians and pseudo-politicians talked about the problem of 'disorder' (some of them even talking as if it were a new problem!) when the big two met, and, of course, Celtic fans being Celtic fans, a 'conspiracy' was detected. In fact, it was simply incompetence.

In their wisdom, the SPFL decided that the Celtic v Rangers game would be in the second round of fixtures, the idea being that

Celtic would win the league against Hibs at Easter Road the week before, and that therefore the league title would not depend on the Old Firm fixture. Critics pointed out, however, that Celtic fans would possibly be in a position to gloat at the Rangers fans, and who was to say that this would not make the situation a lot worse? In any case, the week before that Celtic had beaten Rangers in the Scottish Cup semi-final, and was there 'disorder'? Well yes, there was, but no more than usual!

The whole soap opera got a lot worse when Celtic in fact lost at Easter Road to Hibs, thereby declining to win the league title in Edinburgh. Maybe just as well, because Celtic were wearing the pink rubbish and did not look like Celtic. They did not play like Celtic either, and maybe it was all a plan so that, after all, Celtic could win the SPFL at Celtic Park against Rangers on Sunday, 29 April! 'The best laid schemes of mice and men gang aft agley...' was the way Robert Burns put it over 200 years ago! Certainly, there was a distinct lack of tears from the Celtic fans at full time at Easter Road as the Hibs fans indulged themselves with a rare celebration – 'Sunshine On Leith' – in fact, a curiously moving rendering of it. A couple of them in the car park wished me all the best of luck next week against Rangers, whom they did not seem to like very much!

And so we all assembled at Celtic Park for the lunchtime kick-off. A major source of merriment was the arrival of the Rangers fans, police escorted up London Road, no longer even defiant or aggressive, more dejected and disgraced. It reminded the learned of a Roman triumph when the victorious general was allowed to exhibit some of those he had conquered as he paraded them through the streets of Rome to allow people to jeer and laugh at them! A few silly things were said, and at one point they were all herded by police horses into the wall of the Emirates building, before they were allowed in to Celtic Park. It was almost as if the police were laughing at them as well.

Celtic played Griffiths on the bench and gave Odsonne Edouard a start. Quite a few fans had been none too impressed by the Frenchman so far this season, but today he would silence his critics. Rangers were managed by a likeable fellow called Graeme

Murty. Like his predecessors, Warburton and Caixinha, he simply had not got a clue how to deal with the impossible element of his own support and some of his bosses, about whom eyebrows were still being raised. The task was unachievable; most of his players were decent, honest players who might have done a good job for Hamilton Accies or Ayr United. Against this mighty Celtic team, they were simply outclassed. They had as much chance as the early Christians did against the lions of the Roman Colosseum.

The mocking and the ridicule of the Celtic fans was cruel, and even a little embarrassing. Alfredo Morelos, who had missed an open goal at Ibrox a month before, was laughed at when he came on, and Andy Halliday, who had several times allowed himself to be quoted saying he was a 'big Rangers fan', was cheered to the echo, whereas those who had Celtic-sounding names like Murphy and Docherty were booed for their perceived treachery. And, of course, Steven Gerrard, the manager-elect, was similarly ridiculed. Apparently he was not at Celtic Park today.

The goals came at regular intervals. Celtic, playing towards the Lisbon Lions stand, simply took control. Following several corners and near misses, they took the lead in the 15th minute when Kieran Tierney made ground down the left and crossed for EDOUARD to score fairly easily. Odsonne had to work harder for his next goal in the 40th minute. Rangers conceded possession, James Forrest picked the ball up, then threaded a lovely pass for EDOUARD to run in and score a brilliant goal; 2-0 and that seemed to be it as half-time approached. Already some Rangers fans were showing signs of wanting to go home; just on half-time a lot of them did just that when James FORREST scored a third, threading his way through the weak Rangers defence and evading what challenges there were from them to hammer home. 'No contest, no contest whatsoever,' bellowed Dave Crocker on SKY TV, as Mikael Lustig committed what used to be called a 'felony' by stealing a policeman's hat (which he duly returned).

And so it was 3-0 at half-time. One recalled how in the 1969 Scottish Cup Final Celtic were 3-0 up and how the delirium was mixed with a certain fear that Rangers might yet make some kind of a fightback. There was no such fear here, for the outclassing was so pronounced. Rangers supporters certainly thought so. This game must have seen the biggest-ever half-time exodus of supporters, and London Road saw a trickle of Rangers fans enjoying the pleasant spring sun.

The second half had hardly started when Tom ROGIC made it four, lobbing the ball almost nonchalantly past a static Rangers defence, with the goalkeeper and all the others about six yards out of their goal! It was astonishing, and about five minutes after that Edouard made space on the left to pass to Callum McGREGOR to make it five.

There now seemed to be no limit to what Celtic could do here. 7-1 could have been dwarfed, double figures was even a possibility, but Celtic probably decided that the carnage and humiliation should now stop. 'Don't ever humiliate your fellow professionals,' Jock Stein used to say to Tommy Gemmell and Bertie Auld when the showing off got out of hand, and this sort of thing seemed to happen here. There would have been no point. Even the Celtic fans realised that there should be some sort of a limit. Celtic were so far ahead that there was a danger of it not being a contest at all. Humanity and compassion, rare emotions in Celtic v Rangers games, took over – but the mockery, ridicule and laughter were still there.

The result was that the game petered out. Had Rangers scored, the Celtic fans would have given them a cheer. After all, Rangers had hardly any fans left and there was a precedent of how John Greig once got a cheer from Celtic fans at Hampden in 1972 when he scored a late consolation goal! As it was, the last few minutes were spent with everyone looking at the clock until eventually Craig Thomson ended it all. Celtic had now won the Scottish League for the 49th time, and, although last year was a great deal more emphatic, 2017/18 had only seldom looked as if it were likely to go any other way. The previous Rangers visit to Celtic Park between Christmas and New Year had seen a draw. It was a disappointing game. 'Crisis' was brought out by the press, and even by some of the Celtic supporters that day in the context of Celtic's performance (unbelievable, but true!).

Celtic were so far ahead today that it was even possible to feel sorry for Rangers' supporters. There were, after all, some decent people among them – in fact most of them are – but nevertheless Nemesis, for all that they had done before, had now visited them with retribution and pain for the past several years. Some of us who could recall 1963 and 1992 knew a little of what they were going through, but this was 2018, and ecstasy and rapture were the order of the day.

ACKNOWLEDGEMENTS

MANY thanks to Paul and Jane at Pitch Publishing, and to Andrea Dunn and Duncan Olner.

My thanks also to all Celtic supporters (too numerous to mention) and a few Rangers supporters who have contributed to my researches, particularly my friends on the Joseph Rafferty Celtic Supporters Bus.